Commission of the European Communities

Library Automation in North America

A Reassessment of the Impact of
New Technologies on Networking

Charles R. Hildreth

K·G·Saur   München·New York·London·Paris

EUR 11092

Publication No. EUR 11092 of the Commission of the European Communities, Directorate-General Telecommunications, Information Industries and Innovation, Luxembourg

Charles R. Hildreth, READ Ltd, Springfield, Illinois, USA

CIP-Titelaufnahme der Deutschen Bibliothek

Hildreth, Charles R.:
Library automation in North America : a reassessment of the impact of new technologies on networking / Charles R. Hildreth. Comm. of the Europ. Communities. — München ; New York ; London ; Paris : Saur, 1987
    ISBN 3-598-10735-8

© ECSC-EEC-EAEC, Brussels-Luxembourg, 1987
Publisher: K. G. Saur, München
Printed by WS-Druckerei, Werner Schaubruch, Mainz
Bound by Buchbinderei Schaumann, Darmstadt
Federal Republic of Germany

ISBN 3-598-10735-8

CONTENTS

PART III

AUTOMATED SYSTEMS AND SERVICES IN LIBRARIES

LIST OF ACRONYMS

AI	Artificial Intelligence or Authorities Implementation.
ALA	American Library Association.
AMIGOS	AMIGOS Bibliographic Council.
ANSI	American National Standards Institute.
ARL	Association of Research Libraries.
ASCII	American Standard Code for Information Interchange.
AVIAC	Automated Vendors Interface Advisory Committee.
BALLOTS	Bibliographic Automation of Large Library Operations Systems.
BLIS	Biblio-Techniques Library Information System.
BNB	British National Bibliography.
BRS	Bibliographic Retrieval Services.
BSDP	Bibliographic Services Development Program.
CARL	Colorado Alliance of Research Libraries.
CD-ROM	Compact Disc Read Only Memory.
CISTI	Canada Institute for Scientific and Technical Information.
CLASS	Cooperative Library Agency for Systems and Services.
CLR	Council on Library Resources.
COM	Computer Output Microfilm.
CONSER	Conversion of Serials Project.
CRL	Center for Research Libraries.
DRA	Data Research Associates.
DRANET	Data Research Associates Network.
DRAW	Direct Read After Write.
EBCDIC	Extended Binary Coded Decimal Interchange Code.
ESTC	Eighteenth Century Short Title Catalog.
IAC	Information Access Corporation.

IAIMS	Integrated Academic Information Management System.
IFLA	International Federation of Library Associations.
ILL	Interlibrary Lending.
ILLINET	Illinois Library Network.
ILS	Integrated Library System.
INCOLSA	Indiana Cooperative Library Services Authority.
ISBD	International Standard Bibliographic Description.
ISBN	International Standard Book Number.
ISO	International Standards Organization.
ISSN	International Standard Serial Number.
ITOL	International Thomson·Organisation, Ltd.
LAN	Local Area Network.
LC	Library of Congress.
LCS	Library Circulation System or Library Control System.
LOCIS	Library of Congress Information Systems.
LSCA	Library Services and Construction Act.
LSP	Linked Systems Project.
LSSI	Library Systems & Services, Inc.
MARC	Machine Readable Cataloging.
MEDLARS	Medical Library Analysis and Retrieval System.
NAC	Network Advisory Committee.
NACO	Name Authorities Cooperative Project.
NAL	National Agricultural Library.
NCLIS	National Commission on Libraries and Information Science.
NELINET	New England Library Information Network.
NISO	National Information Standards Organization (U.S.).
NLC	National Library of Canada.
NLM	National Library of Medicine.

NOTIS	Northwestern Online Technical Information System.
OCLC	Online Computer Library Center.
OND	Office for Network Development (National Library of Canada).
OPAC	Online Public Access Catalog.
ORBIT	Online Retrieval of Bibliographic Information Time-Shared.
OSI	Open Systems Interconnection.
PACNET	Pacific Network of OCLC.
RECON	Retrospective Conversion.
RFP	Request for Proposal (or Bid).
RLG	Research Libraries Group.
RLIN	Research Libraries Information Network.
SNI	Standard Network Interconnection.
SOLINET	Southeastern Library Network.
SPIRES	Stanford Public Information Retrieval System.
SUNY	State University of New York.
TRLN	Triangle Research Library Network.
UTLAS	UTLAS International; formerly University of Toronto Library Automation System.
VAN	Value Added Network.
VTLS	Virginia Tech Library System.
WLN	Western Library Network.
WORM	Write Once Read Many.

PART I

OVERVIEW OF LIBRARY AUTOMATION AND COMPUTER-BASED NETWORKING IN NORTH AMERICA

1. Introduction: Conditions at the Beginning of the 1980s

At the beginning of this decade, it would have been appropriate to begin an overview of the state of the art of library automation and networking in North America with an account of the organizations and activities of the four major bibliographic utilities. In 1980, OCLC, RLG/RLIN, WLN, and UTLAS dominated the library automation scene in North America. Among these four "bibliographic utilities" (as the organizations that operate computerized library networks are commonly called), each of which utilized a centralized bibliographic database, OCLC was the largest and most influential. Since most libraries' first experiences with automation involved joining one of the utilities to acquire online cataloging and interlibrary loan (ILL) services, the utilities exerted the major influence on the pattern of library automation and networking development into the early 1980s. Most of the computer terminals in libraries in 1980 were dedicated terminals connected solely to the remote, central computer system of one of the four utilities. Each utility stood alone, operating separate and unlinked private telecommunications networks to connect its member or client libraries to its centralized processing facilities and database.

The years leading up to and including 1980 have been called "the golden age of library cooperation and cooperative networking" (DeGennaro, 1983*). These were the years the large, mainframe-based centralized online network systems and databases to support shared cataloging and ILL activity were developed and established with seeming permanence on the library landscape of North America. The growing acceptance and use of the MARC formats for the creation and maintenance of catalog records, along with the Library of Congress' MARC tape distribution service, facilitated the development of the utilities. Each utility began network operations with online shared cataloging facilities, each exploiting the easy availability of LC MARC records and cataloging formats for this purpose.

*For citations, see the Bibliography at the end of this book.

As DeGennaro (1983) has said, "the coming of powerful but expensive online systems and telecommunications capabilities provided both the technical means and the economic incentives for librarians to band together to develop large cooperative networks." The application of new information technologies to automated library functions has always been shaped by the existing capabilities and costs of available computer and communications technologies. In the 1970s, online networking systems were too complex and costly for individual libraries to develop and operate. Thus, non-traditional library organizations (e.g., OCLC) built the expensive centralized bibliographic resource systems, and libraries joined computerized networks or entered into agreements with these new bibliographic utilities to share the high costs and risks of computerization. Few libraries had the capital resources or staff with the sophisticated technical skills needed to mount large, advanced computer technology projects. As Malinconico (1986) points out, "a principal function of shared network systems is to assist libraries to surmount the capital investment hurdles, and to control the risks associated with high technology ventures."

By 1980, OCLC RLG/RLIN, WLN, and UTLAS had brought online computer technology, through their shared cataloging systems, to thousands of libraries in North America. Some viewed this networking development as a culmination, as the case "par excellence", of applying computer technology to library functions. Others, more visionary, saw it as merely the beginning, the foundation of the coming pervasive use of diverse new technologies in libraries, including entirely new solutions to the problem of providing affordable and effective computerized networking systems for libraries.

A brief look at the context of library automation and networking in North America in 1980 will prove useful as a point-of-departure for two reasons: 1) many librarians in Europe believe this context represents current realities, and (2) such an account will provide a contrasting backdrop to the presentation of present realities and dominating trends. At almost every dimension of the computerized library service and networking environment, major, fundamental, structural and functional changes have occurred during the 1980s, up to the present time.

Any state-of-the-art survey of library automation and networking at a given time must identify the major components of the environment and the forces and conditions which determine its unique characteristics. The components of the library computer networking environment include the participating organizations (e.g., libraries and utilities), the functions to be automated and provided as services, specific network configurations (physical and organizational), and the <u>current technologies</u> that support the automation of library and network functions. The dominant forces which interact to shape the networking environment have been, in this century, at least, economic exigencies, the capabilities of new technologies, and the commitment to resource sharing ideals and other motivations of the networking participants. Other factors, such as "politics" and the level of technical knowledge and skills achieved by librarians, also play an important role in defining the limits of the possible.

In a landmark paper published in 1980 by Avram and McCallum of the U.S. Library of Congress ("Directions in Library Networking"), the authors explain that computer technology available in the 1970s "pushed the community toward centralized automated systems." Large centralized facilities which exploit mainframe computer systems and available "inexpensive" telecommunications options to serve hundreds or thousands of libraries were required to achieve the necessary economies of scale and to distribute the high costs of computer technology among the large number of users. Thus, explain Avram and McCallum, the large centralized utilities and their regional service networks came to dominate the library networking environment by 1980. The primary functions they performed included the provision of machine-readable cataloging records for various forms of local catalogs, and the provision of holdings or location data needed to facilitate interlibrary lending and exchange of materials. In a companion piece on "Cooperation and Competition among Library Networks," Robinson (1980) reminds us that OCLC was the first of the "local" non-profit networks to extend its service and network to libraries on a nationwide basis. "Indeed, it is my contention," says Robinson, "that OCLC's success gave rise to competition from RLIN, UTLAS, and WLN." (Robinson's paper provides an overview of the utilities' member library sites and the geographical territory covered by each of the four major networks in 1980. Also included is an account of the emergence of state and regional networks or consortia as OCLC service centers and brokers of OCLC products and services.)

Avram and McCallum (1980) provide a summary of the participants and the basic network structure among libraries in the U.S. at the beginning of the decade. The participants are of two types: <u>libraries</u>, which, as always, need cataloging records and location information, and the <u>bibliographic utilities and their regional service centers</u>, which supply these bibliographic services to libraries. The inclusion of "service centers" in the second category of participants is interesting, because this applied mainly to OCLC in 1980; but this shows that even at the Library of Congress,

OCLC has been viewed as the "model" North American bibliographic utility. (Other significant differences between the four utilities will be described in Part II of this book.) Noticeably absent from this account of network participants are the commercial suppliers of library systems and catalog records.

MARC cataloging records made available through the LC MARC tape distribution service provided the original resource data upon which the centralized utilities were built. But from the start, OCLC and the other utilities provided online, shared, contributed cataloging facilities, which enabled libraries to input their cataloging into the central, remote databases, when LC MARC records could not be found. Thus, the databases maintained by the utilities began their rapid growth, and now LC MARC records constitute much less than half of OCLC's millions of bibliographic records. Hundreds of libraries which had previously acquired their catalog records on cards or machine-readable tapes from LC now joined the new utilities to acquire catalog records, online cataloging capabilities, and electronic ILL support.

Avram and McCallum refer to the advent of the bibliographic utilities in the 1970s as "the independent development of major networks." What they mean by "independent" is that the major utilities, which came to define the library networking environment by 1980, were not formally created or sanctioned by any act or agency of the U.S. or Canadian federal governments, including the Library of Congress and the National Library of Canada. They are correct in pointing out that the rush of libraries joining-up with the independent utilities led to the proliferation of new "intermediate" agencies in the networking environment, and ever-greater dependencies by libraries on external agencies. The use of remote, centralized bibliographic facilities, whether as a contributing member of a cooperative or as a client paying for commercial services, required contracts, support, and special training. The need for some agency to manage these new processes and operations led to the creation of state and regional service centers. More than twenty such centers were in operation in 1980, brokering the services of the utilities, and otherwise standing between libraries and the major bibliographic utilities.

In 1980, Avram and McCallum, along with many other library leaders, expressed fearful concern about several "negative" consequences of the new networking developments: the duplication of bibliographic services to the nations' libraries, the overlapping territories and competitive structure of the world of the utilities, loss of control by individual libraries, and the absence of rational (read "national") coordinaton of networking activities which has led to the "current (1980) disjointed developments in library networking." The authors also signal the emerging controversy over the ownership of records which was to become the most debated networking issue of the early 1980s.

At the risk of oversimplification, it suffices in this introduction to say that the major, most influential "players" in the library automation and networking world of 1980 were the four large, centralized utilities and their supporting service centers. Indeed, Martin (1968) observes, "in that time, it was difficult to discuss library automation without mentioning library networks or vice versa. Even libraries with local systems usually required a link to a bibliographic utility and its database." The utilities were the first to introduce automation into very large numbers of North American libraries, and thereby, to demonstrate its efficacy. The cost-effective support of utility-based automated cataloging and electronic ILL activity was well-established in 1980, and serials control, union listing, and acquisitions systems were either operational or undergoing testing and development by the utilities. The dream of a centralized, total library system was still alive (including even the local function of circulation control supported on the remote computer system of the utility). In 1980, the governors and managers of the utilities gave little thought or direction to the opportunities inherent in local, distributed library computer systems and the interlinking of their separate, large-scale computer systems and databases. Furthermore, "integrated library systems" (ILS) and "online public access catalogs" (OPACs) were not familiar phrases in the common parlance of library networkers.

With a welcome touch of realism (perhaps the benefit of hindsight), Malinconico (1986) reminds us that "the development of computerized bibliographic networks in North America has been the result of pragmatic responses to prevailing circumstances, not the logical consequences of coherent strategies or grand designs." He goes on to say that the services they provide and the manner in which they are organized is determined by economic realities, current technological capabilities, and the "urge toward self determination." I would add that librarians' demands for new services from the utilities also play a determining role in the provision of services and products. If the demands (e.g., for subject access to library collections and OPACs) go unheeded long enough, librarians will turn to suppliers other than the utilities for these services and products. Unfortunately, until recently, as Markuson (1985) documents, library networkers have designed and implemented models of networking that optimize bibliographic control rather than facilitate bibliographic access through advanced computer technology, and have developed systems that serve the needs of librarians more effectively than the needs of library users.

Making the same point in her critique of centralized bibliographic networks and electronic union catalogs – namely that librarians have concentrated their efforts on the creation and processing of bibliographic records in ever larger systems, utilities, and union catalogs – Beckman (1982) cites the comments made by Bregzis (National Librarian of Canada) and Wright in 1979:

> The original objective, to harness technology for the benefit of the information user, was soon displaced by the substitute and less complex objective to apply technological innovation to the manipulation of bibliographic records.

The perceived requirement of librarians for more cost-effective bibliographic control, plus the marriage of the mainframe computer and machine-readable cataloging records, largely explains the golden era of the development of the large bibliographic utilities and their centralized processing centers.

2. Networks in Transition: the Eclectic Computerized Library Networking Environment of the Mid-1980s

The four North American bibliographic utilities are still major participants in the library automation and networking environment today, but almost everything in that dynamic environment has changed, including the utilities themselves.

Martin (1986) summarizes the dramatic change in the automated networking environment with this passage:

> With the more conservative political and economic climate of the country, libraries have shifted from the enthusiasm of total cooperation to a strong support of local systems with a more cautious embrace of the cooperative.

Martin identifies three determining factors responsible for this change: 1) microcomputers, which enable libraries to accomplish locally what once could be achieved only by joining with others, 2) the preference of librarians for the autonomy afforded by a local system, and 3) the wide availability of services and products provided by the private, commercial sector that compete with the network (utility) services.

New "players", new technologies, more knowledgeable and skilled librarians, and new networking models and configurations have led to radical changes in the basic network structure among libraries in North America. With the addition of new participants who have in many areas taken the initiative and leadership away from the utilities, the pattern of development of library automation and its adoption by libraries has also changed.

To convey an understanding of today's networking and automated resource sharing environment in the U.S., it is necessary to point out that two grand visions still alive in 1980 are now completely dead ideas: 1) the concept of a national bibliographic network, and 2) the dream of a network-based "total library system" developed and operated centrally by one of the bibliographic utilities.

A national network?

In the mid- and late 1970s, many U.S. library leaders spoke with confidence and optimism about the coming national network. Proponents of the national network agreed that it should have a central, coordinating agency at the national, that is, federal level. The basis for much of the discussion and early planning was the 1975 NCLIS report "Toward a National Program for Library and Information Services: Goals for Action." The report proposed a political structure for organizing the national network, designating the role of the federal government agency as one of coordination, incentive funding, and even management and operation of key network components and functions. Most proponents of the plan assumed that planning and coordination for a national network should take place at the national level, and the Library of Congress was often recommended for this role.

In her overview of this period, Markuson (1985) points out that the plan was never put into action; the proposed federal agency was never created. To many, LC was the natural and most feasible choice to be the federal agency responsible for coordinating the national library network. Though not the official national library of the U.S., LC had developed and continued to maintain the MARC cataloging formats, and was the principal distributor of MARC tapes containing machine-readable catalog records. These tapes provided the data resource basis for the early successes of bibliographic networking systems like OCLC. A frequently discussed network model placed LC at the center of a vast national bibliographic network system linking major research libraries and the large bibliographic computer networks as regional nodes. Some hoped that LC would build this network, or at least administer its operations and maintain its resource database. However, federal legislation and funding never materialized to set-up this program, and LC chose not to pursue the role of national network center. No other national library agency was able or willing to achieve a broad mandate for this role. So, the centrally administered national network never materialized.

During the late 1970s, the bibliographic utilities became well-established as providers of MARC cataloging services and experienced a rapid growth in membership. Hundreds, then thousands of libraries joined these independent, non-governmental network organizations. OCLC's membership and central database grew to make it the largest network, with libraries across the nation using its resources and contributing records to its ever-growing bibliographic and holdings (library locations) database. In the eyes of many, OCLC had become the de facto national network. This development was viewed with alarm in some quarters. Those who still held to national network objectives believed that the leaders of OCLC, RLG, and WLN were assuming roles that properly belonged to national planners.

Apparently this was a minority view, because talk of a unified national network and a national coordinating agency for such a network has all but disappeared from the scene in 1986. Martin (1986) explains: "it became clear that the loss of autonomy suggested by such a structure, together with the perceived bureaucracy, made a national network less desirable than orginally thought. Librarians began to question whether they really needed to know everything about collections nationwide...A physically centralized national network is a fading dream and is being replaced by ideas for connecting networks and local systems to provide access to networks throughout the nation."

In retrospect, it can be seen that the forces of decentralization (and especially anti-centralism) were already having an effect on the networking environment, as the four major utilities flourished and became more competitive among themselves. In the early 1980s, even some of OCLC's regional networks ("brokers" and "service centers") began to plan or actually offer the computer services formerly supplied by the central OCLC system.

Additional forces and consequences of decentralization in the networking environment will be discussed later in this book. It will suffice to say here that in the first half of this decade, efforts to establish a national network were replaced by calls for greater voluntary coordination and cooperation among the major, independent utilities in the U.S. The very notion of a "national network" has now been replaced in discussions with the reality of "nationwide networks." The Linked Systems Project (LSP), a program to link the computer systems of LC, RLG/RLIN, WLN, and OCLC, utilizing standard communications protocols to create an "open sytems interconnection" environment, has materialized to become the major cooperative networking effort at the national level ("across the top") in the U.S. A single physical national or continental bibliographic network will not come into existence in the foreseeable future.

A centralized, total library system?

Automating all the functions of a library in a central system that could be shared by many libraries participating in an online network was another ill-fated, but understandable, dream of library automation innovators in the 1970s. When most libraries could not afford to buy computer hardware and mount major system development efforts on their own, this dream had a certain validity. Under the leadership of Kilgour, OCLC had developed by 1980 several of the components of a "total library system" on its central computer system in Ohio, and had extended access to these functions to libraries through its nationwide online network. In addition to cataloging on OCLC, member libraries could choose to use OCLC's online ILL system and serials control system. Acquisitions was being field-tested, and circulation control was under development. Thus, the "total" library system (for libraries' "housekeeping" functions) was almost completed, in a time-sharing, online network mode.

However, as other affordable options for automating local functions such as circulation and serials control became widely available to libraries from the commercial sector, librarians began to question OCLC's reasoning that local transaction and data files could be maintained reliably and economically on the central, remote system. Major concerns of users centered around poor response time between the local OCLC terminal and the central system (OCLC was experiencing major problems with system stability and response time at this time), and adequate access to and control over data that is entirely local in nature. Subsequently, OCLC abandoned the goal of providing a total automated library system on its large network system. None of the other utilities chose to pursue that goal.

3. New Realities, Wider Options

Today, most medium and large public and academic libraries in the U.S. have installed computer systems to automate circulation functions and local catalog maintenance. Many have also automated one or more of serials control, acquisitions, and the public access catalog. Most formal plans for acquiring a local automated library system now specify a multi-function, integrated library system (ILS) that can be operated entirely at the local site. Typically, these integrated library systems are minicomputer-based and are supplied as "turnkey" systems by commercial vendors. In addition, microcomputer systems and products are flooding the entire library community. They are bringing significant computer processing power to even the smallest of libraries. More data will be provided on this rapidly expanding local automation phenomenon in Part III of this book.

In the early 1980s, the locus of initiative and influence in determining the direction of library automation and networking shifted from the bibliographic utilities to the commercial vendors of local systems, and to librarians more interested (and now better qualified) in using the new commercial systems and software to solve access and resource sharing problems closer to home. De Gennaro (1983) documented this trend toward the "rapid proliferation of a variety of powerful and versatile mini- and microcomputer systems in individual libraries and clusters of related or affiliated libraries." By 1980, several commercial firms like CLSI and GEAC had brought to market affordable turnkey local library systems. "Turnkey" systems represent an arrangement whereby a single vendor provides all the software and hardware for the functions to be automated and assumes the responsibility for system installation and maintenance. Most of the early turnkey installations were circulation control systems, and they provided librarians the opportunity to use automated technology in their own environment to exercise control over the materials in their collections.

Malinconico (1986) reminds us that in the late 1970s and early 1980s, "the bibliographic utilities entirely missed the opportunity to develop and market turnkey systems." This fact accounts in part for the structural and functional changes in the automated networking environment. Competition and new products from the commercial sector have provided librarians more sources for automated systems and services. Functions formerly automated at the network level are now being distributed and supplied to the local level. As a result, a larger number of librarians at all levels have become sophisticated in their knowledge of computer technology applied to local library functions and resource sharing activities, such as interlending and reciprocal borrowing practices, based on shared or linked automated circulation systems.

Recent decisions by the utilities to market mini- and microcomputer-based systems, and to distribute some of their traditional network-based functions to the local IBM PC-based workstation, may be viewed as an attempt to regain their former position of dominance and leadership in the library automation and networking environment. More likely it is a rational approach to remaining viable in a dynamic and highly competitive marketplace. However, in this new <u>decentralized</u> environment, two trends (at least) are irreversible: more and more computer processing power will be brought within the budget range of all sizes of libraries, and librarians will increasingly be driven by the urge toward self-determination and control to exploit locally available technology to solve local problems.

Libraries no longer need to join large networks to get the benefits of automation. The automated services and products provided by the utilities will be purchased by libraries only if they are competitive in quality and price. The role and functions of the large utilities in today's decentralized and commercialized library automation and networking environment are undergoing rigorous reexamination within the library community. The responses of OCLC, RLG/RLIN, WLN, and UTLAS to this period of examination and adjustment will be summarized below in Part II.

To understand the changing environment of computerized library networking and automation in North America, it is necessary to gain some insight into its dominant themes: decentralization and commercialization, a resurgence of regionalism and local initiative, and the democratization of computer expertise in the application of new information technologies to library functions and activites. As these themes are being played-out, a new pluralistic, multi-layered library networking environment is rapidly emerging.

4. Decentralization and Commercialization of the Networking Environment

In their 1980 state-of-the-art review of new networking technology, Avram and McCallum observed that "the most significant point about this new technology is that after pulling the community toward large centralized facilities for 10-15 years -- in order to use large machines with accompanying economies of scale -- it is now pushing toward decentralization." The authors had in mind primarily the new technology of very large scale integrated (VLSI) circuits which made possible very powerful mini- and microcomputers at greatly reduced costs.

From a broader perspective, Segal (1985) argues that networking efforts in the library world have always been shaped by two sets of countervailing forces: forces pulling toward centralization, and forces pulling away from it. Forces driving toward centralization include:

    1) the desire to build large databases to provide universal or "global" electronic union catalogs,

2) the perceived need for national or international holdings data to support interlibrary loan activities,

3) the need to impose and maintain standards,

4) the availablility of inexpensive telecommunications and advanced technology,

5) the proliferation of machine-readable records, and

6) the reduction in costs achieved by a reduction in duplicate efforts.

Forces pulling away from centralization include:

1) fear of the loss of autonomy and the urge for self determination,

2) an increase in telecommunications costs,

3) technological advances in distributed computer processing (e.g., powerful mini- and microcomputers), and

4) increasing costs and overhead associated with acquiring and supporting network services.

DeGennaro (1983) believes these countervailing forces explain the existence of two parallel and sometimes conflicting lines of development in the history of library automation: one focused on local systems, the other on network systems. He believes that in the 1980s these two lines are coming together in a "synergistic way":

The interest, energy and resources that went into network building in the 1970's are now going into buying and installing mini- and microcomputer-based local systems...These local systems may eventually acquire the capability to link to each other and to the utilities for shared cataloging and ILL purposes.

The latter promise has been realized. Growing numbers of libraries in North America have been able to afford and install multi-function local systems. Commercially-supplied turnkey systems have become more reliable and acquiring support directly from the vendor has made them attractive to librarians. Vendors acquired experience early with providing local systems and support services, such as retrospective conversion, local database maintenance, etc. And now they are providing systems capable of supporting groups of libraries in local clusters or statewide network services. As Malinconico (1986) observes, "the result has been a decreasing dependence on shared (remote) computer facilities, and increased instances of cooperation carried out on a small scale, among libraries with a very high affinity of interests" (or I might add, with a very close proximity to one another).

Vendors have had a major impact on the library environment greater than that of the utilities in the 1980s. They have exploited low-cost minicomputer technology and have offered libraries affordable turnkey automated systems: systems which include all hardware, software, installation, training, and ongoing support from a single source. Unlike OCLC (in its role as a remote utility), they became directly involved with library management and staff, and proved to be more responsive than OCLC to demands for new design features, such as online subject access and authority control. By quickly upgrading their systems to take advantage of the expanded power and flexibility of superminicomputers, turnkey system vendors will continue to shape the pattern of library automation development. The massive processing and storage capacity of the new multi-processor systems provide the capability of supporting multi-functional, integrated library systems (in which a single bibliographic file supports all functions) for large public and academic libraries, or even local or state-wide library consortia. As Boss (1984) observes: "The sharing of systems based on large minis may not reduce the costs of automating, but it will facilitate resource sharing in local areas." Shared or linked local automated circulation systems are able to provide precise, timely, online information to staff and patrons regarding the status of materials in all the linked collections.

OCLC and UTLAS have recently begun to compete with the turnkey system vendors by marketing their own integrated library systems. This development, plus that fact that UTLAS is now owned by a for-profit international corporation, may have a far-reaching impact on the way libraries perceive and do "business" with these utilities. Martin (1986) points out that more and more the large utilities "are increasingly viewed as vendors that are vying for the library's business rather than as partners in an effort to reach a common goal." The logic and motives involved in doing business are different than those required for shared, cooperative efforts. A business relationship is by its very nature more transient. Contracts replace shared commitment and reciprocal loyalty. If a new vendor offers better services at less cost, the library customer is likely to change vendors. In its recent expansion of its network and services into the U.S., UTLAS undoubtedly has this possibility in mind. One must conclude, however, that this increased competition in the library systems marketplace has provided more kinds of options for automated services to libraries in North America.

It is too early to measure the impact of this decentralization and multiplicity of options on the traditional bibliographic products and services provided by the utilities. But trends can be anticipated. Even two years ago Boss (1984) reported that:

> The development of local, integrated, multi-function systems has led a
> number of libraries to limit the role of their bibliographic utility to

that of a resource database supplier. After obtaining a machine-readable record from a utility's database, many libraries do all subsequent searching and editing locally. As interfaces are developed among the local library systems in a region, the use of the utilities' databases for interlibrary loan also changes. Already some libraries use the utiities' ILL subsystems only to access out-of-state locations.

The number of commercial suppliers of bibliographic records has exploded in recent years, and some are offering optical digital disc-based cataloging systems at prices far lower (per unit) than those incurred in using a utility.

5. Regionalism and Local Initiative

During this period of decentralization, library resources and efforts to apply new information technologies to library functions are being redirected to the local level of the library community. Medium and large libraries are installing (or planning to install) turnkey integrated library systems. All libraries, large and small, are purchasing a diverse variety of microcomputer software products and are using it for a variety of local administrative and resource sharing needs.

This trend toward decentralization and local initiative must not be seen as a reduced commitment to cooperation and resource sharing among libraries. Librarians are very much aware of the continuing need to share limited resources, and maintain a professional allegiance to cooperative goals and programs. The former enthusiam for national or large centralized networking activities has clearly diminished, and may not exist at all as a common spirit in the U.S. As DeGennaro (1983) predicted, librarians have moved to regain the control over much of their technical operations that they gave up to the utilities in the 1970s. They have learned that "they cannot be totally dependent on external and sometimes fragile technical systems over which they have little or no control." Transferring responsibility for key library functions to external agencies is not appreciated or understood by the local political and governing bodies that support and oversee their libraries. With the rapid proliferation of turnkey systems and wide availability of microcomputers and software, librarians are shifting their priorities to the development, maintenance, and extended use of their own automated local circulation systems, machine-readable databases, and online public access catalogs (OPACs).

There is no need for alarm or pessimism. Resource sharing and networking activities are not diminishing. We are witnessing a return to the local, "grass roots" level of networking, using a variety of local computer-based technologies and arrangements. Robinson (1980) reminds us that networks began as grass roots organizations, and probably "ought to remain so." In her report to LC's Networking Advisory Committee (NAC), Markuson (1985) argues that local network interests should retain their primacy. The wide access to interlibrary information in the U.S. has been based on local funding and local initiative:

> The reality is that the majority of library collections, services, and
> access are provided by local, not national, agencies using local, not
> national funds, and that any extended access to these local collections
> has come about through professional cooperation and operational
> necessity. The reality is that our tremendous system of nation-wide
> access to library holdings would stop dead in its tracks without
> constant local commitment and financial support.

It must be said that librarians in North America have no natural desire to engage in expensive, computer-based cooperative activities on a large scale, across vast geographical distances. The need for local control and the urge for self-determination position them against remote, centrally controlled and administered networking organizations, whether they are private or public, for-profit, or not-for-profit. Librarians did not, upon shared deliberations and driven by a positive spirit of cooperation, join together in the 1970s to develop large, centralized, nationwide bibliographic networks. The utilities provided the technology of the day; the incentives to join were largely economic or of "operational necessity." Experience is teaching us once again that librarians' commitment to operational cooperation is inversely proportional to the geographical and political distance separating the participants, and directly proportional to the natural or logical affinity of group interest and goals.

Most libraries cannot satisfy all their patrons' needs from their own stock. Thus, resource sharing is very much alive. But for many libraries this need can be satisfied with an arrangement to share resources with libraries in the local vicinity or within the state or province. Malinconico (1986) speaks of the emergence of computerized mini-networks. More and more small groups of cooperating libraries are purchasing one or more systems from a single vendor. Whether through sharing a common database or through the vendor-supplied linking of the separate systems, such "clustered" systems support either reciprocal borrowing agreements or interlibrary lending.

Bibliographic records already in the database can be adapted and used by libraries in the local group to catalog new acquisitions, making it possible to bypass the utility's network. An example of this can be found in a group of public libraries in Cleveland, Ohio which use turnkey systems supplied by Data Resources Associates (DRA). The systems are linked together using the vendor's DRANET linking and datacommunications facilities.

Several state library agencies have instituted plans to select a single commercially-supplied, multi-function turnkey system to serve as the basis for a statewide resource sharing network. Either through incentive funding or legislative mandate, systems are acquired and installed at the libraries within the political jurisdiction. The separate computers and databases are linked via a variety of telecommunications technologies, incuding cable and microwave. Examples include the use of VTLS (Virginia Tech Library System) in the West Virginia State Library Network, and the decision to install GEAC systems in Indiana's public libraries.

Other libraries in a region, within a state or across state boundaries, are joining together voluntarily to share a powerful, locally-developed network system and its database storage and circulation control capabilities. Local catalog records are typically tape-loaded into the central system, but direct entry is being planned. The central computer system may have been developed originally by a single university (as is the case with the Illinois Statewide LCS System -- Sloan, 1984), or by a college and university consortium, for example, CARL, the Colorado Association of Research Libraries (Culkin & Shaw, 1985), and TRLN (Triangle Regional Library Network) in North Carolina (Byrd, 1985). In two of these cases, (CARL & LCS) public libraries have been included in the state network systems. In other local regions, commercial vendors have supplied cataloging, circulation, and ILL systems to small groups (often newly formed) of libraries (see Freund, 1985 and Heinemann, 1986). In some cases, these locally developed or installed systems are replacements for a utility. In other cases, the utility still serves as the resource bank for the local, automated cooperative.

Two other "local" networking developments that must be mentioned are 1) the increasing use of mini- and microcomputer communications and ILL software to support interlending among libraries within a state, province, or local consortium, as an alternative to using the utilities' ILL systems (see Givens, 1982 and Abbott & Kavanaugh, 1986), and 2) the integration on large university campuses of the library's automated system via a local area data communications network (LAN) with the wider computing environment of the university community. Access to the library's system and resources through the OPAC is thereby provided to anyone having access to the larger network on the "wired campus." As McCoy and Davison (1985) observe "the information accessible through online catalogs ranks near the top as an attractive resource on campus local area networks." When linkages to other local, regional, and national online information systems are established, the library will have the opportunity to position itself in the university environment as a gateway to diverse information resources, and a "facilitator of access to local, national, and international information." The impact of this development on the utilities is not yet visible, but leaders at both OCLC and RLG are carefully analysing this growing phenomenon as part of their strategic planning activities.

6. The Democratization of Computer Literacy and Expertise

Librarians in ever-increasing numbers are both contributing to and benefiting from the decentralization occurring in the library automation and networking environment. Not many years ago, the broad "rank and file" of librarians had little exposure to, or training in, computer and communications technologies. Before the 1980s, few libraries had computer systems in-house. Individuals possessing both knowledge of library operations and computer expertise as applied to library functions constituted a small, informal elite in the library profession.

This is no longer the case, as we have witnessed in North America what can be characterized as a democratization of computer literacy. Among librarians, this spread in knowledge and competence with library computer systems and applications occurred gradually in the 1970s and 1980s. Three major, evolutionary contributing factors can be identified. They represent conditions that have appeared successively with some overlap over the years, and that together have had a progressively propelling impact on the increase of technological sophistication and computer expertise in the professional library community.

One of the positive consequences of the success of automated bibliographic utilities and networks, as Malinconico (1986) points out, is that thousands of librarians gained first-hand experience with new computer technologies. Even in library schools, the first lessons in automation typically involved training on the use of a utility's terminal. Malinconico observes that, as a result, an increasing number of librarians "have developed a sophisticated understanding of the potential of library applications of computer and telecommunication technologies." They are, thus, a motivated force working vigorously for the implementation and improvement of these services.

The second factor responsible for the increased technological sophistication among librarians is the rapid proliferation of local multi-function turnkey systems in libraries since 1980. Specific data on these installations is provided in Part III of this Report. A recent survey of the top large public and academic libraries in the U.S. disclosed that 65% use turnkey systems and most of the rest are planning to automate (Peat, Marwick, Mitchell and Co. 1986). This development has brought entire computer systems, not terminals alone, into large numbers of libraries. As a result, librarians have become very literate and comfortable with regard to computer technology. Furthermore, a new professional specialty and role has emerged for librarians who wish to assume responsibility for the management, coordination, and operation of local library systems. These specialists, also growing in number, are variously called "systems librarians", "automated systems coordinators", etc. These librarians constitute a highly trained, progressive force for change in today's library community.

The third factor is the microcomputer revolution sweeping across all professional and business sectors of the U.S. and Canada, including libraries. Hundreds of thousands of microcomputers have been acquired by American libraries. Hundreds of microcomputer software products for library functions are available in the marketplace. Unlike the dedicated turnkey sytem, micros can be found in all corners and units of the library. It is the pervasiveness of microcomputers throughout the library that has completed the democratization process. They are now common tools in the administrative offices of libraries; they are used to support or backup a variety of "housekeeping" functions, from cataloging to circulation management activities, and they are increasingly being introduced in public service areas as OPACs or "end-user" reference search stations. Librarians are learning to select and use off-the-shelf microcomputer equipment and software, both for their own needs, and for new services to their patrons. Many libraries provide public access microcomputers and software for on-site use. Therefore, many librarians have acquired computer education and training skills to support this new service.

This democratization of library computer knowledge among librarians is having a major impact on the ways new information technologies are being put to use in libraries and networking activities. Uses range from managing administrative tasks (e.g., budgeting, statistics, report generation) to improving patron access to library information files. Micros have enabled (rather, empowered) the librarian to take automation directly to library and information users.

No longer is there a concentration of computer knowledge resources or leadership in the organizations of the utilities and a few universities. At the beginning of the 1980's, most librarians were _passive_ network participants. They were involved in library bibliographic networks primarily as recipients of the utilities' services and products. Today, more librarians across the U.S. and Canada are _active_ network creators and managers, using local turnkey systems and micro-based ILL and communication software for local and regional resource-sharing programs and activities. In the last 2-3 years, local system vendors have created linking and networking software for their products, in response to demands from librarians in local institutions and local library consortia. Local initiative and the urge for self determination and autonomy are forces network planners and coordinators in North America will have to reckon with as never before, now that affordable, flexible information technology is making its way into all areas of most of our libraries.

7. A Pluralistic Mosaic of Networks and Cooperative Activities

No single model of computerized library networking will suffice to adequately characterize current library networking and computer-based resource sharing activities in the U.S. and Canada. The networking environment today is decentralized, multi-layed, increasingly populated at the local level with distributed processing systems, and resplendent with a resurgence of local, grass roots networking and linking initiatives.

It is no longer accurate, if it ever was, to hold up OCLC's centralized star-configured network system of the early 1980s as the paradigm of library networks in the U.S. Clearly, the "big four" utilities are still major forces in the library automation and networking environment. However, in today's competitive, mixed library market environment, the utilities no longer dominate in the development and distribution of automated products and services. It is easy to make a case that they have lost the initiative (at least temporarily) in introducing new technology and computer-based support services into libraries. Other commercial organizations are leading the way with the introduction of turnkey, multi-processor, integrated local systems, networking software, advanced OPACs, and optical disc, microcomputer-based end-user reference systems. While continuing to grow by most measures (e.g., database size, online terminals, member/client libraries, etc.) and in combination serving thousands of libraries in North America, each of the four large utilities differs in significant ways from the others. Furthermore, OCLC, RLG/RLIN, and UTLAS are pursuing their separate plans for decentralizing their networks and exploiting distributed processing in ways they deem viable and otherwise in their best interests.

Since the late 1970s, library leaders in Canada have advocated the development of "an electronic decentralized nationwide library and information network" for their country (Durance, August 1985). They have been very vocal and visible in their oppositon to a centralized, nationally administered network for Canadian libraries. At times, they have proudly set themselves apart from, if not above, the national leadership and "policies" of the U.S. library networking community. In the late 1970s, the Canadians perceived quite correctly that in the U.S. a push for a centralized national bibliographic network was taking place at high levels, and that in reality, OCLC with its centralized system was rapidly becoming the de facto national network.

The Canadians steadfastly opposed both developments, and pursued their own policy of developing a decentralized network configuration in which hundreds of different library computers and databases across Canada would be linked in an open systems environment, based on the developing ISO/OSI standard protocols for connection and communication between different computer systems. The National Library of Canada, through its Office for Network Development, assumed the role of coordinator of OSI standards development and system interconnection pilot and field tests, such as the well-known 1981-82 iNet field trial. It was foreseen that the National Library's DOBIS-based union catalog database at Ottawa would be a major, but not the only, node in the Canadian library network.

Ironically, most of the reasons listed by Durance, Director of the Office for Network Development, to explain Canada's rejection of a centralized network approach apply equally well to the U.S. (Durance, August 1985). Rationalism aside, actual networking developments in the U.S. are bringing reality closer to the Canadian wish. U.S. library leaders in the bibliographic utilities have reached near unanimity in their support for the implementation of ISO/OSI protocols. The Linked Sytems Project (LSP) undertaken by RLG, WLN, OCLC, and the Library of Congress is an outstanding example of this commitment to OSI-based open systems interconnection, although this program is correctly viewed as a "linking across the top" by other participants in the U.S. library networking environment.

Commercial vendors and state and regional networkers are viewing this development (LSP) with caution. Centralized, "top down", national coordination of the new "open" nationwide bibliographic network by LC, CLR (The Council on Library Resources) and the three large U.S. utilities is likely to meet as much resistance from the commercial sector and the "grass roots" as did earlier plans to create a national network. In their enthusiasm for expanding the library applications and scope of the LSP project throughout the library community in the U.S. and Canada (see McCoy, 1986), the LSP leaders run the risk of being perceived as elitist "officials" (self-appointed) handing down policy from the top. The current environment is not hospitable to that approach. It should be pointed out that the current LSP National Policy Committee, which is extending the scope of its efforts to include all segments of the computerized library networking community, has no members respresenting public libraries, smaller academic libraries, or the commercial library system sector.

Summary

Local, state, provincial, and regional bibliographic databases supported by a variety of computer systems are populating the library landscape in North America. A wide variety of computer networking and linking arrangements can be found for sharing cataloging, holdings, and reference information resources. As Markuson (1985) says, "New technology now allows us to pose many alternative network models from highly centralized to highly distributed systems." In his landmark 1983 paper, DeGennaro observed the reaffirmation of local autonomy which was producing local and regional networking arrangements to "supplement, modify, or even supersede the familiar star networks (utilities)." He predicted correctly that the utilities' networks, regional, state and local online catalogs would be linked and coordinated in a variety of ways:

> There will be no single hierarchical National Library Network in the
> U.S.; nor will there be a central government agency planning and
> directing the pluralistic, multifaceted and ever-changing mosaic of
> library and commercial systems and networks that will be the national
> library and information network in reality, if not in name.

This largely uncoordinated, "disjointed", decentralized networking situation may be viewed with alarm by some leaders in the U.S., Canada, and Europe. On the positive side, the environment is rich with new, innovative uses of computer and communications technology, devised by knowledgeable, public service-oriented librarians to better facilitate resource sharing and provide needed information and materials to library users. Whatever one thinks of the changes in networking that have evolved in this decade, their reality, as summarized succinctly by Segal (1985), must be accepted:

> The ideal of a national network gave way to the proposal that networks,

clusters, systems, consortia, and cooperatives of varying sizes and functions might be linked via the Open Systems Interface (sic) reference model, allowing for local network development and control to be combined with resource sharing at national and even international levels.

8. The Bibliographic Utilities Respond: Distributed Processing, Product Diversification, LSP, and Internationalism

A rigorous and lively reexamination of the role and proper functions of the traditional utilities in a decentralized, increasingly competitive automated networking environment is taking place at all levels in the library community, and within the corporate organizations of the utilities themselves. In the community at large, the need for the utilities' massive databases as national resources to support shared cataloging and ILL activities is a matter of some debate. As we have seen, the dream of a single, national bibliographic network that all libraries could use for shared cataloging and ILL was replaced in the late 1970s by the successful development and expansion of OCLC, RLG/RLIN, WLN in the U.S., and UTLAS in Canada, each with its own network, database, and group of member libraries.

The current program to link the U.S. utilities and the Library of Congress in the Linked Systems Project (LSP) may be viewed as an attempt to create a "virtual" or "logical" national bibliographic network and national database of catalog (and authority) records and holdings information for thousands of the nations' libraries.

Ironically, this massive, multi-year, expensive endeavor (LSP) is taking place at a time when many library leaders are pointing to the reduced need for the traditional bibliographic services offered by the large utilities, and when some are even expressing concern about the continuing economic viability of the utilities. Furthermore, it would be difficult to make a case that this new "virtual" national database of separately maintained, linked databases is an efficient, cost-effective enterprise. There is an incredible amount of overlap in catalog records and holdings information in these soon to be linked databases. Each contains the USMARC file, and OCLC's and RLIN's databases both include machine-readable records for several of the same large research libraries, due to the cooperative program of tapeloading one another's members records. LSP, supported with substantial funding by the Council on Library Resources (CLR), will be described in more detail in Part II of this book.

In a "Glossary for Library Networking" (Library of Congress. Network Development Office, 1978) prepared for the Network Advisory Committee (NAC), "bibliographic utility" is defined as "an organization that maintains onlinebibliographic databases, enabling it to offer computer-based support to any interested users, including national library network participants."

Out of date, this is a common view of the utilities in North America. It should be easy to understand why OCLC, RLG/RLIN, WLN, and UTLAS have always been uncomfortable with the narrow label, "bibliographic utility". Although initially each network offered online shared cataloging services to its libraries, the four "utilities" developed a variety of additional library systems and services in the late 1970s and early 1980s. These services include electronic ILL, serials management, acquisitions, retrospective conversion (recon) of manual catalog files, and offline products like catalog cards and machine-readable tapes, accession and serials union lists in various formats, and in some cases, COM catalogs. RLG and OCLC point with pride to their support and involvement in national level programs like CONSER and the Major Microforms project.

Will the utilities still be needed?

Yet, today, the major activities of the four utilities are online cataloging (including recon) and ILL, measured either by computer processing power consumed, or revenue generated. In his 1983 article, DeGennaro predicted a diminishing role for the utilities in the decentralized networking environment, but confidently asserted that "the shared cataloging and ILL functions are and will continue to be the mainstays of the bibliographic utilities for several more years in the foreseeable future." In her comprehensive monograph on library networks, Martin (1986) argues that access to the bibliographic utilities is the primary support mechanism for library cooperation, and that libraries still need their large databases to achieve high cataloging hit rates. In response to speculation that the utilities' large centralized databases will not be needed in the future as interconnected local sytem proliferate, Martin states:

> Libraries will undoubtedly wish to continue to support and enhance ILL
> capabilities, document delivery, collection management, and access to
> machine-readable data files. For this reason, the structures that have
> been built in the form of these large databases will need to continue
> and be supported rather than to diminish in importance as local
> systems thrive.

Setting aside issues of national bibliographic policy and the policies of any of the network organizations (DeGennaro and Martin are both directors of RLG libraries), an inescapable conclusion is that there will be a diminishing need and demand for the traditional online cataloging and ILL services of the utilities as the years go by. There are several reasons for this, but these are the basic ones: 1) the utilities are viewed more and more as vendors of services rather than partners in a cooperative endeavor (UTLAS is now a for-profit company owned by International Thomson Organization, Ltd., and OCLC markets a local turnkey system, LS/2000, and has claimed ownership of its bibliographic database.), 2) local network options for these services, especially ILL and OPACs are growing rapidly, and 3) the utilities are facing growing competition from commercial suppliers of cataloging, recon, and other bibliographic services. (The reader is reminded that the opinions of the chief executive officers -- as of fall 1986 -- of OCLC, RLG, WLN, and UTLAS on this issue are contained in Appendix A.)

These trends may lead libraries to reconsider their voluntary membership (and its attendant costs) in the utility-owned networks and their regional service networks. Wetherbee (1984), executive director of AMIGOS, formerly an OCLC regional service network, has observed that because of burgeoning commercial-sector services and local network growth, "Individual libraries will have so many options that advantages for staying in centralized, regional or national systems will decline." Even Martin (1986) concludes that the threat to the utilities of declining membership (or reduced rate of growth in the U.S.) and a decline in the concommitant revenues is real and present:

> In the areas of library systems and support services, the private
> sector is obviously able to provide the same kinds of quality of
> products available to libraries through bibliographic utilities and
> regional networks, although the lower-volume, high-cost transactions
> are less likely to be supported. As more libraries adopt their own
> local sytems, it may be particularly appealing to reconsider a major
> financial commitment to a network and to replace it with private sector
> services instead.

Malinconico (1986), fearful that these developments may "even undermine the economic viability of the national network systems," suggests that the utilities, as holders of national and special bibliographic resources not held by local organizations, may have to be publicly subsidized:

> This clearly is a classic case of a service that needs to be publicly
> supported, i.e., it is a service acknowledged to be of general value,

yet which cannot be made self-supporting.

The utilities grow and thrive with new products

Whether to survive and remain internally viable or to continue their role in assisting libraries achieve their management, service, and program roles, or both, the utilities have demonstrated a remarkable ability to respond and adapt to a changing network environment, increased competition from the commercial sector, and demands from users for new and improved services. In the 1980s, UTLAS and RLG have upgraded their computer systems, and OCLC is in the process of doing so - all at the costs of millions of dollars. In combination, the four North American utilities serve approximately 10,000 libraries. Two things are worth noting:

1) all of the utilities began as university-based or public organizations (WLN is an agency of state government), and
2) all of them are stronger and more stable now than at times in the past.

Many commercial, for-profit library service firms have not fared as well over the past ten years.

For purposes of summation, the responses of the utilities to changing conditions and new challenges can be grouped into four categories: 1) a move to distributed processing systems, 2) participation in the Linked Systems Project (except UTLAS), 3) the introduction of new and improved services, and 4) international programs and strategies.

Distributed processing

Each of the utilities is following its own plan to distribute computer processing power, services, and information products away from their central computer facilities and databases. Not all of the details of the plans are known, but several developments can be reported. Each utility will continue to maintain a central database, as a resource bank to support its members' cataloging, ILL, and program needs. But, some processing functions will be distributed to local systems and microcomputer workstations, and segments of the utility's union database will reside at local or regional sites on magnetic or optical disc storage media. In some cases, portions of the union catalog will be physically dispersed throughout nodes of the utilities' networks. In other cases, portions of the union catalog will be replicated on magnetic or optical mass storage media to serve special local needs.

With varying degrees of success, each utility has accommodated the emergence of stand-alone, local library systems. OCLC and UTLAS have acquired turnkey systems, and continue to develop and market them. RLG has contracted with the turnkey vendors GEAC, NOTIS, and Biblio-Techniques (BLIS) to develop computer-to-computer linkages between their systems and RLIN, recognizing that many of its research library members have installed (or will) one of these systems. WLN had a pilot arrangement with DATAPHASE to link local circulation and central cataloging functions in the state of Washington until the vendor went out of business. UTLAS purchased the DATAPHASE ALIS III Tandem computer-based turnkey system and renamed it the T/Series 50.

It is not yet clear how the utilities will establish and control the data transfer interfaces between the local systems and the central database. As a matter of policy, each utility will require the uploading of new cataloging and holdings data to the central facility, but also must support the downloading of bibliographic data to the local mini- and microcomputers needed for the libraries' circulation, acquisitions, serials management, and OPAC systems. Most of these activities will not take place on the utilities' dedicated terminals connected to their private telecommunications networks. Thus, new linking and interconnection methods must be established.

Currently, OCLC's local system, LS/2000, has no computer-to-computer linkage with the central system via OCLC's private network. Libraries using LS/2000, along with those using GEAC, CLSI, and NOTIS systems, etc., are dependent upon a printer-port connection from the OCLC terminal to transfer online records into the local system (they may also, of course, employ batch tape-loading procedures). This situation will change in the near future, as OCLC and RLG/RLIN establish new linkages between local systems and their new networks. Both OCLC and RLG are planning to install private, packet-switched telecommunication networks to replace their current dedicated, leased-line networks. OCLC seems to be further along in this process, projecting completion in late 1987. RLG hopes to have their packet-switched network operational by mid-1988.

OCLC and WLN have adopted the IBM PC microcomputer (with modifications) as their network-based user workstation. RLG plans to do so as well in the near future. OCLC has taken advantage of its "M300" IBM PC-based workstation to provide more efficient and easier-to-use cataloging and ILL local modules called "Micro-Enhancers." OCLC has also chosen to replace its centralized serials control and acquisitions services with separate, local microcomputer-based systems ("SC350" and "ACQ350"). UTLAS markets an IBM PC-based OPAC, and at another level, the Canadian-based corporation has announced the installation of a new processing center in Kansas City (U.S.), as a "new node" in its North America network to provide more efficient services to its U.S. customers.

The linking issues

Each of the utilities has publicly expressed its support of OSI standard protocols for linking systems and networks (see Appendix A). Yet, the utilities are competitive among themselves, and each assumes it is in control of its future and how its distributed systems and processes will be designed and interconnected. Martin (1986) thinks that this assumption may be false, "since libraries will purchase the local systems that appeal to them and only then will worry about the way the local system will interface with the utility."

Each of the utilities will have network member libraries which have purchased local systems and products from other vendors. More OCLC members, for example, have turnkey local systems of other vendors than have LS/2000 systems. Will OCLC extend the same interconnection technology and methods planned for linkages to its local system to vendors of competitive systems? Fulfilling a commitment to OSI standard protocol-based linkages is at least a three-level program. At the highest level, LSP represents a national program to link the U.S. utilities and LC (for an explanation of LSP, see Part II). Will the LSP participants decide which applications are to be standardized after the initial implementation of the authorities standard? Recently, several vendors of turnkey systems have formed a new standards advisory committee (AVIAC), partly as a show of mutual support for adopting standard system interconnection protocols. They want a voice in the development of application-level standards. Each has expressed a commitment to develop software in compliance with the developing national and international standards to support the interconnection of their different systems at the local level. The third level requires development and facilitation of standard interfaces to permit linking between any of these local systems and one or more of the utilities. The utilities may wish, however, to restrict open access and interconnection at this level to gain a competitive advantage. Today, the only OSI/LSP-based successful linkage between a U.S. utility and a turnkey vendor is the test connection that has been established between RLIN and GEAC. In Canada, a GEAC system and two university systems have established successful OSI-based linkages with the DOBIS computer system at the National Library of Canada for purposes of bibliographic record file transfers.

New services

In recent years, the utilities have introduced many new bibliographic products and library services. Some of the new services are natural extensions to their centralized, online shared cataloging services. These include online ILL, acquisitions and/or serials control, the addition of "special" databases to their MARC files, the support of non-roman alphabets (e.g., Cyrillic, Chinese, Japanese, Korean, and Hebrew), reference searching of their databases, online serials union listing, and retrospective conversion services. OCLC and WLN have adopted the IBM PC microcomputer as their new, more intelligent, multi-purpose workstation, and UTLAS will provide emulation software for its online customers who choose to use an IBM PC. This provides greater flexibility for both the library and the utility. Libraries can use the IBM microcomputer as a stand-alone workstation for a variety of tasks when it is not being used online to access the utility. On the other hand, the utilities can develop software for the IBM PC as a way of: distributing some system functions to the local workstation, e.g., full-screen data entry and editing, error checking and data validation, etc.; streamlining user terminal tasks; and providing user-system interfaces that are easier to learn and use than those required in the central, online system. OCLC markets such microcomputer software for use with its cataloging and ILL systems called "Micro-Enhancers".

The utilities support a variety of services related to their online cataloging services. RLIN, WLN, and UTLAS support subject and keyword searching of bibliographic files using a variety of indexes, and WLN and UTLAS support online name and subject authority control. All the utilities offer a broad array of offline cataloging products including catalog cards, machine-readable tapes of a library's records cataloged online, COM catalogs, printed lists and bibliographies, and book labels. UTLAS offers a batch, tape processing authority control and MARC upgrade service for local catalogs.

OCLC and UTLAS have devised services to further exploit their electronic networks. UTLAS supports an electronic mail service, and OCLC has recently added a gateway service via a direct line from its network processors to the BRS online database search service in Latham, New York. This gateway permits OCLC users who subscribe to BRS' search services to access BRS directly from their OCLC terminals while logged on to the OCLC network. To further expand its gateway services, OCLC has recently licensed the "iNet" intelligent, directory-based gateway and networking software developed by Bell Canada. The National Library of Canada coordinated the participation of several Canadian libraries in the 1981-82 field trial of iNet, declaring it to be the first test of an OSI-based interconnection of different computer systems. OCLC has just begun to offer its new iNet-based "OCLC LINK" online gateway and database resource directory services to its member libraries. OCLC LINK provides automatic connection and logon from an OCLC terminal to a number of independent, online database search services and other information providers. OCLC's iNet facility (the licensed software and a configuration of Tandem computers) will not replace the OCLC network, but will operate in conjunction with it, much as iNet uses the DATAPAC public, packet-switching telecommunications network in Canada for data transmission between separate and remote computer processing centers.

OCLC and UTLAS have been aggressive in their efforts to acquire or develop mini- and microcomputer-based local systems. OCLC's LS/2000 is a multi-function, integrated turnkey system which can be configured to run on minicomputers of various sizes and capacity. Its software design supports clusters of affiliated libraries. UTLAS markets and supports two local library systems. The T/Series 50 system is a multi-function, integrated turnkey system for medium and large libraries, based on Tandem super-minicomputers. The M/Series 10 is an IBM PC-based local OPAC which can be interfaced with a circulation system if the client library so chooses.

WLN had granted a special license to a private firm, Biblio-Techniques to develop and market the WLN software as a local system, and at least six universities have purchased the BLIS system. However recent reports indicate Biblio-Techniques has decided to go out of business. RLG has not developed local library systems or services for its members, but its major broker and distributor, the independent regional network, CLASS (Cooperative Library Agency for Systems and Services), has developed microcomputer-based serials control and database management systems for libraries.

Recent research and development efforts at OCLC, WLN, and UTLAS have produced prototypes of several laser, optical disc-based products. WLN has developed "LaserCat", a CD-ROM-based local cataloging system to be used with an IBM-PC workstation. Three compact discs contain all WLN records with holdings (location) information attached, plus 200,000 of the most recent Library of Congress MARC records. LaserCat was introduced early in 1987. UTLAS has a CD-ROM, microcomputer-based recon system now ready for service. OCLC has demonstrated prototype CD-ROM cataloging and reference search systems at several library conferences in 1986 and 1987. Researchers at OCLC are also exploring microcomputer-based, full-text retrieval and online browsing systems which may use optical mass storage media, and electronic document (text and graphics) delivery systems.

International initiatives

In Appendix A, the utilities respond to this investigator's query about their business and services plans for Europe. It may be useful here to review a few of their current activities in the international arena.

WLN, the smallest of the utilities and an agency of state government, has limited its international activites to licensing its software to interested organizations. Licensees include the British Library, and the national libraries of Australia, New Zealand, and Singapore. The software, which includes online shared cataloging and online authority control and maintenance modules at its core, runs on IBM or IBM-compatible mainframe computers.

UTLAS, a division of International Thomson Organisation, Limited since its acquisition in early 1985, actively seeks expansion into Asia and Europe. It has offices in Canada, the U.S., Japan, the United Kingdom, and Europe. Several libraries in Japan use the UTLAS shared cataloging system, CATSS II, which has the capability of processing cataloging in Asian languages. The Maruzen Company distributes UTLAS products in Japan. UTLAS is willing to provide services in Europe, either via telecommunications or system replication. Marketing efforts for its local library systems products may increase in Europe in the near future.

RLG, the non-profit corporation owned by a consortia of 36 universities and research institutions, owns and operates the RLIN automated bibliographic network. RLIN exists primarily to support the Consortium's programs. RLIN apparently does not seek to be an international online database resource system, and has no plans to install or replicate its system in other countries. RLG's policy is not to compete with national means of bibliographic control, but rather to pursue links among existing and evolving networks and systems. RLG is willing to share its experience and expertise gained from operating RLIN and from its work on the OSI standards-based Linked Systems Project.

RLG seeks cooperative agreements, activities, and data sharing with research institutions and libraries in other countries where such cooperation supports RLG program goals or the shared goals of the participating organizations. A current arrangement with the British Library provides online access via the RLIN network to catalogers in London who are jointly building the Eighteenth Century Short Title Catalogue (ESTC) RLIN database with a special team at the University of California, Riverside, in the U.S. To support this activity, a transatlantic cable link was installed in late 1985 to connect the British Library with RLIN, and both teams use RLIN terminals to contribute information to the database. The British Library and other European libraries have expressed interest in contributing to the RLG "Conspectus Online." The Conspectus is an inventory instrument that describes member libraries' collection strengths and current collecting interests. Online, the Conspectus enables institutions to gain and communicate information about their collections in common terms. Adopted by the Association of Research Libraries in the U.S., it has become the national standard for description of collections. With European libraries contributing, the Conspectus has the potential for becoming an international resource and online instrument for describing collections.

Authorized by its Board of Trustees in April 1980, OCLC began shortly thereafter to make its services available to libraries outside the U.S. Today, OCLC provides services to its member libraries in the U.S. and 16 other countries. In January 1981, OCLC established its "OCLC Europe" office in Birmingham, England to provide OCLC network support services to libraries in the United Kingdom and Europe. The Birmingham facilities are connected via transatlantic cable to the OCLC network and OCLC's computing facilities and centralized database in Dublin, Ohio.

The OCLC bibliographic database contains approximately 16 million bibliographic records in 314 languages. With over 250 million library location listings ("holdings" information) linked to these bibliographic records, indicating that the listed library has cataloged the work represented by the record, the OCLC database may be the largest international online union catalog. Several libraries in Europe have used this resource through the OCLC network-based online ILL system. The Technical Research Center in Finland has been using the OCLC ILL system since 1980, and the British Library Document Supply Center has used the ILL system since 1983. More recently, the Statsbiblioteket at Arhus, Denmark commenced a six-month evaluation of the OCLC ILL system in March, 1986.

It is becoming clear that OCLC is stepping up its efforts to expand its network-based, online database services into Asia and Europe. At its fall meeting in Ohio, September 21-23, 1986, the OCLC Users Council (part of the OCLC governance structure) focused on international networking and the creation of an international database. Barriers and opportunities for international networking were discussed by several speakers. Rowland Brown, OCLC's President, spoke on "OCLC International." The Users Council adopted a resolution urging OCLC to continue its international operations, but requested an opportunity to review OCLC's international plans and their financial implications.

OCLC's global strategy is outlined clearly in its responses to the Questionnaire included in Appendix A. OCLC aims to build and maintain an international database containing "not only the records of our own members' holdings together with those of the Library of Congress and other national libraries, but (records) of significant collections of other libraries throughout the world" (OCLC, 1986). The expanded, ever-growing international database in OCLC's plans will be a "physical" union catalog of "master" records and library holdings information from around the world, "replicated nationally or regionally when the need and technology permits." OCLC makes it clear that it is not speaking of a "logical" or virtual union catalog created by linking independent national and regional systems, but a real, physical OCLC international database, owned, maintained and operated by OCLC.

OCLC has said that it will be "flexible, cooperative, and collaborative" in its present and future dealings with agencies and institutions in other countries. OCLC has copyrighted the OCLC online union database in the U.S., and has said (see Appendix A) that it is currently formulating policies for the use and transfer of OCLC-derived records (machine-readable bibliographic records copied or extracted from the OCLC database via downloading or transferred on magnetic tape or other media) by institutions located in countries outside the United States. Institutions in Europe planning to contribute records to the OCLC database will be watching the development of these policies with great interest. OCLC is likely to deal with each case on its own merits and requirements, but the legal, contractual approach is likely to be the formal mechanism employed by OCLC to establish and define each new arrangement and relationship.

In pursuing new collaborative activities with agencies and institutions in Europe, OCLC has said that it does not wish to establish "local" OCLC offices, and "assumes that our 'partners' will provide the continuing support once a central group has been trained." Curiously, this approach appears to be similar to OCLC's position in the U.S. in the 1970s when many libraries nationwide wished to join the Ohio-based network. OCLC chose not to engage and support these libraries directly (e.g., billing, terminal installation, training, support, etc.), but required them to "cluster" together and create regional OCLC networks (i.e., broker organizations and service centers), or to use existing state library agencies or regional library consortia to perform this role. This permitted OCLC to deal with a single agency representing many libraries.

OCLC's cooperative relationship with its state and regional service centers (also called "OCLC Networks") has evolved over the years, and now the terms of the relationship are defined in separate contracts between OCLC and each of its regional networks. Renegotiation of long-standing arrangements are currently underway, and fewer than half of OCLC's networks in the U.S. have been able to reach an agreement and execute a new contract with OCLC. The difficult issues being discussed have mainly to do with policies on the use and distribution of records derived from the OCLC database, and the marketing and support of OCLC's newer local library systems and products, vis-a-vis similar products supplied by competing vendors or the regional networks themselves. OCLC is a non-profit membership-based organization, but its dealings with its traditional state and regional service centers are increasingly perceived as legalistic and a matter of "strict business."

OCLC, the largest of the North American utilities, is a dynamic organization actively seeking new databases and participants (ILL, cataloging, recon) in Europe. Two developments to be watched are the recent 1986 agreements with two French government agencies and the Deutsches Bibliotheksinstitut in Berlin. France's DBMIST and DLL, agencies of the Ministry of Education and the Ministry of Culture, respectively, have entered into an accord with OCLC to explore mutual interests in building and sharing online bibliographic files. During an evaluation period, OCLC terminals will be placed at the Bibliotheque Nationale, various university libraries around Paris, and at the BPI at the Pompidou Center in Paris and other public libraries. The terminals will communicate with the OCLC database in Ohio via a packet-switched service to the UK, then to OCLC via the transatlantic cable. The aims of the program include a determination of the usefulness of OCLC records in building computerized catalogs in France, and an attempt to discover French library records or files which may increase the usefulness of OCLC's database for libraries in the U.S.

The agreement between OCLC and the Deutsches Bibliothekinstitut will explore the cost-benefits to both U.S. and German libraries of shared cataloging and retrospective conversion using each country's major machine-readable union databases. Access to each other's data and systems is the basis of the evaluation. Seven German research and university libraries have been selected to participate in the evaluation of the OCLC database. Samples from the libraries' catalogs will be searched in OCLC's database to determine if there is sufficient data to support or contribute to the retrospective conversion of the German catalogs. OCLC members will search the serials and monograph union databases maintained by the Institut for similar evaluative purposes. Each party to the agreement hopes to substantially enrich their electronic union catalogs with the addition of bibliographic records and location information from each other's databases and contributing libraries.

PART II

LIBRARY NETWORKS AND BIBLIOGRAPHIC UTILITIES: MAJOR ORGANIZATIONS, SYSTEMS AND PARTICIPANTS

1. Profiles of the Major Bibliographic Utilities

OCLC (Online Computer Library Center, Inc.)

Location: 6565 Frantz Road
Dublin, Ohio 43017, USA
(614) 764-6000

Organizational Status, Governance, and Funding:

OCLC is a non-profit library service and research membership organization that makes available computer-based processes, products and services for libraries and other educational organizations. From its facility in Dublin, Ohio, OCLC operates an international computer network that libraries use to acquire and catalog books, order custom-printed catalog cards and machine-readable records for local catalogs, arrange interlibrary loans, maintain location information on library materials, and gain access to other databases. Over 6,000 libraries in the United States and eighteen other countries contribute and use information in the OCLC Online Union Catalog, the world's largest database of library bibliographic information. OCLC also provides local decentralized computer systems and stand-alone, microcomputer-based systems for individual libraries or clusters of libraries.

Chartered in the state of Ohio, OCLC is a non-profit educational and scientific corporation organized to establish, maintain, and operate a computerized network of bibliographic cataloging services for libraries and to promote the evolution of library use, of libraries themselves, and of librarianship. The corporation has federal income tax-exempt status under Section 501(c)(3) of the Internal Revenue Code of 1954.

OCLC's charter states: "the purpose or purposes for which this Corporation is formed are to establish, maintain and operate a computerized library network and to promote the evolution of library use, of libraries themselves,

and of librarianship, and to provide processes and products for the benefit
of library users and libraries, including such objectives as increasing
availability of library resources to individual library patrons and reducing
rate-of-rise of library per-unit costs, all for the fundamental public
purpose of futhering ease of access to and use of the ever-expanding body of
worldwide scientific, literary and educational knowledge and information."

Governance:

Governing powers necessary to the administration of the affairs of the
organization are accorded to a 16-member Board of Trustees, including the
president of OCLC; five members from the professions of business, law,
government, and/or finance; three board-elected members from the library
profession; and six members from the OCLC Users Council. The founder of
OCLC, Frederick G. Kilgour, is a permanent member of the Board of Trustees.

Delegates to the Users Council represent those networks, systems,
consortia, or groups of libraries participating in the OCLC Online System.
They are elected by member libraries of OCLC that participate in the Online
System. The OCLC Users Council, a body of sixty delegates, serves to reflect
and articulate the interest of the member libraries. In addition to electing
six Trustees, the Users Council must approve any change in the corporation's
documents of governance.

Funding:

OCLC is a self-supporting membership organization. At various times, OCLC
has received grants for specific research and development projects from the
U.S. Office of Education, the Council on Library Resources, Inc., the State
Library of Ohio, and the National Agricultural Library.

OCLC does not issue stock, pay dividends, or share earnings. Although OCLC
is a non-profit corporation, it is a self-sustaining organization. It
derives it operating funds from fees for products and services provided to
its users. Therefore, its income must exceed expenses so that it can finance
expanding services, purchase additional equipment, fund research and
development projects, cover inflationary increases in the cost of replacement
equipment, and meet the obligations of bond issues used to finance capital
equipment requirements.

Online System Use Pricing Structure:

The pricing structure for the Cataloging Subsystem is based on the access
and use of records and location information already in the Online Union

Catalog, rather than on system resources (connect time or computer time) used.

A library is charged for its access and first-time use of a bibliographic record in the database. Charges are lower for libraries that add their holdings to existing records as part of a recognized retrospective conversion project; a credit is given for original cataloging (entering new bibliographic records) and the enhancement of minimal-level records.

Other expenses include dedicated-line or dial-access telecommunications costs and the price of catalog cards, OCLC-MARC tapes, terminals, service fees, and any network charges.

OCLC-related charges for using the Interlibrary Loan, Acquisitions, and Serials Control Subsystems are levied on a per-transaction basis. A credit is given to libraries filling ILL Subsystem requests for materials. Requests for bibliographic and location information from the Online Union Catalog are charged separately. In addition, each serials union list group is charged a small start-up fee. Hardcopy products carry separate charges based on quantity ordered and, in some cases, frequency of receipt. A discount is available to libraries that use both the Cataloging and Acquisitions Subsystems.

In addition to access to OCLC via its dedicated terminals, dial-access to OCLC is available to libraries through CompuServe (a value-added network) or direct dial (via local telephone company). CompuServe bills OCLC for users' dial access on a connect-hour basis; OCLC passes these charges on to regional networks, which then bill the libraries. Libraries using direct dial are billed directly by their phone companies.

Recently, changes have been made to the OCLC pricing structure to more accurately reflect each library's actual system use and resource-sharing contribution. For example, credits for original cataloging and interlibrary lending are given, and searches above a free searching threshold, based on the amount of online transactions performed in all OCLC subsystems during each fiscal year, incur a charge.

Membership:

OCLC users are classified into two types, participants and nonparticipants. A participant is a library that, among other things, does its cataloging online or by tapeload. As General Members of OCLC, they participate in its governance by electing delegates to the Users Council.

Nonparticipants may use one more of the OCLC subsystems, receive OCLC products, and access the Online Union Catalog. Prices and access vary from those of participants. Examples are national libraries, library schools, processing center clients, group access users within the Interlibrary Loan Subsystem, Serials Union List libraries, and partial users.

OCLC currently has over 5,000 active participating libraries. Many kinds of libraries are OCLC members: academic, research, community and/or junior college, corporate, federal, law, library school, medical, municipal and state government, public, school, state, and theological. Directly and indirectly, OCLC serves over 6,700 institutions.

Many libraries outside the United States, including libraries in Australia, Belgium, Canada, China, Denmark, the Federal Republic of Germany, Finland, France, Iceland, Japan, the Netherlands, the Republic of Ireland, Saudi Arabia, Spain, Sweden, Switzerland, Taiwan, the United Kingdom and the Vatican City, use the OCLC Online System.

Participating Libraries* by

Type:	Number:
Academic	1,312
Research	114
Public	909
State	60
State and Municipal Government	106
Processing Centers	129
Law	262
Medical	413
Corporate	498
Theological	120
Federal	541
School	106
Community/Junior College	350
Other	468

*Does not include libraries that participate in union lists or group access projects. (Source: OCLC Annual Report, 1985/86)

OCLC-Affiliated State and Regional Networks:

State and regional networks are organizations that contract to provide OCLC services to OCLC-member libraries. Some of these networks are private, not-for-profit organizations; others are public, state-owned and state-operated. One, FEDLINK, is a network of federal government libraries. Of the twenty networks listed in OCLC's 1985/86 Annual Report, some began their existence in the 1970s as brokers of OCLC's services; others were existing consortia that assumed this role for their members. OCLC owns PACNET (Pacific Network) and OCLC/Europe. These networks may be viewed as OCLC service centers, in that they provide brokerage, support, and training services to member or user libraries. Many networks have diversified their offerings, and now-offer non-OCLC automated services and products as well. Recently, several state and regional network organizations have executed new contracts with OCLC. This is being done on a case-by-case basis. The rest of the networks are in various stages of discussion or contract negotiation with OCLC.

Program Activities, 1986-87*:

Member libraries (includes serials union list participants)	6,738 (6/87)
Dedicated terminals online	7,872 (6/87)
Total bibliographic records in the OCLC Union Catalog	15,173,088 (11/4/87)
Library locations listed in database	258,106,416 (11/4/87)
LS/2000 Local System agreements	95 supporting 173 libraries
LS/2 (formerly DataPhase) sites under maintenance	46 libraries

(Totals for year 1985-86)	
Books and other materials cataloged online	24.6 Million
Custom-printed catalog cards ordered	131 Million
Online interlibrary (ILL) loans transacted	2.7 Million
Cataloging records added to database	1.17 Million
Titles ordered online from publishers	834,826
Catalog records generated for tape subscribers	44.0 Million
Serials holdings modified to reflect receipts	2.04 Million
Online serials union lists (4,537 libraries)	72 Lists

*Source: OCLC Annual Report, 1985/86; and OCLC Services for Libraries: Questions & Answers, Spring/Summer 1987

Current Programs, Products, and Services:

The central online system supports what OCLC calls it major "subsystems" and their associated files: cataloging (online in 1971), serials control (1975), interlibrary loan (1979), and acquisitions (1981). The LC name-authority file is available online, and serials union listing and the name-address directory became generally available in late 1980. The online union catalog, at the core of the central system, grows by about 30,000 bibliographic records weekly. Most of these records are contributed by member libraries cataloging their materials online. The rest are by tape loading records from the Library of Congress, the National Library of Medicine, and the British Library.

When cataloging library materials, OCLC users find, on the average, records online for 94% of the items they search. For the remainder, they must enter new records, using workforms displayed on the terminal screen. Modifications made to the existing online records to reflect local practices and to incorporate local data are not stored in the online union catalog. Therefore, libraries do not have access to their uniquely local catalog records via the OCLC system. If the library has it own machine-readable database, currently OCLC terminals cannot be used to search and maintain that local database. When cataloging online with OCLC to create, derive and/or edit an online record, users have access to the LC name-authority file to aid in the choice and form of name headings. The authority records include established headings, cross references and notes. This online file is not linked to the bibliographic database.

The interlibrary loan (ILL) system supports electronic library-to-library communication over the OCLC telecommunications network. The procedures for creating, transmitting, and filling loan requests (and status tracking) are highly formalized through pre-formatted display screens and automated functions. Bibliographic and local data can be transferred automatically to the online request forms, and users may access the linked name-address directory to discover another library's lending policies. The name-address directory is an online, interactive file that contains listings for thousands of libraries and publishers. ILL users can also search and create loan requests from online serials union lists, and electronically request documents from suppliers like the Center for Research Libraries, University Microfilms International, and the British Library Document Supply Center. OCLC has extended use of the ILL system to non-OCLC libraries if they are part of a cooperative or consortium some of whose members are OCLC libraries. This is called the "Group Access Capability," which permits the members of a local cooperative to interact among themselves for ILL purposes. Non-OCLC members use dial-access terminals to connect to the OCLC ILL system.

OCLC's Serials Union List Component enables members of a union list group to enter and display summary serials holdings efficiently and economically. The component automatically builds union list displays from information in member institutions' local data records, and printed union lists are available in paper, microfiche, and tape versions. The Union Listing Component also provides serial volume holdings information through the Interlibrary Loan Subsystem. Serials Control users can belong to an unlimited number of union list groups and use the displays of any union list group and its members. The serials holdings of nearly 1,500 non-OCLC Union Listing participants are entered into the Union Listing Component by 107 OCLC members called agents.

The Standard Union List Tapeload capability allows union list group members and individual institutions to tapeload serial holdings. This one-time process creates Local Data Records (LDRs), which form the foundation of Online Union Lists. OCLC provides the standard tape format specifications to enable participating and nonparticipating institutions to format their tapes for loading into the OCLC Online Union Catalog.

OCLC offers a variety of offline products and services. These include sets of customized catalog cards (which are requested online), archive tapes in the MARC II communications format, a library's cataloging transactions accumulated over a period of time, and through an agreement with Blackwell North America, print or microform (COM) catalogs, shelflists, indexes, etc.

Recently, OCLC has added a number of microcomputer-based products and services to its offerings. The OCLC network "terminal", the "M300 Workstation", is an IBM Personal Computer (PC) to which OCLC has added special hardware and software features that enable libraries to use the OCLC online system through dedicated-line or dial-access connection. The M300 performs both as an online terminal and as an IBM PC with thousands of programs for general purpose and library applications. More than 5,500 of the over 7,800 OCLC terminals installed are M300 Workstations.

OCLC has developed "Micro Enhancer" packages for use the with online cataloging and ILL systems. The Micro Enhancer packages are microcomputer software programs that provide special features to increase efficiency and ease of use of the OCLC Online System. They support automatic, unattended processing that streamlines library operations while reducing repetitive, time-consuming online activities.

The Interlibrary Loan (ILL) Micro Enhancer package supports interactive access to the Online System, batch updating, and the downloading and printing of records in the message file. The Cataloging Micro Enhancer package supports batch searching with local editing capabilities. Both Micro Enhancer packages are available for use with the M300 Workstation. Over 900 copies of the ILL Micro Enhancer package had been installed through April 1986.

OCLC supplies several additional hardware and software products for microcomputers.

Following the trend toward distributed processing, OCLC has developed microcomputer-based local serials and acquisitions systems. Serials Control 350, a microcomputer-based local serials system, is now available to OCLC members. The SC350 system is a full-function serials control system, facilitating handling of bibliographic control, check-in, claiming, binding, routing, ordering, and fund management. The SC350 system runs on the OCLC M300 Workstation and is linked to the OCLC Online Union Catalog, Name-Address Directory, and state and regional Union Lists.

The ACQ350 Acquisitions Processing System, first made available in early 1987, is a complete microcomputer-based acquisitions system. It will handle all bibliographic formats and order types. Users will be able to upload order information to OCLC for centralized printing and direct transmission of orders to vendors via the DX system.

The OCLC Direct Transmission system (DX) is an electronic order transmission service for vendors and publishers. This service provides for daily transmission of orders via a dedicated communication system. As of May 1986, fifteen vendors receive orders via the DX system, which permits vendors to retrieve a library's purchase orders directly from OCLC computers saving libraries the expense and delays of mailing.

Since 1984, OCLC has marketed the LS/2000 system, a turnkey, integrated local library system. Based on the "ILS" system developed in the late 1970s at the National Library of Medicine's research center, the OCLC-developed and enhanced local system provides circulation control, bibliographic file maintenance and authority control, an online public access catalog, and an administrative subsystem for management reports. Acquisitions and Serials Control are being provided to LS/2000 users through links with the ACQ350 and SC350 systems.

OCLC supports over 95 LS/2000 computer installations serving more than 173 libraries in the United States and the United Kingdom (mid-1987). The system software runs on a full line of Data General and some DEC minicomputers, accommodating libraries of many sizes. A timesharing option is available in Washington, D.C., Dublin, Ohio, and Southern California to meet the needs of libraries for which a minicomputer-based system is not economical. Each LS/2000 installation receives the full-service assistance of OCLC's support staff, which provides libraries conprehensive documentation and support in training, implementation, and ongoing operations. In addition, OCLC now owns and has 46 "LS/2" (a turnkey system formerly owned by the defunct DataPhase Co.) sites under maintenance agreements.

OCLC offers three options for libraries that wish to convert manual catalogs to machine-readable form (retrospective conversion). The library may perform its own conversion using the online system, or contract to have OCLC perform the service according to local requirements.

The OCLC RETROCON Service converts records directly from shelflist or other card files according to customized instructions. OCLC also can enter and edit local information, convert headings into AACR2 or AACR2-compatible form,and enter new records into the Online Union Catalog.

The MICROCON Retrospective Conversion Service, a microcomputer-based alternative that allows libraries to provide much of the labor and thereby lower their costs, is also available. With this new servive, OCLC lends M300 Workstations to members at no charge. Library staff enter search keys and local data onto diskettes, which are then returned to OCLC for transfer to magnetic tape. The tapes are run against the Online Union Catalog for actual conversion of the libraries' records. Nonmembers may also take advantage of this service using their own IBM PC-compatible hardware.

TAPECON, OCLC's newest retrospective conversion service, enables libraries to obtain full OCLC-MARC records for retrospective conversion after reformatting existing tapes according to specifications provided by OCLC.

OCLC currently offers two reference-related services--OCLC EASI Reference and the OCLC Gateway Service. The OCLC Electronic Access to Subject Information (EASI) Reference database, which is made available through BRS Information Technologies, provides subject access to a special subset of the OCLC Online Union Catalog. Approximately one million bibliographic records from the OLUC are retrievable from the OCLC EASI Reference database using BRS/SEARCH. These records have imprint dates spanning the most recent four-year period and represent recently published items in all eight bibliographic formats acquired and cataloged by OCLC participants. The database is updated quarterly.

The OCLC Gateway Service increases access to bibliographic information at a modest charge. Gateway subscribers can access alternately the OCLC Online Union Catalog and all BRS databases from a single terminal using the entire range of searching capabilities of the OCLC Online System and the BRS/SEARCH Service.

OCLC participates in a number of national projects and programs, including CONSER, the Linked Systems Project, the Major Microforms Project, and the United State Newspaper Program.

The CONSER (CONversion of SERials) Project is a cooperative effort undertaking by the library community to build a machine-readable database of quality serials cataloging information. The information may be used for ordering, cataloging, interlibrary lending, check-in, other serials operations, and as a basis for union lists and bibliographies. Institutions participating in CONSER can upgrade the records and add missing information to the OCLC Online Union Catalog in accordance with CONSER bibliographic standards and agreed upon conventions.

The Linked Systems Project (LSP) involves computer-to-computer links between the Library of Congress, the Research Library Information Network, the Western (formerly Washington) Library Network, and OCLC. OCLC has acquired computer hardware for its computer link in the name-authorities phase of LSP, in which OCLC-affiliated NACO (Name-Authority Cooperative) libraries will have online input via the OCLC Online system into the Library of Congress Name-Authority File.

Through the Major Microforms Project, OCLC provides cost-effective cataloging services and products for libraries with large, uncataloged microform sets. Authorized participants enter all cataloging for available major microform sets at no charge using the OCLC Cataloging subsystem. Other institutions can then order cataloging products for these sets at a substantial savings.

The United States Newspaper Program (USNP) is a national program established to organize, preserve, and make available United States newspapers with the assistance of computer automation. Participants enter their bibliographic and holdings records into the OCLC Online Union Catalog and Serials Control Subsystem. Bibliographic records are authenticated by participants and distributed as part of LC's MARC Serial Distribution Service. LC and the National Endowment of the Humanities (NEH) jointly administer the United States Newpaper Program. NEH provides grants management, LC provides technical management, and OCLC, through, CONSER, provides the facilities for the bibliographic phase of the program.

System Environment:

Database

Nearing 16 million bibliographic records, OCLC cataloging users contribute over 80% of the records in the "Online Union Catalog"; the national libraries contribute the remainder.

The percentage of records by type in the database is (May 1987):

84.76% Books
6.17% Serials
2.91% Sound Recordings
2.42% Films (AV)
2.03% Music Scores
1.23% Maps
0.40% Archives and Manuscripts
0.08% Machine-readable data files

The language distribution of those records, by percentage, is:

69.37% English
6.62% German
5.39% French
4.35% Spanish
14.27% Other

The bibliographic database is not partitioned into separate files.

Terminals/Telecommunications

Nearly 5,000 libraries have OCLC terminals. Approximately 2,200 libraries have dial-access terminals, accessing OCLC through CompuServe or direct dial. Some libraries have several terminals, some share terminals with one or more other libraries, and some are customers of processing centers.

Over 7,800 OCLC terminals - including over 5,500 M300 (modified IBM PCs) Workstations - are linked to the online system. Terminals are added at the rate of approximately 100 per month.

Currently, the OCLC terminals, including the M300 Workstations, are linked to the online system via OCLC's proprietary telecommunications network which employs leased lines to support 2400 baud, full-duplex, synchronous, multidrop lines. A new, private, packet-switched telecommunicatons network is being planned to replace the leased-line system.

<u>System Hardware/Configuration</u> (Source: OCLC Services for Libraries: Questions & Answers, Spring/Summer 1987)

The OCLC online system is a unique configuration of several different kinds of computers that are linked by communications equipment to form the aggregate system.

Thirty-five Digital Computer Control Model D-116 minicomputers serve as line concentrators to 327 2400-baud, full-duplex, multidrop synchronous lines and 33 asynchronous lines. These communications are managed functionally through the Distributed Communication Processor (DCP), which consists of two Tandem TXP systms (called DCP01 and DCP02). Both DCP01 and DCP02 are eight-processor systems. The DCPs communicate with multiple (currently 15) Xerox SIGMA 9 computers through an OCLC-developed custom interface device. The SIGMA 9 computers serve as the applications or host processors and are linked to two expandable database systems through the same kind of interface device used for linking the DCPs. The database systems consist of three Tandem TNSII/TXP systems having a total of 41 processors. The bibliographic records in the OCLC Online Union Catalog are stored on 112 Ampex 300-megabyte removable disks and 92 Tecstor 300-megabyte fixed disk drives. One Data General S140 computer system has been installed to support the Linked Systems Project.

OCLC also has a Tandem TNSI six-processor system and two Tandem TNSII/TXP systems (comprising 14 processors) that serve as administrative and development systems and support a facility that simulates the OCLC Online System for testing purposes.

Other systems include three Data General MV/10000 computers supporting financial applications and administrative support functions and two Data General MV/6000 computers supporting the LS/2000 development facility.

Administrative, production, and software development computing needs are served by the Production Data Center. Here, the production environment includes one Sigma 9 computer, one Data General MV/4000, and an IBM 4381. Attached to the IBM production mainframe are a Xerox 8700 laser printer, state-of-the-art IBM 3480 cartridge tape devices, a large disk storage subsystem, and seven IBM 3203 impact printers used to print catalog cards.

<u>New Projects and Developments</u>:

OCLC is currently undertaking a massive modernization of its entire online system. A new private, packet-switched telecommunications system is being installed to enable information in many forms to be transmitted over the OCLC network directly between workstations, computers, and other networks, and will provide service alternatives to leased private lines. Modernization will enable OCLC to exercise greater control over telecommunications and to incorporate the most cost-effective telecommunications and new computer offerings available.

The OCLC publication, "Questions & Answers: New OCLC Online System" (June 1986), provides a detailed overview of OCLC's comprehensive redesign of the online system. This modernization project will replace old computers such as the Xerox Sigma mainframes, with state-of-the-art fault-tolerant computers. Generally speaking, the applications software is being rewritten to run in a UNIX operating system environment. The system redesign aims to take OCLC further down the road of distributed processing, as well as replace outdated equipment. This will enable OCLC to offer more services to a greater number of users worldwide, and to maximize computing resources at local, regional, national, and international levels. Most notably, the redesign will advance OCLC to the status of a full bibliographic retrieval system, with the ability to search by subject and to use Boolean operators in keyword searches. With this development, OCLC will join RLIN, WLN, and UTLAS in supporting conventional keyword and Boolean search methods.

OCLC has been developing and testing CD-ROM compact disc products for both cataloging and reference services. The catloging system will use subsets of the online union catalog stored on compact discs. The system will run on an OCLC M300 Workstation and communicate with the online system to search for additional records, update records, and produce catalog cards, labels, and MARC records. Using the Compact Disc Cataloging System, users will be able to search, udpate, and add records to the Online Union Catalog in both online and batch modes. The package will include a local save file, where users will be able to store records for local manipulation. The Compact Disc Reference Service is a microcomptuer-based reference service that makes use of unique reference databases on compact discs. OCLC's Compact Disc Reference package will run on an OCLC M300 Workstation or IBM PC or PC-compatible hardware with a compact disc reader attached. OCLC will distribute on compact discs a variety of local reference databases created from records in the OCLC Online Union Catalog and other bibliographic sources.

The prototype, compact disc, micrcomputer-based reference workstation has just begun its first field test at Vanderbilt University, providing local access to a database of citations from education-related journals. OCLC, as a turnkey vendor, supports the entire workstation -- hardware, software, and data on compact disc.

OCLC has recently added the capability to support cataloging activities in the Chinese, Japanese, and Korean languages. The CJK350 Program is the OCLC Chinese, Japanese, and Korean language automation program, which is composed of three separate software packages: CJK350 Online Cataloging, CJK350 Card Production, and CJK350 Word Processing. These packages run on the CJK350 Workstation, an enhanced OCLC M300 Workstation that processes CJK vernacular data elements. The CJK350 Program is intended for users abroad as well as in the U.S.

The CJK350 Online Cataloging package interacts with the OCLC Online System and allows users to catalog library materials in the three major East Asian scripts. The CJK350 Card Production package allows users to produce catalog cards at the workstation site via a local printer. And the stand-along CJK350 Word processing package provides editing and file manipulation capabilities in the three languages.

OCLC's research group is exploring a variety of technologies in the areas of full-text retrieval and online browsing of tables of contents, book indexes, and pages of text; electronic rapid delivery of full documents (text and graphics) from local or central storage banks; and mass storage optical media.

OCLC's international initiatives have been discussed in Part I, and are reported on in Appendix A, was well. UK MARC records are now loaded into the OCLC database, and OCLC ILL users now have access to the holdings of the British Library cataloged since January 1984. OCLC is exploring similar arrangements with libraries and agencies in other European countries.

Policy on Data Ownership and Use:

In 1982, OCLC began procedures to copyright the OCLC database. In March 1984, the U.S. Copyright Office registered OCLC's copyright of the OCLC Online Union Catalog as a compilation of data. During the early 1980s, OCLC announced a number of restrictions on the transfer (by tape, downloading, etc.) and use of records "derived" from the online database. In some cases, these restrictions applied even to contributing, member libraries and their OCLC-affiliated regional networks. OCLC libraries and networks claimed ownership of their records in the OCLC database, and others questioned how OCLC could copyright public MARC records supplied to the OCLC database by the national libraries. Nonetheless, OCLC threatened to invoke copyright against any member library or network which violated these restrictions. Some library consortia registered their portion of the database with the Copyright Office, or claimed their records were in the public domain, protected as such by state law, as counter moves to OCLC's copyright action.

After much controversy and discussion in the library community, and, specifically, among OCLC members, networks, and their representatives on the OCLC Users Council, OCLC removed or relaxed most of these restrictions for its member libraries and non-member libraries who use OCLC-derived records for resource sharing purposes (e.g., union catalogs and OPACs) within their local, state, or regional cooperatives and consortia. However, OCLC has stated that projects involving the transfer and use of OCLC-derived records in machine-readable form by the OCLC-affiliated service networks will be dealt with contractually, on a case-by-case basis.

OCLC's current policy, as it is known, is published in "Principles and Guidelines for Transfer of OCLC-Derived Machine-Readable Records, May 13, 1986" (see Appendix A for a related statement). One of the few explicit restrictions remaining has to do with the use of OCLC records by "third party" commercial organizations in profit-making, competitive enterprises. It should be kept in mind that these policies are guidelines only, and that OCLC retains the right to invoke copyright when and where it so decides. OCLC policies for the use and transfer of OCLC-derived records by institutions located in countries outside the U.S. are being formulated as needed on a country-by-country basis, to meet the needs of both OCLC and the agreeing institution or agency.

RLG (Research Libraries Group, Inc.)

Location: Jordan Quadrangle
        Stanford, California 94305, USA
        (415) 328-0920

Organizational Status, Governance, and Funding:

The Research Libraries Group, Inc. is a non-profit corporation owned and operated by its members: major universities and research institutions in the United States. In addition, RLG has many "programmatic members" – institutions that participate in one or more of the corporation's programs. These programs, together with RLG's technical resources, support libraries in meeting their commitments to collect, organize, preserve, and provide the information necessary to education, research, and scholarship.

RLG, a consortium of 36 "owner" members (as of June 1987) that are universities and research institutions rather than libraries, operates an integrated set of cooperative programs to aid members in the areas of collection management and development, shared resources, materials preservation, general bibliographic access and control, and access to and management of specific forms of research information. RLG's automated information system, RLIN (Research Libraries Information Network), combines databases and computer systems to support these these programs. RLIN, a nationwide network, serves both RLG members and non-member institutions, including public, academic, and special libraries.

RLG was established in 1974 by Harvard, Yale, and Columbia Universities and The New York Public Library. One of the objectives in establishing RLG was to create a computer-based bibliographic processing system that would improve efficiency in library operations, link RLG programs, and afford library patrons searching for bibliographic information an increased and more flexible set of access points than is possible in conventional card catalogs.

In 1978, following an investigation of available systems for automated bibliographic control and cooperative technical services, RLG concluded an agreement with Stanford University to acquire BALLOTS, the system developed in the late 1960s and early 1970s for the Stanford libraries. By this agreement, Stanford became a member of RLG as well as the host institution for RLG's central staff and central computer facility. BALLOTS became the technical base for the Research Libraries Information Network (RLIN), RLG's wholly owned automated information system. These changes transformed RLG from a regional association into a national partnership.

Membership:

Full membership and ownership in RLG is restricted to a small number of relatively large university and research institutions. Only 67 would qualify presently for full membership. The criteria for full, associate, and special membership in RLG, effective January 1, 1986, are listed below:

Full, owner membership --
An institution applying for full membership must be a member of the American Association of Universities (AAU) and the institution's library must qualify for membership in the Association of Research Libraries (ARL);
or the institution/library must be a member of the Independent Research Libraries Association (IRLA);
these alterations in criteria do not alter the membership status of current members in good standing.
Associate membership in RLG is extended to libraries belonging to institutions that qualify for full membership but have not joined the consortium.
Special membership is open to institutions/libraries that specialize in one or more of the areas in which RLG has made or is making a particular program commitment; whose collections are genuinely unusual and, therefore, likely to enhance RLG's union database; and that will be likely, by their nature, to find the use of RLG's automated bibliographic information system combined with program activities especially useful or even essential to their operation.

Associate and special memberships allow specialized research institutions such as museums and archival repositories to participate in programs that expand the range of materials under national online bibliographic control. (From the "Responsibilities and Obligations of RLG Membership, " Research Libraries Group, Inc., October 1985.

Governance:

RLG is governed by a Board of Governors composed of one representative from each owner-member institution. Special standing advisory and program committees are composed of appointees from participating institutions and report to the president. As necessary, the Board of Governors or these standing committees create steering committees and subcommittees or task forces.

The Board of Governors is the ownership group of RLG and has ultimate authority for all programs and activities. Each owner-member institution has one vote in the formal governance of RLG. Associate and special members, and libraries affiliated with CLASS (Cooperative Library Agency for Systems and Services), RLG's broker and service network organization, do not have a formal voice in the governance of RLG.

Hundreds of non-RLG academic, public, and special libraries use the RLIN system for searching, cataloging, and ILL functions, providing RLG a significant source of revenue. (Some of these libraries were BALLOTS users before RLG selected it and renamed it RLIN.) Under contract with RLG, CLASS functions as a network coordinator and service center for the non-RLG users of RLIN, much as twenty other state and regional networks do for OCLC. CLASS provides start-up, training, billing, and other support services for these users. CLASS, a California-based organization will be described in the next section.

Funding:

RLG income is based in part on a partnership fee established by the Board of Governors to support programs and management and also in part on fees charged for use of the RLIN database. When a library bases its cataloging on a record in the RLIN database, it pays for the use of that record. If, however, a library contributes a new original cataloging record to the database, there is no charge. In addition to support from consortium members and RLIN users, RLG has received substantial financial support from the following foundations and agencies:

Atlantic Richfield Foundation
Carnegie Corporation of New York
Conoco, Inc.
Council on Library Resources
Exxon Education Foundation
Sherman Fairchild Foundation
Ford Foundation
J. Paul Getty Trust
William and Flora Hewlett Foundation
Lilly Endowment
Andrew W. Mellon Foundation
National Endowment for the Humanities

National Historical Publications and Records

Commission of the National Archives

Pew Memorial Trust

RLG's owner-members have made substantial financial commitments in the form of grants and loans to ensure the organization's survival in difficult times in the past. Approximately 25% of RLG's revenues derive from the non-RLG RLIN users. Also, RLG has a management agreement with Stanford University to host business, personnel, and program activities at that institution; there are approximately ninety staff members on the Stanford campus.

RLIN's fee structure includes charges for transactions, equipment, telecommunications, and offline products, and, thus, is comparable to that of OCLC and its regional networks. Martin (1986) provides a useful comparison of 1985 RLG and selected OCLC-network charges:

Product	AMIGOS	BCR	NELINET	PACNET	PALINET	RLG
Cataloging (per title)	$1.67	$1.85	$1.86	$1.69	$1.47[1]	$2.13
Catalog cards	.056	.062	.061	.067	.0495	.039
ILL create request	1.25	1.30	1.57	1.34	1.10[1]	1.70
forwarded	1.31	1.42	1.64	1.40	1.16	.71
Recon (per title)	1.12	1.15	1.33	1.12	1.15	.70
Tapes (1000/wk)	n/a	105.00	99.72	92.00	92.00	72.60
Terminal	3,590	3,590	3,590	3,590	3,590	1,72?
Maintenance term/month	171.00	43.00	48.58	43.00	43.00	36.00
Communications term/month	183.00	307.00[2]	285.49	192.00	126.50[3]	290.00
Acquisitions	1.24	1.30	1.59	1.10	1.10	1.99
Prepayment discount	9%	2%	varies	10%	5%	8%

[1] Additional monthly service fees for acquisitions, cataloging, ILL.
[2] One terminal only; additional terminals are less expensive.
[3] Does not include data set rental of $225/month for up to 15 terminals.

Source: PALINET.

Program activities, June 1987:

Member (owner) libraries	36
Associate members	12
Special members	39
Special affiliates	3
RLIN users through CLASS	250
Total bibliographic records in the RLIN database (does not include 2 million LC name-authority records)	24.6 million
Records in special databases	332,000 (approx.)

(Totals for year September 1985-August 1986)

Books and other materials cataloged online (includes 723,133 recon titles)	1.79 million
Catalog cards ordered	21.1 million
Online interlibrary loans transacted	120,000 (approx.)
Acquisition records generated	712,947
Technical services maintenance transaction	2.5 million

RLIN does not have a serials control system, and does not market and sell local automated system products. RLG reports having 335 "search-only" accounts on RLIN.

Current Programs, Products, and Services:

RLG now operates four principal programs: Collection Management and Development; Shared Resources; Preservation; and Library Technical Systems and Bibliographic Control. These programs are independent but interrelated; they also may support more specialized programs and task forces that cut across program boundaries.

In addition to the broad programs that address issues of interest to all kinds of research libraries and to the constituencies they serve, RLG has developed several specialized programs in East Asian studies, art and architecture, law, music, medical and health sciences, and archival and special collections.

The Collection Management and Development Program's basic goal is to achieve the broadest possible coverage of relevant materials across the membership while reducing duplicative purchasing costs. To achieve this goal, RLG has supported collection reviews, analyses, and verification studies among its members, and has developed the RLG Online Conspectus to support these activities and goals.

The RLG Conspectus is essentially an inventory instrument that describes members' existing collection strengths and current collecting interests. The Conspectus-Online (it is also a searchable database) enables institutions to communicate information about their collections in common terms, and to make local decisions in light of other members' holdings. It can also be used to relate collection policy to preservation policy.

RLG's special subject-based programs include the Art and Architecture, Archives, and East Asian programs.

RLIN, RLG's automated information system, supports RLG's principal resource sharing programs as well as the technical processing requirements of research libraries.

RLIN is primarily a mechanism for material procurement and processing, catalog or archives management, and reference use. Acquisitions and cataloging are done in machine-readable form at computer terminals, with the information stored in an online database. The system prints catalog cards for libraries that continue to maintain card catalogs and will generate book or microform (COM) catalogs to supplement or replace card catalogs.

Because the central databse accommodates all users' individual records. RLIN is also a mechanism for shared cataloging, interlibrary loan (ILL), and collection management, which reduces participating libraries' operating costs. Libraries cataloging online search the database for records already entered by other institutions or by the Library of Congress and use copies of such records as the basis for their own cataloging rather than entering entire new records; a copied record can be modified in numerous ways to suit local practices or special requirements. The RLIN ILL subsystem allows members to request and send each other cataloged holdings as well as photocopies.

The central RLIN database integrates eight files representing archival materials and manuscripts, books, machine-readable data files, maps, sound recordings, musical scores, serials, and visual materials (films, etc). Other "special" databases for scholarly access include the Avery Index to Architectural Periodicals, an index to art sales catalogs (SCIPIO), and the Eighteenth Century Short Title Catalogue (ESTC).

In summary, the RLIN-based services are:

- Online acquisitions and cataloging in eight material formats
  (including recon),
- Data entry and retrieval in all Roman-alphabet languages and trans-

literations plus Chinese, Japanese, Korean, and Cyrillic characters,
- Cataloging services - cards, work sheets, machine-readable tapes,
- Acquisitions services - order forms, claims, cancellation notices,
  printed by the user or RLG; requestor notices and department reports
  printed by RLG,
- Online access to Library of Congress MARC records and to the users'
  online union catalog, which includes holdings and local data such as
  purchase decisions,
- Public service reference support through flexible searching of the
  entire database,
- Automatic notification of newly entered LC MARC or member data for
  specified titles,
- Ability to pass data retrieved at an RLIN-programmed terminal to one's
  local system through the terminal printer port,
- ILL requests transmitted via the RLG ILL subsystem in RLIN,
- Membership collection strengths and collecting policies available
  in the RLG Conspectus-Online,
- Creation and searching of special databases such as the Avery Index,
  ESTC, and SCIPIO.

System Environment:
Database

The central RLIN database is divided into eight files:

Books	21.3 million records
Serials	2.2 million
Visual materials	102,000
Maps	116,000
Sound recordings and scores	500,000
Archives and manuscripts	97,700
Machine-readable data files	3,300

Other files are:

Avery Index	42,000
ESTC	188,600
SCIPIO	73,000
LC name-authority	2.5 million

(May 1987. Source: Jennifer Hartzell, RLG)

Because records in the central database combine bibliographic, acquisitions, and holdings data, an item can be ordered, received, and cataloged all in the same record. Unlike in OCLC, a library's data, with any local modifications, always remains accessible as a part of the RLIN record.

RLIN offers both keyword/Boolean and phrase (heading) access to records through 22 general and local indexes as well as 18 character and exact character indexes to CJK (Chinese, Japanese, and Korean) materials.

Terminals/Telecommunications

As of October 1986, 1031 RLIN terminals provided access to the central system via a dedicated, synchronous telecommunications network. The network, which links the RLIN terminals with five PDP-11/60 front-end processors at RLIN's Network Control Center in Palo Alto, California, is a 2400 baud, polled, multi-point, leased line network.

The customized RLIN terminal, the RLG84, is an intelligent, programmable terminal built to RLG's specifications by the Zentec Corporation. It supports the ALA character set and RLIN's polled, link level communications protocols. The terminal also supports full-screen editing and formatting functions, and may also be used as a basic asynchronous terminal for general-purpose communication with other systems. Transtech International has developed RLG's terminals that support the Asian languages (CJK). Software has also been developed to permit standard IBM PC microcomputers to emulate RLIN Zentec terminals. The success of this software led to the decision late in 1986 to discontinue production of the Zentec RLIN terminals in favor of personal computers. The RLIN database can also be accessed using "dumb", asynchronous terminals with modems via the Telenet packet-switched network, or by dialing-in directly.

System Hardware/Configuration

The central host hardware configuration located at Stanford University consists primarily of these components:

- A dedicated Amdahl 5890 mainframe computer (32 channels & 80MB memory with the basic operating system, IBM's MVS/XA 3.8,
- Two STC 4305 2x6 solid state paging devices including controllers (12 logical devices, 168MB), using 3380 image mode,
- 24 IBM 3380 disk storage modules and controllers; 9 Amdahl 6380 disk drives and controllers; and 4 National Advanced Systems 7380 disk drives and controller,
- 4 IBM 3420 tape drives,
- 3 IBM 3480 cartridge tape drives,

- Communications between terminals and the RLIN system controlled and
  facilitated by five PDP 11/60 minicomputers and related communications
  equipment (e.g., modems, multiplexors, lines, etc.),
- Additional PDP 11/series computers supporting development and the
  Linked Systems Project,
- One IBM 1403 impact printer for product printing,
- One Xerox 9700 xerographic printer,
- Use of the University's IBM 3800 laser printer.

(From "A Technical Overview of RLIN", 11 April 1986. RLG)

New Developments and Products:

RLG is planning to evolve RLIN's centralized, star network into a
distributed network. The former central facility would be primarily a data
resource node on the new network. Microcomputer software is being developed
to permit the transfer of some central processing functions to the local
microcomputer-based workstation.

Development is also underway to establish links with university local area
networks and their libraries' local systems. A test link has been established
with the GEAC system at New York University. RLG, along with OCLC, WLN, and
LC, participates in the ISO/OSI-based Linked Systems Project (LSP), and has
successfully tested a computer-to-computer link with the Library of Congress'
system to exchange authorities records. Using the new LC-RLIN link, 1986 was
the first full year throughout which the Library of Congress routinely used
the LSP protocols to send its authority records to RLG online. An average of
2,000 authority records were added to the RLIN database each week. The time
for such records to appear for RLIN users was reduced by several weeks.

RLG is well underway with its plans to purchase and install a private,
packet-switched data communications network to replace its existing leased-
line, synchronous telecommunications network. The vendor selected was
NCR/Comten. Installation began in mid-1987, with completion projected for mid-
1988. The new network will support intersystem communications between many
different local systems and RLIN.

Additional "special" databases are likely to be added to the RLIN database,
and support for additional non-Roman alphabets, such as Hebrew, is under
development. In May 1987, RLG announced the new ability to catalog and search
RLIN in Cyrillic, specifically in the modern alphabets of the Russian,
Belorussian, Bulgarian, Macedonian, Serbian, and Ukrainian languages. This
capability requires the IBM PC RLIN terminal. (The Research Libraries Group
News, Issue No. 13, May 1987)

Policy on Data Ownership and Use:

The machine-readable bibliographic records of the RLIN databases are co-owned by RLG and the institutions which have created them whether through original or copy cataloging activity. RLG places no restrictions whatever on the use which the creating institution may wish to make of its own records.

Conversely, the consortium may use the records to serve its purposes, which include exchanging record sets with others for mutual benefit and providing reasonable means of access to others who are not members. The consortium elects not to distribute subsets of records which would compromise primarily the holdings of an individual member (or other RLIN cataloging institution) unless so directed by that institution. It reviews requests for subsets of records with individual institutions which may have a substantial stake in the subset before a decision to share them is made. No individual institution's advice on how to respond to such a request has ever been ignored.

WLN (Western Library Network)

Location: Washington State Library
         Mail Stop AJ-11
         Olympia, Washington 98504, USA
         (206) 459-6518

Organizational Status, Governance, and Funding:

WLN is a multiservice, regional bibliographic network and database, and the smallest of the bibliographic utilities. WLN is an agency of state government, created in the early 1970s by the legislature of the state of Washington. Created as the "Washington Library Network" to serve libraries within the state, over the years it expanded its services and network to surrounding states in the Pacific Northwest of the U.S. WLN also has member libraries in British Columbia, Canada. Nonetheless, WLN still functions as a division of the Washington State Library. A review of its governance in 1985 led to the change in its name to the Western Library Network and somewhat more independence in its operations.

Governance:

With a staff administered on a daily basis by the Executive Director of WLN, the organization is overseen by the Washington State Library Commission (WSLC), a lay group appointed by the governor of Washington. The Commission is advised by WLN's Computer Service Council, a user council composed of delegates from the various states within WLN's regional service area. The chief executive officer of WLN is the State Librarian who is appointed by the WSLC. The executive director of WLN reports to the State Librarian. In late 1987, a formal review of WLN's status and governance was underway which could lead to greater autonomy and separation of WLN from the State Library Commission.

Membership:

WLN serves all types and sizes of libraries, but recognizes three types of member: principal, associate, and "cluster" members. Principal members are primary, direct users of the WLN online system who contribute their cataloging and holdings data to the WLN database. Associate members are libraries that contract with principal members to acquire specified WLN

Computer Service services for charges agreed upon between the principal and associate member, and approved by the Commission. A cluster member is a library that contracts with a principal member to use WLN records which reside on the principal member's local system. The cluster member must participate in the same local system used by the member. WLN sets the fee for the use of WLN records by cluster members. WLN also serves "search-only participants" and "recon-only participants."

Funding:

WLN staff are employees of the Washington State Library. WLN revenues are derived from a complex fee structure for its services and products. Fees are charged for a variety of online system transactions and command usage in the cataloging, acquisitions and ILL "subsystems." Charges are also incurred by members for telecommunications and WLN equipment purchases (modems and terminals), installation, and maintenance. WLN also sells offline products, including catalog cards, label sets, COM catalogs (to members) and magnetic tapes of records in the MARC communications format. WLN staff provide, for a fee, full MARC cataloging services for libraries who choose to contract with an outside frim for current cataloging services. Retrospective conversion services are also available. WLN also licenses its entire software package to interested parties. Libraries will be charged a flat, annual subscription fee for WLN's new CD-ROM cataloging product.

Program activities, as of September 30, 1986:

Principal and associate members	159
Search-only participants	79
Recon-only participants	116
WLN terminals	265+
Total records in bibliographic file	4.25 million
Total records in authority file	4.75 million
Titles with holdings	2.03 million
Holdings statements	9.98 million
Acquisitions in-process file records	131,646

Records are added to the database
at the rate of :

MARC CATALOGING:
- 28,000 books/month
- 14,000 serials/month
- 200 films/month
- 2,500 Canadian books/month
- 1,600 GPO books/month
- (GPO= U.S. Government Printing Office)
- 700 music/month

LOCAL CATALOGING
- 11,000 records/month reviewed by WLN central staff.

Current Programs, Products, and Services:

WLN offers the traditional services of an online bibliographic utility: shared cataloging (under complete authority control), catalog maintenance by WLN staff, batch and online recon, reference searching capabilities, acquisitions control with links to vendor and publisher directories, and interlibrary loan.

In addition, WLN offers a variety of special services and products for libraries. Offline products include printed catalog cards and bibliographies, magnetic tapes of members' cataloging records in the MARC format, and tape processing to put bibliographic records into the MARC format. WLN's "Cataloging/Inputting Service" provides MARC cataloging process and input services for individual libraries. A recent service for member libraries is Micro-Recon software for IBM PC microcomputers. Libraries create search keys for their catalog records that can be matched against the central database in a batch process. For libraries that cannot afford online services, WLN offers a microfiche union listing of all records in the database which contain holdings information.

WLN has always taken pride in the quality of the bibliographic records in its database. A central staff is employed to perform quality control. Records contributed by members are reviewed by WLN staff (unique among the four utilities), and the entire bibliographic file is maintained under strict authority control. The authority file containing all authorized name and subject headings used in WLN records and their associated cross references is linked online to the bibliogrpahic file. UTLAS is the only other utility which supports this capability. The excellent centralized database maintenance capabilities has made the WLN software very attractive to national libraries in other countries.

WLN has completely converted its terminal population to IBM PC microcomputers which may be used for multiple purposes in members' libraries, offline, as well as online to WLN. WLN offers microcomputing consulting services, and plans to offer software products in the future.

System Environment:
Database

The WLN database contains records in both U.S. MARC and Canadian MARC bibliographic formats. The complex database structure includes fully linked bibliographic and authority files.

Terminals/Telecommunications

WLN's polled network is based on dedicated multi-drop leased lines, over which access is provided to the central computer. The WLN PC terminals support WLN'S synchronous communications protocols and the ALA character set. The network can also be accessed by IBM 3270 terminals, and general-purpose inquiry terminals via Telenet or direct dialing. However, the dedicated lines are needed for catalging online. Front-end processors manage access to the central computer by dedicated network, Telenet, and dial-access users.

System Hardware

The WLN central computer is an AMDAHL 470/V8 mainframe, with 16 megabytes and sixteen channels. It operates under OS MVS/SP 1.3.5, and uses the ADABAS (4.1) database management system to manage the database files.

New Developments and Projects:

WLN has been a participant along with RLG and LC in the national Linked Systems Project (LSP) since its inception. Development staff have made major contributions to the successful completion of the Standard Network Interconnection (SNI) facility for linking differenct computer systems. WLN has implemented the SNI phase (data communications protocols) of the LSP project, but has postponed further work on the authorities function until after 1987.

Development continues on the ILL subsystem, and the recent addition of the capability to provide full-screen data transmission via regular dial-access lines facilitates dial-up use of the WLN ILL subsystem.

With financial support from the Fred Meyer Charitable Trust Fund's LIRN (Library and Information Resources for the Northwest) program, WLN recently undertook a major development project to produce a CD-ROM local cataloging system called LaserCat. Introduced early in 1987, LaserCat includes three compact discs containing recent LC MARC records and all WLN records having member libraries holdings (about 2 million records). The package runs on an IBM PC (or WLN PC) as a stand-alone system, but can be linked to the central WLN system for searching and downloading bibliographic records, and for uploading holdings data. LaserCat users will also be able to print catalog cards, book labels, and bibliographies. WLN now offers LaserCat to both members and non-members on a fixed-cost, annual subscription basis ($900.00 for one copy). The subscription will include the retrieval and support software plus quarterly cumulative updates to the data discs.

Policy on Data Ownership and Use:

The WLN bibliographic database is owned by the Washington State Library Commission. The Commission accords certain rights in the use of records from the database to WLN member libraries. Member libraires may use copies of records from the database which have their holdings data attached in local systems. But if non-members belong to the local system, the "Cluster Membership Policy" applies. Non-members must pay WLN a fee for each record used in the local system. Generally speaking, WLN members may not sell records obtained from the WLN database, or independently profit from their use (this does not apply to a members original cataloging). Members may provide their WLN- derived records to vendors only for non-profit resource sharing purposes, or to obtain products or services (e.g. COM catalogs) from that vendor. WLN wishes to prevent the accumulation of its records by a vendor to be used for the vendor's own interest. However, WLN has established a liberal "data sharing" policy with RLG and other not-for-profit networks.

UTLAS (Utlas International Canada)

Location: 80 Bloor Street West
            Toronto, Ontario M5S 2V1, Canada
            (416) 923-0890

Organizational Status, Governance, and Funding:

UTLAS is a computer-based service organization for libraries and the information industry. As a bibliographic utility, UTLAS maintains a large online bibliographic database and operates a centralized online system accessible throughout the world. Based in Toronto, UTLAS is a wholly-owned subsidiary of International Thomson Organisation, Limited (ITOL). Early in 1985, ITOL purchased UTLAS, Inc. from the University of Toronto, where UTLAS came into being in 1971 as the "University of Toronto Library Automation System." The UTLAS network is the result of two decades of research and development at the University of Toronto.

UTLAS can trace its origins back to 1963 when the University of Toronto Library set out to explore the potential of the computer in library operations. From 1965 to 1967, the Library participated in a research project using computers to prepare and publish a catalog in book form of the initial collections of five new institutions of higher education. This project was called the Ontario New Universities Library Project (ONULPO).

In 1967, a separate Systems Department was established within the University Library, and a dedicated computer facility was procured. Already underway was a massive project to convert most of the Library's catalog to machine-readable form, an undertaking that was completed in 1975.

The Systems Department was charged with developing automated systems for the library community in general - and not solely for the University Library. This mandate was made easier by the reorganization of the Department in 1971 into a separate administrative unit named UTLAS. Two years later, in September 1973, the online Catalogue Support System (CATSS) was inaugurated; it remains at the heart of all of UTLAS' systems. Network organization efforts paralleled system development efforts. Initial external users included several public libraries in Ontario and a consortium of eight Ontario and Quebec university libraries.

With growth came significant changes in UTLAS' organizational status. In 1977, it became an ancillary enterprise of the University, reporting to the

Chief Librarian. Two years later, a reorganization took place whereby it began reporting to the Vice-President, Business Affairs, and received its own Board of Directors.

In 1983, UTLAS was incorporated as a company under the laws of the Province of Ontario. This new status reflected the University's recognition that UTLAS Inc. had evolved from a small research project into a true commercial enterprise.

Until 1980, UTLAS restricted its services to Canada. In the early 1980s, UTLAS began to expand its network services to libraries in the U.S. and Japan. In January 1985, a redesigned version of the online cataloging system (CATSS II) was implemented. Maruzen, a Japanese library publications and information retrieval services firm, became in Tokyo the first user of CATSS II. UTLAS has appointed the Maruzen Company Limited as the distributor of its products and services in Japan.

UTLAS' goal is to automate "the whole spectrum of library services," which includes continued operation of the network and the central online system, plus the offering of mini- and microcomputer-based local, distributed systems and services. This goal places it closer to OCLC than RLG or WLN, and explains several recent acquisitions and agreements with other organizations.

In May 1985, an agreement was executed giving UTLAS exclusive rights to Data Phase's ALIS III local system software. ALIS III was renamed T/Series 50. The T/Series 50 system runs on Tandem computer equipment, giving UTLAS a large, powerful, turnkey multi-function library system. In June 1985, UTLAS integrated Carrollton Press' REMARC database (representing LC pre-MARC cataloging) into its line of products and services. UTLAS entered the microcomputer area with its development of an IBM PC-based OPAC, named M/Series 10. The PC-based OPAC, designed for small libraries includes full authority control with cross references, and can be coupled with a circulation module.

To supplement its online acquisitions system, ACCORD, which supports book ordering, UTLAS recently acquired the marketing rights in Canada and parts of the U.S. to Innovative Interfaces' INNOVACQ microcomputer-based acquisitions system. This system includes fund accounting and management reports modules, and may be interfaced with the central ACCORD and CATSS systems.

Reflecting its expansion into the U.S. (and perhaps a desire to compete more aggressively with OCLC), in 1986 UTLAS International U.S., Inc. maintained five offices across the U.S. The U.S. headquarters were located in Arlington, Virginia. Other offices were located in California, Kansas, and Missouri. Recently UTLAS has contracted directly with two large OCLC regional network service centers, AMIGOS (southwest) and SOLINET (southeast), to provide authority control services to their members (OCLC libraries) at discounted prices. The agreement with AMIGOS also provides UTLAS' Canadian customers access to the AMIGOS Collection Analysis Service. Provided the leadership and resources of ITOL, UTLAS is rapidly expanding its services and markets to "remain an international leader in the field of computer-based library services." However, in mid-1987, reports circulated that ITOL was seeking a new buyer for UTLAS.

Funding:

UTLAS, a division of International Thomson Org. Ltd., is a private sector, for-profit business enterprise. Although complete financial information is not available, almost certainly most of UTLAS' revenues must be derived from the selling of its online database services and related products. It is unlikely that UTLAS has recovered its recent investments in the purchase and development of local automated systems and products. UTLAS has a complex fee structure applied in the use of its centralized online cataloging, acquisitions, and ILL modules. For example, users incur a per terminal network access fee which covers connect time, communications, and related charges. Fees are assessed for either full time terminal use (monthly) or part-time use (an hourly rate). Although there is no membership fee (as with OCLC), a one-time charge is levied for training and catalog system (CATSS II) profiling. Fees are also charged for card, label, and magnetic tape profiling, as well as costs for these products themselves. Online system-use transaction charges are "unbundled" and vary. The user is charged for individual search and display commands, as well as for record creation and update. UTLAS offers a rebate for original cataloging contributed to the database. Uses of special features like authority records incur separate charges. Users access the UTLAS central system with any general-purpose asynchronous terminal, including microcomputers with terminal emulation software. Users assume their own costs for purchasing and maintaing these terminals.

Program Activities, June 1987:

UTLAS' customer base is made up of libraries of all types and sizes. Over 500 institutions, members of consortia, and government agencies, representing over 2,000 libraries, maintain user-owned databases through UTLAS' facilities. The large majority of cataloging done in Canada is supported by UTLAS. More than 70% of the research and university libraries in Canada, including most of the major universities, belong to the user network. Libraries of this type constitute more than 31% of the customer base. Nearly 38% are special libraries, and more than 12% come from the public library sector. Over 7% are schools of library science. Commercial customers, such as book suppliers, represent almost 7%; national libraries, slightly over 1%; and school boards, over 3%.

UTLAS' database contains over 40 million records in various MARC, REMARC, authority and other bibliographic files. The estimated number of unique bibliographic records in the database is 12.5 million. The database comprises files from the Library of Congress, National Libraries of Canada, Britain, and France, the U.S. Government Printing Office (GPO), the REMARC file, and the files of its customer libraries. Each library's database is contained in the central database; this largely accounts for the large number of duplicate records.

Current Programs, Products, and Services:

UTLAS offers online cataloging, book ordering (with electronic transmission to cooperating vendors), ILL and electronic mail, batch and online authority control, in-house or micro-based recon ("ReQuest") and the usual array of cataloging products, such as card sets, book labels (printed while online), and COM catalogs. CATSS II supports cataloging in English, French, and Japanese. Reference access is supported by a separate information retrieval module with a variety of display formats.

A major advantage of the UTLAS database is that it retains all unique contributions of its client libraries and national library MARC files. This permits a library a broad choice of records for copy cataloging, ranging from records with specialized subject vocabulary (e.g. MESH), to records from libraries which have modified LC subject headings or added their own. UTLAS also maintains the French language version of the LC subject headings. Unlike OCLC libraries, UTLAS' clients always have online access to copies of their records for editing and updating purposes. A customer's file cannot be altered in any way by another user.

Mention has already been made of UTLAS' local system automated products: M/Series 10, a micro-based OPAC and circulation system for small libraries with collections up to 25,000 titles; T/Series 50, a Tandem nonstop computer-based local circulation system with an OPAC for large libraries; and the INNOVACQ micro-based acquisitions system. The T/Series 100 product has been announced recently. It consists of the local system product linked to the central UTLAS online cataloging system. UTLAS is one of only two vendors in North America which offer local system database upgrades to full MARC standards under full authority control for names, series, uniform titles, and subjects (Blackwell North America is the other). Libraries send their magnetic tapes to UTLAS for this upgrade service.

System Environment:
Database

UTLAS' file structure provides each library its own file of catalog records created by copy or original cataloging. Thus, the library always has access to its own version of a record containing its unique local modifications and local data. Copies of a library's records may be used by another library, but only the owning library can alter records in its file. Unique holdings codes are assigned to bibliographic records in the database, reflecting the libraries which have used a record for cataloging purposes. National libraries constitute the other primary source of bibliographic and authority records in the database. The following represents the approximate size of UTLAS database source files as of April 1987:

Bibliographic Source Files Distributed By The Library of Congress

File	No. of records
LC Books	2,261,828
LC Serials	367,527
LC Maps	104,183
LC Music Scores	17,442
LC Visual Materials (e.g., film)	76,632
LC Minimal Level Cataloging	164,774
COMARC (discontinued contributed MARC)	35,779
COBRA (Art and Art Catalogs)	2,563
U.S. Government Printing Office (GPO)	242,804
TOTAL LC:	3,273,532
REMARC TOTAL:	4,600,000

Other Bibliographic Source Files

CAN/MARC Books	259,503
CAN/MARC Music	3,421
CAN/MARC Serials (CONSER records)	409,053
National Library of Medicine Books and Serials	662,794
UK MARC (British Library)	451,264
Inter MARC (France)	85,903
MARC Quebecois (BNQ)	69,649
CIHM (historical microreproductions)	27,790
Centrale des bibliotheques	199,999
TOTAL OTHER:	2,169,376
TOTAL BIBLIOGRAPHIC SOURCE FILES:	10,042,908

Authority Source Files

LC Names	1,812,762
LC Subjects	189,894
CAN/MARC Names (English)	216,604
CAN/MARC Names (French)	225,379
RVM (French)	70,542
SHARAF (Customer contributed)	412,340
TOTAL AUTHORITY RECORDS:	2,927,521

TOTAL DATABASE SIZE: 40,000,000, exclusive of REMARC

ESTIMATED NUMBER OF UNIQUE BIBLIOGRAPHIC RECORDS: 13,000,000

Terminals/Telecommunications

Use of UTLAS does not require a dedicated terminal, and UTLAS does not sell terminals. Any general purpose asynchronous terminal with a 1200 baud modem can be used to access the central system. UTLAS does provide software permitting access and enhanced cataloging (full-screen, cursor-controlled editing mode) on an IBM PC microcomputer owned by the user.

Customers are provided network access to the central system in one of five ways, depending on the location of their library. Canadian customers in Toronto dial-in directly. Customers in other high usage areas use UTLAS' own packet-switching network. Other remote Canadian customers use Canada's public data network, DATAPAC. U.S. customers use Telenet, and satellite telecommunications provide access to customers in Japan.

Hardware

The central UTLAS computer facility consists of a configuration of Tandem computers and equipment.

New Developments and Projects:

Most of UTLAS' product expansion and diversification has taken place in the past two years. The company has made a major commitment to using Tandem equipment, both as a basis for the central computer facilities (the CATSS II conversion to Tandem was completed in January 1985) and the T/Series 50 local library system product. This decision provides UTLAS a great deal of flexibility for distributed processing scenarios and the linking of its central and local systems, represented by the new T/Series 100 product. A Tandem-based network node has been installed in Kansas City in the U.S. Some processing formerly done in Toronto (or that would have been for U.S. customers) will be distributed to the new node, and some files are likely to be stored there as well. This could be a model for future international expansion of the UTLAS network.

UTLAS has demonstrated an optical disc-based retrospective conversion service, and early in 1987 introduced a CD-ROM, microcomputer version called "M/100 with DisCon". DisCon consists of four CD-ROM discs of 1.8 million MARC and 4.2 million REMARC records mounted simultaneously in four CD-ROM players connected to an IBM PC computer.

Policy on Data Ownership and Use:

UTLAS claims no copyright to records in its database, or to entire files, including REMARC.

Customers own the records they create through UTLAS' facilities. The records may be loaded for the customer's use into other automated systems which the customer may own or license, or to which it subscribes.

Each UTLAS customer creates its own database of bibliographic records by copying records from other databases which UTLAS provides. Customers may also key records directly into their database , or arrange to have them loaded via magnetic tape.

Customers may at any time request an up-to-date copy of their database on magnetic tape in one of several commonly used versions of the MARC Communications Format. Where online interfaces to local systems exist, the customer's own records may be downloaded online.

2. Automated Cataloging and Networking Support: Extensions and Alternatives
   to the Bibliographic Utilities

A. Regional and State Library Networks

<u>Origins and evolution</u>

In the beginning there was OCLC (then, the "Ohio College Library Center");
and for all practical purposes, OCLC created the phenomenon of regional
networks. OCLC's online service began in 1971 as a shared cataloging utility
for the 54 academic institutions that were the original members of OCLC. When
libraries outside the original consortium, including libraries in other
states, wanted to join the computer network and benefit from its online
cataloging services (and order catalog cards from OCLC), OCLC did not have
the resources to provide them direct support and training. These libraries
were encouraged to "cluster" into regional-area groups (not pre-defined in
most cases) or to use existing cooperatives or agencies to represent them.
Therefore, OCLC could deal with a few intermediate organizations, each
representing many libraries which comprised the "regional" networks'
memberships. OCLC regional networks sprouted quickly, if haphazardly, in the
1970s, to serve almost solely as service intermediaries between OCLC and
libraries throughout the U.S.

Regional networks are a fuzzy phenomenon. There are many kinds. Some are
voluntary, private organizations created by librarians, and include libraries
from several states in a region. Others are state-owned and state-operated;
that is, they are public agencies or divisions of state government. Thus,
the notion of "regional networks" includes <u>state</u> networks. In summary,
regional networks are formal, membership cooperatives, which provide computer-
based library and resource-sharing services to their members by contracting
with another organization such as OCLC.

Most of the regional networks have never owned or operated their own computer facilities, thus, they do not offer primary database services to their members. OCLC terminals in libraries have connected, generally speaking (OCLC-Europe is an exception), directly to the OCLC central system via OCLC's physical, dedicated telecommunications network, and not through nodes at the state or regional network offices. The latter have existed primarily to offer local training and support for OCLC's centralized services.

In their short history, the regional networks have become an endangered species. There are two reasons for this. First, OCLC is changing its stance toward the regionals as its needs, abilities, and products change in an era of distributed processing and local systems. Contract renewal negotiations have been bitter and controversial in the early and mid-1980s. OCLC failed in its attempt to redefine the regional networks as marketing agents of OCLC, and thus, as part of the corporation itself. Some public, state networks were restricted by law from assuming this new role. Others fiercely defended their organizational independence as local or regional membership organizations, closer to their libraries than to OCLC. OCLC's copyright of the online union catalog also muddied the waters. Most of the networks and their member libraries believe they are co-owners of the database. This has caused a great deal of dispute, and at least one "OCLC network" (AMIGOS) has also applied for copyright co-ownership of the database. In another case, the state of Wisconsin has countered with an official ruling that the OCLC data is in the public domain, not owned by OCLC. These disputes, and recent network contract negotiations, are redefining the relationship between OCLC and its networks.

Second, with the explosion of new automated systems and services available from the commercial sector, libraries no longer have to turn to the regional networks for "one-stop shopping" and support. Vendors and new local and state-level groups are joining to support resource sharing through the linking of local circulation systems and OPACs. Other vendors are supplying cataloging and ILL products and services. Regional networks, whose existence has been tied to OCLC central services, are in danger of becoming superfluous in the changing environment.

OCLC has already announced the removal of its serials and acquisitions services (from which networks gain revenue) from the central system. Micro-based systems are replacing them, and just recently, all microcomputer products and services at OCLC have been placed within the organizational domain of the Local Systems Division. This is the OCLC group which, as a turnkey system vendor that deals directly with client libraries, markets and supports the OCLC local library system, LS/2000. The development of OCLC beyond its early role as a remote bibliographic utility to that of a direct vendor of local systems and products to libraries will continue to have a major impact on the regional networks. Some will fare better than others.

Most regional networks offer additional services to their member libraries; services not offered by OCLC, and services that compete with OCLC's. Two networks, SOLINET and AMIGOS (both large, multi-state networks) operate their own computer facilities. Their non-OCLC services include: the provision of discount contracts and training for online database search services (e.g., DIALOG, BRS), microcomputer consultancy and training, the management of members' OCLC archive tapes, authority control services for local databases, and the production and maintenance of union lists, COM catalogs, and the network's own regional union catalog. However, regional network organizations will increasingly experience assaults on and threats to their survival, not only from OCLC in its attempts to wean them (now that it can't absorb them), but from the commercial sector which offers automated products and services to libraries that compete with both the regional networks and the utilities.

The public, state agency-based "OCLC" networks are in a stronger position than the private cooperatives. Already the state library agencies are looking inward, planning linkages of local circulation systems and OPACs, or online, statewide union catalogs. Some are planning optical disc-based union catalogs as well. In short, local libraries and state agencies look to OCLC, if at all, as a data resource bank. Libraries are joining in new "clusters" and cooperative arrangements to exploit new, cheaper technologies at the local and state level. The locus of initiative and control in the use and management of computer resources is shifting away from the traditional OCLC regional networks. Some of these networks are aligning themselves with commercial vendors -- even another utility -- placing themselves in direct competition with OCLC. Clearly, an era of OCLC-defined cooperative, computer-based networking has come to an end. It lasted about fifteen years.

The new environment: case studies
ILLINET

The Illinois Library and Information Network (ILLINET), a long-time OCLC broker and service center, is an agency of the state of Illinois, headquartered at the Illinois State Library. About 300 of the 2,500 libraries in the state are members of ILLINET, receiving OCLC services.

ILLINET also coordinates other cooperative programs within the state. Many communities share the same or linked minicomputer-based circulation systems. The University of Illinois' online library system (LCS) supports resource sharing among 27 academic institutions across the state. LCS terminals at these locations provide access to their combined bibliographic and holdings data, and support borrowing and interloan activities (Sloan, 1984).

In recent contract negotiations, ILLINET redefined its role as a service center in relation to OCLC. It will not serve as a marketing agent for OCLC's "local" library products, and it will not offer many of OCLC's new products. ILLINET will coordinate the development of an OCLC-derived statewide online union catalog which will reside on the University of Illinois' online system. This mainframe-based system has been enhanced with the linking of the LCS circulation system to the WLN software to provide better database maintenance facilities and improved online catalog searching. This LCS-WLN union catalog will give the state of Illinois a powerful, online resource sharing facility. The online union catalog will include the bibliographic and holdings information for hundreds of libraries of all types in the state. Each year tens of thousands ILL transactions are conducted on the LCS statewide system. Illinois state plans include a CD-ROM version of the new union catalog, to eliminate some in-state telecommunications costs now required to access the LCS-WLN computer system (Clark, 1986). OCLC will serve primarily as a supplier of bibliographic records.

INCOLSA

The Indiana Cooperative Library Services Authority (INCOLSA) was established by a joint agreement of the governing library authorities in the state of Indiana. As a traditional OCLC network, INCOLSA brokers and supports all of OCLC's online services. Indiana libraries receive help with installation of OCLC equipment, training, and ongoing support. The Indiana union list of serials is provided by the OCLC online system. INCOLSA offers a number of non-OCLC services. Group discounts and training are offered through INCOLSA to DIALOG, BRS, and the SDC ORBIT online database search services, and electronic mail is brokered to libraries through several vendors. INCOLSA operates a processing center to provide cataloging and book processing for all types of libraries.

INCOLSA has taken on a new role in coordinating the selection and purchase of turnkey circulation systems for single libraries or clusters of libraries in the state. One aim is to provide group discounts for system purchases. Another aim of this state network agency is to control and manage the eventual linking of local systems throughout the state. At this time, INCOLSA's vendor of choice to supply local automated circulation and OPAC systems, is GEAC, not OCLC.

AMIGOS

The AMIGOS Bibliographic Council originated in 1974 when 22 institutions in Texas and New Mexico joined to contract for access to the OCLC online system. Over the years, AMIGOS became an independent corporation and grew to include almost 300 libraries in the southwest U.S. and Central America. Through the years, AMIGOS has been a full-service OCLC broker and regional support center, but has supplemented these services with additional offerings stemming from its own computer facilities. One of the first services offered was maintenance of its members' OCLC archive tapes (which contain the library's catalog records created from using the OCLC cataloging system). AMIGOS has built a regional database ("SHARES") from these tapes, which is used to provide its own recon services, bypassing the OCLC database unless a match cannot be found in the regional database. From this database and facility, AMIGOS provides customized tape and database services for local libraries, including the conversion of OCLC records to formats required by other vendors' local systems, such as CLSI, DataPhase, NOTIS, and Data Research Associates (DRA). These tape processing and recon services, used even by libraries outside the region, have recently been enhanced by an agreement reached between AMIGOS and UTLAS. AMIGOS and its libraries gain UTLAS' authority control and maintenance services, and UTLAS gains recon and tape processing services for its local system customers. (There is more to the formal agreement.)

AMIGOS has strongly and publicly opposed OCLC's claim of copyright to its database. Fearing future action by OCLC that might restrict the use of records in its regional database, in 1985 AMIGOS' Board of Directors filed a claim of co-ownership with the U.S. Copyright Office. AMIGOS' relationship with OCLC is under review by both parties with the major issues still to be resolved. OCLC may sever all contractual relationships with AMIGOS, if the latter refuses to drop its claim to co-ownership of the database.

SOLINET

Another large OCLC regional network, SOLINET (Southeastern Library and Information Network), provides access to OCLC services and products to almost 400 member libraries. At times in the past, SOLINET has considered replicating the OCLC system and operating independently in the southeast of the U.S. (other networks have had similar aims; none have succeeded - see Kruger, 1984, on the history of NELINET). Short of this goal, and similar to

AMIGOS' efforts, SOLINET desired to establish its own computer facility to provide "regional support services" to its member libraries. In the late 1970s, SOLINET purchased a Burroughs mainframe and acquired the WLN software in order to reprogram it to run on the Burroughs computer. Thus, a regional support system was developed. Later named LAMBDA, SOLINET's new system provided a regional database, and a public access online union catalog. It also supported regional services for tape handling, recon, and ILL.

SOLINET has experienced major financial difficulties in supporting LAMBDA over the years. In 1980, OCLC came close to joining SOLINET as a partner in the effort by supporting the development of the regional system. After lengthy discussions which took place over many months, no agreement could be reached between OCLC management and SOLINET's Board. Vital, unresolved issues included ownership of the data and the system, and who would control system development. SOLINET managed to proceed on its own and ultimately established LAMBDA as an online, regional database network supporting public access and ILL activities.

The computer facility still supports SOLINET's recon, tape, and batch data processing services, but a recent announcement discloses that the online access LAMBDA network will be discontinued. Many member libraries have elected to spend their limited funds on the purchase or development of their own local, online systems. Some state library agencies in the SOLINET region have developed plans to coordinate the purchase, installation, and ultimate linking of the local systems for groups of libraries within their jurisdiction. Also, the state of North Carolina has reached an agreement directly with OCLC whereby the utility will maintain the state's online union catalog (including the holdings of non-OCLC libraries) at its center in Ohio. Non-OCLC libraries in North Carolina will have access to the state's online union database via dial-access to OCLC. A statewide union list of serials will be placed online in the coming months. This is one of many cases where state library agencies are seizing the initiative in automation planning from multi-state regional networks. In the case of North Carolina, the state dealt directly with OCLC. In other states, library planners are teaming up with vendors from the commercial sector.

CLASS

CLASS (Cooperative Library Agency for Systems and Services), a membership-based library service organization, was established in 1976 by a joint exercise-of-powers agreement among several state, academic, and public library authorities in the state of California. Its original name was California Library Authority for Systems and Services. Thus, it its origins,

CLASS is similar to Indiana's INCOLSA. But the history and present role of CLASS set it apart from most library network organizations. CLASS never exercised its option to become an "OCLC network", and never became an OCLC service center. With the help of federal funds administered through the California State Library, CLASS quickly offered several major products and services without establishing ties to either OCLC or RLG. Its early products were California library union lists for monographs and serials. CLASS also provided discount contracts and support services for online database search services to its member libraries.

CLASS developed three computer-based products that it markets to its members and other libraries. "On Tyme II" is CLASS' electronic communication network which provides access to databases and electronic mail to libraries across the U.S. "Checkmate" is a microcomputer-based serials control system, and "Golden Retriever" is a database management system specially developed for librarians.

CLASS brokers online database search services for DIALOG, BRS, and WILSONLINE, and provides discount contracts to CLASS members. Wishing to offer the services of a utility to its members, CLASS eventually reached an agreement with RLG to become the broker of RLIN services throughout the U.S. to any library that wanted access to RLIN but did not qualify for membership in RLG. At this time, approximately 400 libraries of all types use RLIN's cataloging, acquisitions, ILL, or search-only services through CLASS. CLASS also offers recon services through either RLIN, WLN, or REMARC (now affiliated with UTLAS), and CLASS libraries may choose to use the WLN system for cataloging.

Although founded as a state library agency, as CLASS expanded its services to libraries outside the state of California, its governance and scope of activities were reexamined in the early 1980s. This led to new "Bylaws" for the organization and a change in name. As Martin (1986) has said, "CLASS is highly unusual among networks, utilities, and vendors. It falls into none of these categories readily, yet it contains some of the characteristics of each." CLASS offers a wide variety of discount services and products, automated and non-automated, to its members. It has a strong microcomputer software, equipment, and training program, and it brokers the online services of utilities and commercial information retrieval services, all the while retaining its independence and close ties to its membership. Martin believes CLASS may be the model regional network of the future. But as CLASS continues to grow and expand, it will surely face the same pressures and challenges of other networks: primarily, how to compete in the local system marketplace; and how to remain a cooperative, membership-based organization as more and more libraries with differing needs join CLASS, and CLASS itself becomes more commercially oriented.

State library agencies

Most states in the U.S. have governmentally-based state library agencies or divisions. In addition to operating the state's library, increasingly these agencies are given responsibility and authority for administering library development and resource sharing programs throughout the state, especially for school and public libraries. The state of Illinois has recently passed legislation permitting participation by all types of libraries in state network and development programs. The trend is clearly toward multi-type library participation in state-level programs.

With a solid, public, organizational basis and existence independent of the utilities, these state library agencies are taking the lead in planning, developing, and administering computer-based services and resource sharing activities at both the local and statewide level. Typically, they are using the systems and services of commercial suppliers of cataloging and local turnkey systems to establish and support these activities and programs. A few cases are worth mentioning.

In the early 1980s, the West Virginia (State) Library Commission decided to purchase and install the VTLS integrated, local library system at several public library centers throughout the state. Each center would support the databases and circulation activities for a local cluster of libraries, and the centers would be linked to create the statewide VTLS network and a logical, distributed online union catalog. VTLS, originally developed for an academic library, supports automated circulation control, bibliographic database maintenance (including authority control), an OPAC, interfaces to cataloging utilities, and also has acquisitions and serials modules.

The West Virginia VTLS network has been successfully installed, and the Library Commission supports many recon projects aimed to expand the size and holdings of the online union catalog. A recent announcement reports the successful testing of a VTLS interface to a commercial, stand-alone, videodisc MARC cataloging system (LSSI's MINI MARC "LaserFile"). The videodisc contains LC-MARC records that can be transfered instantly into a VTLS system, avoiding telecommunications costs to online utilities. A single LaserFile system can support multiple and remote users accessing a single videodisc. VTLS also offers online cataloging interfaces with the utilities, and supports copy cataloging within and across the linked VTLS centers throughout the state. In summary, some of the West Virginia libraries are OCLC members, but the state library agency has contracted with other commercial vendors of automated systems (VTLS and LSSI) to build its computerized state library network and database.

The state of New Hampshire has taken a more piecemeal approach, establishing "regional nodes" in a planned five-node distributed library network. The state's plan calls for the clustering of public and academic libraries in an area to use a single automated local system. Two such nodes have been established, and ultimately all nodes will be linked through telecommunicatons' (dial-access at first) to create the statewide network. The State Library is responsible for planning and coordinating these efforts. It is also headquarters of the first node, where a single online catalog supports the State Library and 40 public libraries. So far, OCLC's LS/2000 local turnkey system has been selected as the basis for the state library network. A second node was recently installed at the University of New Hampshire. This node will also support five public libraries and one high school library, and will connect to the statewide database at the State Library in Concord, New Hampshire. A third node in the planning stages will be located at the Manchester City Public Library, and will include a cluster of three academic and seven public libraries on the same minicomputer.

The state of Massachusetts is moving in a similar direction, if along different paths. Until recently, the state library agency limited its automation efforts to funding the installation of circulation systems at four local cooperatives, serving over 60 libraries of various types. Libraries in each local cooperative share a single computer and its disk storage to create a bibliographic database with their holdings data attached to the bibliographic records. The circulation system supports their day-to-day resource sharing activities. Many other academic and public libraries in the state have installed stand-alone systems using their own funding.

Concerned about the lack of communication among the shared systems of the local clusters, and these systems with the stand-alone systems, in August 1983 the Massachusetts Board of Library Commissioners approved a plan for the establishment of a statewide automated resource sharing network of libraries (Dugan and Bjorner, 1984). The plan includes a conceptual and organizational (largely voluntary) framework for a statewide, coordinated library network to support linked databases, document request and delivery procedures, and computer training for librarians. The plan focuses on the need for statewide coordination of the application of bibliographic and communications standards to achieve the goals of the distributed, multi-system-based state computerized library network.

Other states are beginning to utilize optical disc technologies to support their union catalogs and other resource sharing efforts. At this early stage, the state library agency typically contracts with one of several vendors of videodisc or CD-ROM-based cataloging systems or OPACs. "ACCESS PENNSYLVANIA" is a project of the state library to develop a union catalog on a CD-ROM disc containing 653,000 unique bibliographic records of 153 school, public, and academic libraries across the state. The contract to produce this optical disc union catalog was awarded to Brodart, Inc., which markets the CD-ROM OPAC called "Le Pac". The initial project was successful, and the state library of Pennsylvania is now supporting the extension of the union catalog to include the holdings of many more libraries, including the State Library itself and the Pennsylvania Union List of Serials. The problem being addressed needs to be highlighted: the state of Pennsylvania has nearly 5,000 libraries with over a million volumes. Only 240 libraries in the state are members of OCLC, and, currently, access to the resources of these 240 libraries is limited to OCLC members. By distributing the expanding union database on compact discs, local libraries will need only a microcomputer and compact disc player to gain interactive access to the state's library resources.

The state of Louisiana has recently announced plans for a statewide network using a CD-ROM system developed by LSSI ("MINI MARC") to support MARC cataloging, the development of a union catalog, and intrastate ILL activities. Maine has announced plans for a statewide CD-ROM system, and Connecticut has engaged a consultant to study the feasibility of linking existing "regional" circulation systems within the state.

In 1985, 13 academic and public libraries in Maryland began the operation of MILNET (Maryland Interlibrary Network). Supported by funding from the state's library services agency, MILNET is based on the computer system, AGILE II, Auto-Graphics' online system. Auto-Graphics is a full-service, commercial utility based in California. To qualify for state funds, in the early 1980s Auto-Graphics was formally defined by the California Library Services Board as a bibliographic utility, placing it in the circle with RLIN, OCLC, and WLN. Back on the U.S. east coast at Maryland, the AGILE II ILL subsystem supports MILNET's interlibrary loan network. Operating in a centralized mode much like OCLC, AGILE II maintains the online union database of nearly a million records from 64 Maryland libraries at Auto-Graphics' headquarters in California. MILNET libraries are provided microcomputers to access the database and conduct loan transactions via Auto-Graphics' dedicated telecommunications network.

Many other examples like these could be listed. More and more local cooperatives are acquiring mini- and microcomputer systems and software from commercial vendors to support shared cataloging and circulation systems. State library agencies are beginning to plan and administer the coordination of these local automation efforts in at least two ways: 1) concentrating efforts on linking local systems in a distributed statewide network, and 2) exploiting new microcomputer and optical technologies to support online, local access to union catalogs stored and distributed on optical discs. In the second case, the state library agency will likely maintain and exercise administrative control over the online union catalog and statewide resource sharing based on the union catalog. However, administration and operation of the linked-system online networks is likely to be decentralized and based primarily on voluntary agreements between local library boards or municipal agencies and the state library authority. It is the local library boards and agencies that approve most expenditures for automated systems and services at and among their libraries.

B. Cataloging and Networking Support Services from the Commercial Sector

Automated local library systems

The impact of the commercial sector on library automation and networking is discussed at several points in this book. A variety of turnkey, multi-function automated library systems, microcomputer products, and new services using mass storage optical media offer libraries many alternatives to the traditional services of the utilities and their regional service centers.

As discussed in Part III of this book, libraries continue to buy and install local automated library systems at a rapid rate. The 1984 growth rate of installed turnkey systems was 69%; for 1985 the growth rate was 41%. More than 300 new installations of local systems took place in 1985, but this figure is somewhat misleading; the number of libraries served is much larger. Both vendor-supplied turnkey systems and software-only systems may be used by single institutions with library units at multiple locations, or shared among several institutions. A comparable growth rate has been reported for 1986 (Walton, 1987). As discussed in the previous section, there is a definite trend toward sharing local systems for networking activities.

Until recently, however, most libraries were dependent on a utility as the source of machine-readable catalog records for their local systems. Local system vendors have had to supply interfaces to the utility's terminals so current cataloging data could be transfered directly into the local system. Delayed tape-loading from a library's utility-supplied archive tapes has been the other option. For years, machine-readable cataloging and retrospective conversion (recon) services were almost the exclusive domain of the utilities. This is no longer the case, as many cataloging and recon products and services are now available from commercial sources. A few of these products will be reviewed, but first, a parallel development must be described.

Today's automated local systems include cataloging and database maintenance capabilities, along with the circulation control system, online public access catalog, etc. In a shared system environment, this provides for copy cataloging and even recon among the libraries in the group, through the utilization of the system's central, union database, or by accessing linked databases throughout a region. A record derived from a utility, once in the shared local system, can be used many times for copy cataloging or recon activities. The turnkey vendors have enhanced their multi-location systems with precisely this possibility in mind. The case of VTLS in the state of West Virginia has been reviewed. VTLS supports interfaces to the utilities and to the new optical disc catalog files, but also supports shared cataloging among multiple users of its system or linked VTLS systems. A recent advertisement reads: "Current networking capabilities include several options for multiple libraries using a single VTLS system, networking across VTLS systems, copy cataloging within and across systems, and union catalog development and maintenance."

Data Research Associates (DRA) a turnkey vendor of a minicoputer-based integrated library system, also offers its customers DRANET, a bibliographic networking facility that provides access to the complete LC MARC file and to the databases of other DRA libraries. A DRA library can catalog from the LC file or from other library databases using a computer-to-computer link.

Whether the bibliographic records are maintained in a statewide online union catalog, the shared database of a local cooperative, or in the vendor's files, the attractiveness of this local system cataloging and networking capability is obvious: a group of libraries which purchases one of these systems and builds a common database creates, in effect, a self-contained mini-utility. The scope of coverage of the online union catalog expands when several local systems and their databases are linked across an entire state.

Following DRA's lead, other local system vendors are providing their customers access to LC MARC cataloging, reducing the need for libraries to join a cataloging utility. Some of the options are much cheaper on a per record basis than cataloging on OCLC, and eliminate the required telecommunications costs.

This local system-based, shared cataloging activity may be viewed as a forerunner to the decentralized networking environment that may result when system vendors adopt and implement OSI protocols, permitting the linking of different computer systems -- those of local and state consortia, as well as those of the major utilities. Viewed only as suppliers of cataloging services and bibliographic records, the utilities have more to lose than gain in the new decentralized, open systems environment. OCLC will stress the importance of contributing local records to its database for the "common interest" and international resource sharing. Libraries may not listen.

Commercial sources of machine-readable cataloging and retrospective conversion (recon)

The reasons why libraries want cataloging data in machine-readable form, in a standard format, are now commonly understood. Machine-readable catalog files are the basis of COM catalogs, local, computer-based automated filing and maintenance procedures, and remote-access to catalog records. Machine-readable files of bibliographic and holdings data make it possible for state agencies and regional cooperatives to cost-effectively develop and maintain union catalogs to support reference queries and interlibrary lending. The growth in the number of local automated systems in libraries has been a major factor in the increased need for machine-readable bibliographic records. Almost all U.S. libraries have converted, or plan to convert, their catalog records into machine-readable form, for both current and retrospective cataloging. The major reason?: the library has, or will soon acquire, a local, online system for, at least, circulation control and online public access.

These local systems generally lack a resource database from which to obtain bibliographic records (DRA is an exception). All of the local system vendors, therefore, provide interfaces for loading records into the local system from other sources. Most vendors support the immediate transfer of records from the major utilities into the local system on a record-by-record basis, typically through the printer port of the utility's terminal.

In the mid-1980s, local systems have improved immensely in the quality of database content, maintenance, and access. The LC MARC formats have become de facto standards for machine handling and respresentation of bibliographic data in local systems. In whatever manner they internally store bibliographic data, local systems are now required to accept input, support record maintenance, and produce output in the MARC formats. Many local systems support authority control maintenance of the bibliographic file -- with cross-reference capabilities -- and current cataloging and record update procedures.

Automated cataloging and retrospective conversion which requires creating records locally is not cost-effective in most cases unless done in single-system, shared environment; libraries still need access to a large resource database, and other cataloging support services. Libraries now have a number of options for these services. A recent report by McQueen and Boss (1985) individually describes 22 sources of machine-readable cataloging and recon services in North America. The group includes LC and the utilities, and commercial cataloging services. The nature of each organization, its services, and their prices are described. The McQueen and Boss report is highly recommended, and was heavily relied upon for information to support this study.

The point has been made that OCLC, RLG, WLN, and UTLAS no longer stand together as a clearly identifiable and distinct group of cataloging support services. UTLAS is now a commercial firm, and both UTLAS and OCLC compete directly against other vendors in providing cataloging, recon, and local systems. Auto-Graphics, whose former major service was the production of COM catalogs, is now a full-service utility. OCLC-affiliate networks AMIGOS and SOLINET compete with OCLC and with the commercial sector in offering recon and authority control services. Turnkey system vendors are beginning to provide online, shared cataloging facilities, and even large resource databases in some cases. No longer are the four traditional utilities unique in their services or mission.

Most of the commercial vendors offer both online and offline batch cataloging and recon services. Some offer only batch services (e.g., Blackwell North America, and Inforonics). The online cataloging services of three popular commercial vendors are reviewed briefly here. One, Auto-Graphics, operates in an online network environment, much like the traditional utilities. The other two, The Library Corporation ("BiblioFile") and Library Systems & Services, Inc. (LSSI, with its Spectrum Series --

formerly MINI MARC and "LaserFile"), provide stand-alone, optical disc-based cataloging and recon systems which use LC MARC files.

The process of cataloging is essentially the same in online and stand-alone systems. A library searches for a record in the vendor's databases, inspects and amends the retrieved "copy" with local data or required modifications, and then "extracts" that record from the system to be transferred to a local system, or onto magnetic media such as tape or floppy disks. When no match is found, the system provides formatted screens for entry of original cataloging. New records are validated before they are added to the file, then the extraction process follows. Of course, many libraries still receive catalog cards as the ouput of machine-readable cataloging. It is estimated that more than 2,000 U.S. libraries have COM (computer output microform) catalogs.

Most online cataloging vendors charge for usage on a transaction basis, with fees also assessed for membership (or sign-up), access, terminals, communications, and products, such as cards, labels, tapes, printed and COM lists. Costs vary greatly from vendor to vendor: start-up costs for equipment and membership range from $1,650 to $6,000, with monthly maintenance, access, and telecommunications fees of $250 to $1,200. A few vendors do not charge for transactions, but charge for the number of terminals and functions supported. Terminal installations can cost several thousands of dollars a year.

Stand-alone systems operate much like the online network systems, except that all work is performed locally against a file of LC MARC cataloging data stored on videodisc or CD-ROM discs. The records used and any original cataloging are stored on magnetic media (at this time) or transferred directly into the local system. Tapes or floppy disks containing new cataloging may also be sent to the vendor for addition to subsequent updates on optical discs. Stand-alone systems are gaining in popularity because they do not incur telecommunications and transaction charges, and they can be used any time of the day or week. Their optical disc databases typically contain only LC MARC cataloging copy, but the vendors are beginning to find solutions to this problem, including the use of write once-read many (WORM) optical storage media.

Auto-Graphics

751 Monterey Pass Road

Monterey Park, California   91754

(213) 269-9451

For many years, Auto-Graphics has been a supplier of book and COM catalogs to libraries. It produces the statewide COM union catalogs for several states, including California, Colorado, Delaware, Maryland, Mississippi, and New Jersey.

In 1981, Auto-Graphics expanded its services to the online environment with the AGILE II system for shared cataloging, retrospective conversion, database maintenance, interlibrary loan, union listing, and electronic mail. AGILE II operates on a large centralized computer facility, like the other utilities, located at the utility's headquarters, in this case Monterey Park, California. Also, like the other utilities, Auto-Graphics offers libraries an offline option, its AGILE I microcomputer-based system for cataloging and database maintenance. Auto-Graphics offers libraries a range of retrospective conversion options and services. Most Auto-Graphics' customers are public libraries, but several academic libraries have selected the service in recent years.

The AGILE II Online System

Libraries access the AGILE II bibliographic system computer by dedicated terminals linked to 4800 baud leased lines or by dial access. Dial access is accomplished through Tymnet using any ASCII terminal or microcomputer and a modem. Libraries employing dial access can fully search the database, use ILL, and electronic mail. However, dial access users must limit bibliographic record maintenance to the holdings field.

AGILE II parallels UTLAS in allowing the library access to its own database. The library may choose to keep its database private or enter into reciprocal access relationships with other libraries whereby they share access to each others' databases. The database formats among libraries may differ from full MARC to brief records depending on the library's choice. AGILE II supports both. A library wishing to use another library's record may have to pay for it, a fee usually based on the book budget of the record's user. Auto-Graphics, in contrast to OCLC, believes that libraries own their own machine readable records by virtue of paying for their conversion. AGILE II also gives libraries the capability to create and maintain their own name and subject authority files in LC format. It does not, however, provide authority control of the library's database or support global updates of controlled record fields.

The bibliographic database contains over 8 million records, about one-half of which are unique records. The database includes all LC MARC files in all formats and languages. The LC authority files are not maintained online; however, the authority files of individual libraries are online.

AGILE II allows its clients customization options for: record formats, validation routines, database search sequences, and input workscreens. Workscreens may differ according to MARC record format, as may the record field and subfield definitions. Customizing the search sequence allows a library to first search its own database, and then any other specified files in a specified order.

After moving through its customized search sequence, the library may determine it's found a desired bibliographic record. This record is "claimed" into a workfile for whole record, not field by field, editing. If copy cataloging is not available, the library chooses one of its customized workscreens upon which to enter the original cataloging. AGILE II allows transfer of these bibligraphic records to a local system through its interface software on an IBM or Sperry PC. The transfer may occur online record by record, or through floppy disk or magnetic tape batch loading.

Pricing for AGILE II is based on per terminal charges. Prices run $850 for the first terminal, exclusive of equipment. This price includes the fees for telecommunications and access to the Auto-Graphics' databases. Additional terminals at the same site cost less, usually about half the $850. Required terminals are IBM or Sperry microcomputers or compatibles. There is a database storage charge estimated to be about $.005 per title per month. Installation and training charges are extra and assessed when the AGILE II service begins. Libraries that use AGILE-Link to transfer bibliographic records to their local systems pay a one time fee of $3,200 to implement the link, then an ongoing $200 a month service fee. (All price quotes apply to July 1987 and are provided for purposes of illustration only.)

AGILE I

AGILE I provides libraries an offline microcomputer option for catalog record creation and maintenance. Using an IBM PC and proprietary software, the library "searches" for an LCCN and/or brief bibliographic information and adds local holdings data. These search statements are processed in batch mode against the Auto-Graphics resource files. Original cataloging can also be input using customized workscreens with validation options similar to AGILE II. AGILE I bibliographic information can be transmitted to Auto-Graphics via floppy disks or by telecommunications lines.

Auto-Graphics prices the PC hardware and software at $500 a month leased. No other charges are applicable. Libraries who choose to use their own hardware pay $350 monthly (Heinemann, 1986).

The Library Corporation (BiblioFile)

P.O. Box 40035
Washington, D.C.   20016
(304) 725-7220

In February 1985, The Library Corporation (TLC) began production deliveries of the BiblioFile Catalog Production System. A CD-ROM system, BiblioFile currently stores its database of over three million bibliographic records on four compact laser discs. The database covers all LC MARC records including monographs, serials, Government Printing Office publications, music, films, maps, and Canadian publications. The English language and foreign language cataloging are subscribed to separately. The Enhanced BiblioFile recently became available to offer a multi-workstation capability on a network, maintenance of the library's own MARC records, catalog card printing on a laser printer, and wanding of barcodes to add circulation information to the MARC records.

The BiblioFile database is updated through cumulative discs on which the files have been recompiled, reindexed, and reissued. Subscriptions to the cumulations are available on a quarterly or monthly basis.

TLC also offers its new Book Identification and Ordering System for acquisitions support on CD-ROM . The system accesses the ANY-BOOK database of over one and a half million English language titles on one compact disc. The system provides for order creation and printing, fund accounting, electronic order transmission via modem, and order status and check-in. Cumulative database updates are issued quarterly.

The BiblioFile software is distributed on floppy disk. The access to the records is by author, title, LCCN, ISBN or ISSN. Searches can be narrowed by publication year, material type, or author. Help screens and menus provide user guidance. The system supports creating and entering original cataloging, MARC editing, printing catalog cards and spine labels, and transferring bibliographic records to other computer systems.

The Library Corporation sells limited hardware: only the CD-ROM drive and the necessary cabling to connect it to the user's IBM PC or PC compatible. The PC must have at least one floppy disk drive on which to access the BiblioFile software and the library's stored bibliographic records. BiblioFile uses only one CD-ROM drive with the user changing discs when needed. A multiple CD-ROM player configuration is available. TLC plans to utilize the juke box technology when it becomes commercially available.

The Library Corporation charges $680 for single orders of the International Standard CD-ROM drive with cabling. The Catalog Production application software, user manual, and one set of the LC MARC and ANY-BOOK databases on laser disc is $1750. A package of software updates, user support, and hardware maintenance is priced separately at $540 per year. The drive, applications software, databases, software updates, and hardware maintenance are available at a bundled purchase price of $2930. Database updates are subscribed to separately on an annual basis: English language LC MARC records with quarterly updates for $870, monthly updates $1470; foreign language LC MARC records with quarterly updates for $500; ANY-BOOK quarterly updates for $600. TLC also offers installation and training services for a fee. (Prices current as of July 1987.)

In mid-1987, TLC announced the BiblioFile Intelligent Catalog, a user-friendly OPAC on CD-ROM offering sound, graphics, user guidance, search formulation, and sophisticated search techniques. It may prove to be as innovative and popular as TLC's other products. The complete workstation is $2,495 including computer hardware, software, furniture, printer, and power conditioner. The monthly fee of $37.50 provides an initial database load of 500,000 titles, monthly catalog updates (to the hard disk; when it reaches capacity a CD-ROM is remastered), user and hardware support.

Late in 1986, The Library Corporation announced the 500th installation of its stand-alone BiblioFile CD-ROM MARC cataloging system. Several turnkey system vendors have developed interfaces to transfer records from BiblioFile directly into the automated local system.

Library Systems & Services, Inc. (LSSI)
20251 Century Boulevard
Germantown, Maryland 20874
(301) 428-3400

Library Systems & Services Inc., recently acquired by Gaylord Bros., has offered the stand-alone MINI MARC system for retrospective conversion and cataloging support for a number of years. Initially, the system configuration used floppy disks as the storage medium for LC MARC records. The records were accessed using a microform index. Since mid-1984, the machine-readable records have been stored on laser videodiscs ("Laserfile") accessed directly through a personal microcomputer. With its "Spectrum Series" LSSI now offers a variety of machine-readable cataloging records on videodisc and several different hardware configurations for accessing and editing. It uses its expertise in videodisc publishing to support a "private file" videodisc publication service. The company also offers contract retrospective conversion. LSSI has also recently announced a CD-ROM version of its cataloging system, and a CD-ROM OPAC.

The Spectrum Series

The Spectrum Series product line includes several stand-alone cataloging workstation configurations which use microcomputers and laser videodiscs containing the LC MARC resource bibliographic data. This optically stored database is called "Laserfile". At a minimum, Laserfile contains more than three million LC MARC records for books and serials in all languages, and records in a variety of other MARC formats, published on two 12 inch videodiscs. The Laserfile discs may also contain a library's or a library consortium's own cataloging records. Under an agreement with UTLAS, owner of the REMARC database (pre-1968 Library of Congress cataloging), to help libraries with retroconversion, LSSI also offers a videodisc database of abbreviated REMARC records. This database is used with the Spectrum search software to help libraries identify and order REMARC records from UTLAS. Local data is added to the retrieved abbreviated REMARC record, and a batch of such records is sent to UTLAS where the local data is merged with the full REMARC record and output to tape to be delivered back to the requesting library.

The Spectrum Series 400 is a stand-alone cataloging workstation that offers libraries multiple user capabilities and access to the master Laserfile database. This hardware and software package employs a personal computer, controller and interface card, and a laser disc player, and is available by subscription or purchase. As a local cataloging facility, as many as six users can access the MARC database simultaneously using a network of personal computers. The system can be used for either retrospective conversion or current cataloging, and card and label sets can be produced immediately at the site.

With Spectrum 400, the user can retrieve records from Laserfile by using the LCCN, title or author search key, or ISBN/ISSN. Retrieved MARC records can be edited using Spectrum 400's full-screen editing capabilities. MARC records can be customized to conform with local needs; catalog cards can be designed before being printed locally. Also, cataloging workforms can be modified to meet local requirements. Locally created catalog records are stored on floppy disks for subsequent use.

LSSI prices separately all the items which make up a Spectrum workstation. For purposes of illustration some cost data is given. Annual subscriptions to Laserfile are available at $1,295, with quarterly updates, and at $2,995, with monthly updates. A single-screen configuration with two videodisc players costs $5,695. This does not include the microcomputer (available beginning at around $1,600). The Spectrum software costs $1,000 for a single microcomputer, and hardware maintenance can be acquired for $688 per year for the first videodisc player. Additional equipment needed to expand the configuration for networking is available for less cost than the first components.

In addition to the products offered as part of the Spectrum Series, LSSI also provides a variety of bibliographic and library automation services. These include full retrospective conversion services, database enhancement services (upgrading non-MARC machine-readable records, eliminating duplicate records, etc), and authority services. LSSI will also supply a number of database products generated from stored data. These include classified lists of holdings for collection inspection and analysis, catalogs in printed or COM format, and laser videodisc files of local cataloging to support networked cataloging, ILL, and online public access catalogs. LSSI has produced private videodisc files for the Ramapo Catskill Library System in New York state, and for a group of libraries in Florida (Pezzanite, 1985, and Freund, 1985). SOLINET, an OCLC network and service center, maintains a database of more than 2 million records on its own computer, but has chosen LSSI to produce a Laserfile version of this database to decrease problems with computer downtime and to improve record consistency. SOLINET uses three Spectrum 400 systems, with eighteen terminals, to perform retrospective conversion and other cataloging services for its members.

3. National Libraries and National Programs

A. Library of Congress (LC)

   Earlier in this book, it was explained that the Library of Congress (LC) is
not the "official" national library for the United States, and also that LC
has chosen not to assume the role and responsibilities of operating a
computerized national bibliographic network. Indeed, talk at LC today is not
about a "national network," but about the "nationwide" network and the need
to link different computer systems and networks. LC, through its Network
Development MARC Standards Office and Network Advisory Committee (NAC),
continues to play a leadership and advisory role in U.S. networking
activities.

   Although not the official national library, LC's support of and influence
on libraries in the U.S. is considerable. LC's primary clientele is, of
course, the U.S. Congress, but anyone may use LC's physical facilities and
resources in Washington. In addition, LC supports many programs that are
national in scope and that benefit all libraries. The key programs will be
reviewed here. LC extends its role in two other ways: 1) it represents the
U.S. in matters of bibliographic standards and bibliographic control in the
international community, and 2) LC operates in the commercial sector, so to
speak, as a supplier of catalog records and recon services. Until very
recently, LC has been the major entry point in the U.S. for cataloging from
other countries. Under a recent agreement, for example, tapes of machine-
readable records in the UK MARC format are received from the British
Library. LC converts them to USMARC and makes them available to other
libraries and utilities through its MARC tape distribution service. This
unitary path may change soon, as OCLC, UTLAS, and RLG reach separate
agreements with institutions and agencies in other countries to contribute
catalog records and union lists directly to the utilities' databases. LC has
expressed concern about these international initiatives. One fear is that
existing bibliographic standards may be circumvented, and efforts to promote
the adoption of UNIMARC as an international exchange standard may be damaged.

Once again, LC sees a need for central control over these and related matters to promote data and system compatiblity, and adherence to standards. However, LC does not have the political authority to assume this role. Furthermore, LC is not a member of any network, and it does not administer any network, not even the network of federal libraries (FEDLINK). LC differs even from the National Library of Medicine (NLM), which operates and administers the Regional Medical Library System and MEDLARS, the online information retrieval system. Nonetheless, perhaps because of its sheer size, location, and quality of leadership, LC's influence on networking has been immense and profound. This influence has been realized through the development and distribution of support services, and LC's strong participation in national-level networking and resource sharing programs.

MARC

LC's most significant contribution to computer-based library networking has been the development of the MARC standard formats for bibliographic records. Before MARC, many local formats existed for placing bibliographic records into machine-readable forms. This lack of a standard format made the exchange of records from one computer system to another almost impossible. Software to read and convert the data transferred on magnetic tape would have to be developed for each case. To facilitate the exchange and sharing of machine-readable cataloging records in a world of many different computer systems, a common record exchange format was needed. The MARC format was developed for this purpose.

In the mid-1960s, LC, along with several other libraries, worked to specify a common structure for bibliographic records, a structure appropriate for the computer handling of complex, diverse records of varying length. From the start, the MARC format has consisted of a variable number of variable-length fields (quite radical in the 1960s), which permits its use for almost any type of data and bibliographic records. Following a one-year test of a provisional format (MARC I), in 1969 LC began its MARC II Distribution Service. LC had decided to offer a subscription service of currently cataloged records in machine-readable form. Until 1973, the records distributed on tape included only English-language monographs cataloged at LC. In 1973, the service began to include French-language monographs, and by 1978 the tapes included monographs in all Roman-alphabet languages and all new serials titles, maps and audiovisual materials. Six material formats are supported today, along with the LC name and subject authority files on separate machine-readable tapes.

Intended to allow exchange of data between institutions, the MARC formats are structured "repositories" for the data appearing on catalog cards. The developers of MARC formats aimed for consistency with catalog cards, and to be able to accommodate the data and its structure as found on catalog cards. Thus, the production and output of machine-readable records and catalog cards are closely linked. Intended as a common format for the exchange of records, the MARC format has become the standard format for creating and maintaining catalog records online. The MARC formats, with all their fields, and subfields, and content designators (tags and labels for components of the record), have become the standard workforms for catalogers in North America. This explains the change in name from LC MARC records to USMARC records. The former is a subset of the latter. The utilities and most local automated cataloging systems require the creation of MARC-structured records. The MARC formats are used to interactively, online, edit and update catalog records. LC MARC records now constitute less than half the records in the utilities' databases. The utilities (and others) purchase subscriptions to LC's magnetic tapes, and load them into their databases in a batch process. These LC MARC records are then redistributed to thousands of libraries around the world. Recently, commercial suppliers of cataloging data have based their services almost entirely on the redistribution of LC MARC records. Distributing the LC MARC files on laser discs as part of stand-alone cataloging workstations is gaining in popularity. "Catalog records" and "MARC records" have become nearly synonymous. So thorough is the adoption of the MARC formats for cataloging purposes, most RFP's for local library systems require that the candidate systems support MARC format record creation and maintenance, as well as the batch input and ouput of MARC records.

At various times, LC has attempted to supplement its own cataloging with that of other libraries. These records would be added to its database and distributed with the MARC tapes. A recent program of coordinated cataloging involves a few specially-selected RLG libraries. RLG submits this cataloging to LC on tape, for authentication and subsequent redistribution to MARC tape customers. LC is also now receiving UK MARC records from the British Library and converting them to USMARC. Libraries and utilities wishing these records must subscribe to them separately with the British Library. Oddly enough, the number of subscribers to LC's MARC tapes has declined over the years.

Libraries acquire the MARC records needed for their catalogs from the utilities or other vendors.

The MARC formats expand from time to time to cover new materials, new data elements and new library requirements for data distinctions and relationships. LC does not unilaterally define or change the MARC formats. Recognizing their expanded and broad use, LC calls on two groups to assist in developing the formats: the Bibliographic Information in Machine-Readable Form Committee (MARBI) of the American Library Association (ALA), and LC's own advisory committee, which includes MARBI and representatives from the utilities. The MARC standard is dynamic -- a process as much as a set of record formats. Requests for changes or new formats (e.g., for musical scores, computer software) must undergo an elaborate review procedure by LC and the two committees. Effort is also made to elicit comment from libraries on changes that may have major financial or operational impact. As time passes, this becomes more of a concern, as more and more libraries install and maintain their own automated systems, systems fine-tuned to handle MARC records.

Bibliographic services and products

In 1968, the Cataloging Distribution Service (CDS) of the Library of Congress began distributing machine-readable bibliographic records on magnetic tape for English language monographs. Now, records are available for all Roman alphabet languages, and selected languages in non-Roman scripts for serials, maps, visual materials, and music; for authority data; and for Cataloging-in-Publication. LC also distributes records created by other institutions, such as CONSER, the U.S. Government Printing Office, the British Library, and the National Library of Canada. LC's other commercial offerings include the Select MARC Retrospective Conversion Service, catalog cards, the CDS MARC Retriever Service, and CDS Alert.

New and amended MARC records are available through the Subscription Upgrade Service. For monograph records, the subscription options are Books All (languages)-weekly, Books English-weekly, Books CJK (Chinese, Japanese, and Korean), Books U.S.-weekly, and Books Canada. The monthly LC Serials tapes include records in all languages. They are comprised of: 1) LC cataloged or authenticated serials bibliographic records, and 2) CONSER (CONversion of SERials) authenticated or updated records input on OCLC by CONSER participants. Unauthenticated CONSER records become part of the separate Unauthenticated CONSER Records file. The second CONSER Snapshot file contains authenticated and unauthenticated MARC records for serials through

August 1, 1981. This file contains 339,000 records and is available from LC at the cost of $1,510. The Unauthenticated CONSER records file, also priced at $1,510, is then used as an update to the Snapshot file containing records up to the beginning of the current tape subscription service.

The GPO Monthly Catalog tapes released monthly distribute MARC cataloging for publications listed in the printed Monthly Catalog of United States Government Publications. The Visual Materials monthly tapes provide catalog records for projected media (motion pictures, video recordings, filmstrips, transparencies, slides), two-dimensional non-projectable graphic representations, and kits. The Maps tapes distributed every four weeks produce MARC records for single and multi-sheet maps, and maps treated as serials. The Music service provides MARC records every four weeks for monographs of printed and manuscript music, and for music and non-music sound recordings.

In addition to the MARC bibliographic records, LC distributes authority records for both names and subjects. The Name Authorities weekly service includes new, revised, and converted retrospective headings for personal, corporate, conference, and geographic names; uniform titles; and series established by LC or by a member of the Name Authorities Cooperative Project. The Name Authorities retrospective file includes approximately 1,250,000 records between 1977 and March 1985 and costs $2,300 to purchase. The subject authorities are a machine-readable version of the printed Library of Congress Subject Headings, 9th Edition, cumulating additions and changes through December 31, 1982. The file holds records only for those heading-subdivision combinations appearing in the printed book. In April 1986, CDS resumed distributing updates through a new subscription service.

The LC Retrospective Service handles requests for MARC records prior to the current subscription year. The Complete Service for all records in all formats covering 1968 through March 1985 with 2,340,000 bibliographic records costs $7,050. The Complete Service covers six categories and each may be purchased separately. The number of records included in each category is:

Books	1,940,000
Serials	245,000
GPO	199,000
Visual Materials	70,000
Maps	87,000
Music	5,000

Retrospective Conversion

For retrospective conversion, libraries may load some of the LC tapes described above or use the Select MARC Retrospective Conversion Service by submitting listings of the ISBNs, ISSNs, or LCCNs of the needed bibliographic records. Requests may be submitted on magnetic tape, floppy disks, order forms, or plain paper. A $300 fee is assessed to search each file - for books, maps, serials, visual materials, and music - plus a per-record variable charge based on the form in which the search key is submitted: for records submitted on tape the charge is $.01; on floppy disk, $.02; on a Select MARC Order form, $.03; and on other hardcopy, $.08. Records are output on magnetic tape. The Select MARC Retrospective Conversion Service does not allow the insertion of local data into the records it retrieves.

Other Services

The CDS MARC Retriever Service offers searches on the LC MARC databases based on single or multiple data elements such as author, title, language, date, subject, classification, etc. Catalog cards, page prints, and magnetic tapes may be output.

Catalog cards for LC cataloging from 1898 to the present are available by LCCN for $.60 for a set of eight cards. Non-LCCN search requests incur an $.80 search fee on top of the regular $.60 charge.

CDS Alert provides collection development assistance by weekly running a library's subject interest profile against current LC cataloging. Titles that meet the subject criteria are printed on catalog cards to alert the library to potential new materials.

The Network Advisory Committee (NAC)

With encouragement from the Council on Library Resources (CLR), in 1976 LC formed a Network Advisory Committee (NAC). Membership is at the invitation of LC and NAC, and currently includes 27 representatives of network-related organizations. Membership categories include various library and publishing professional societies, bibliographic utilities, federal libraries, regional service centers/networks, and individual library systems. The objectives of NAC are to provide a forum for discussion of networking issues, to advise LC on its networking role, and to provide input to the Council on Library Resources (an independent, private, library support and funding agency) for its many network-related projects.

The original mission of NAC was to advise LC on its central role in the planned national network. Many meetings and hearings were held in the late 1970s to prepare the way for a national bibliographic network, with LC most frequently suggested as administering agency, imposing programs and standards on U.S. libraries. This concept of a centralized, bureaucratic, top-down network organization met with strong resistance. OCLC resisted the concept, but so also did most librarians throughout the country. As Martin (1986) writes, "The grass roots, pioneering attitude of this country did not allow the country's librarians to accept this concept easily."

In the face of this resistance to its early "grand" plan, NAC redirected its efforts in a piecemeal manner to study and address a series of related networking issues. NAC has evolved from being a prime mover of the national network, to a forum for discussion of divergent approaches to many issues. Over the years, NAC has addressed topics such as document delivery, statewide networks, electronic information delivery systems, telecommunications, and the information economy. Maruyama (1986) has published a review of NAC's first ten years.

In recent years, NAC members have not been able to agree on either a model configuration for a "nationwide" network or how it should be governed. Yet, the effort continues, fueled by fears among top national library network leaders that new resource sharing technologies and alternatives from the commercial sector may lead to a fragmented, decentralized, uncoordinated library networking environment in the U.S. Recent 1985-1986 NAC meetings have addressed the need for "a common vision in library networking." It is still unlikely that NAC and CLR (with new cooperation from OCLC) will be able to set firm networking policy for the entire nation. There are too many countervailing forces. It is an age of local initiative and distributed processing. Libraries will look to the large "national" organizations for standards development, research and education, and data resources not available locally. NAC will probably continue to act as LC's advisory body in presenting to the U.S. library community the issues and options for use of new information technologies and resource sharing.

Council on Library Resources (CLR)

Not an agency of the government nor a part of LC, the Council on Library Resources has had a considerable impact on the use of new technologies in libraries and networking developments. NAC was created on the advice of CLR, and today, CLR joins LC, RLG, WLN, and OCLC in directing the Linked Systems Project. For 20 years CLR has had a major influence on discussions and programs for national network coordination and the linking of systems.

CLR is a private library support foundation originally established by the Ford Foundation. It has a small administrative and program staff. Over the years, CLR has provided support to OCLC, RLG, the New York Public Library and several major universities in their automation efforts. In the early 1980s, CLR funded major nationwide research on online public access catalogs. CLR has brought together large foundations and private funding agencies to address the need for library development and research funding through the Foundations Library Committee.

A major program of CLR is the Bibliographic Services Development Program (BSDP), established to bring some coordination to national bibliographic and networking activites. The program's three primary goals are: 1) the provision of effective bibliographic services, 2) the improvement of bibliographic products, and 3) the control of costs of bibliographic processes in libraries. Lacking the authority of a government agency, CLR must base its influence on strong leadership, research and education activities, and incentive funding. Among the members of the BSDP group are the executive officers of the bibliographic utilities and LC.

Early activities sponsored by BSDP included 1) the creation and evaluation of a system for exchanging data and services between computers, 2) LC's national network configuration design, and 3) the development of standards. CLR spurred the formation of the original LSP groups (LC, RLG, and WLN) to develop a means of linking LC and the utilities. Executives from CLR, LC, OCLC, RLG, and WLN currently constitute the LSP Policy Committee. CLR continues to fund research on OPACs and their use, including user education needs, and co-sponsors, along with the Association for American Publishers, a project to develop standards for incorporating into machine-readable manuscripts the control codes needed by publishers for typesetting. Given its ability to define and support development programs, CLR will probably continue to have more influence than NAC in the introduction and evaluation of new technologies in and among libraries. Its interests range from coordinated networking and improved access, to materials preservation and improved library management.

LC's Optical Disc Pilot Program

In 1982, LC embarked on an Optical Disc Pilot Program, divided into print and nonprint experimental projects, in an attempt to determine the feasibility of using the optical disc medium as a preservation and high-speed access device for library materials. The systems have been developed, and in 1986 the project entered the evaluation stage. Public access terminals and printers have been placed at various points throughout LC, and a systematic evaluation by LC staff has recently been completed (Reich and Betcher, 1986). Early findings indicate the project is meeting with success in several areas. Librarians judge the optical disc workstation as a very effective access and document delivery arrangement (with linked hard-copy printer). Problems with reading text and viewing images on video display units (VDUs) have been identified and remain to be resolved.

LC emphasizes that its optical disc work has been and will proceed as a pilot project through 1987, studying four areas: 1) preservation potential of optical storage media for fragile, rare, or high use materials, 2) improved service through rapid retrieval access stations providing access to the same material at one time to many patrons, 3) the enhancement of images over the source material, and 4) better utilization of library storage space. The current project was stimulated in part by LC's early work with optical disc technology in the Cataloging Distribution Service, where images of catalog cards were digitally scanned for storing and printing of exact card reproductions on demand.

The Print Project

A selected group of periodicals, maps, microforms, manuscripts, and sheet music are to be scanned and stored on digital optical discs at up to 500,000 images per year. Initially, high use current materials will be stored like those used by the Congressional Research Service's Selective Dissemination of Information (SDI) service on public affairs topics; science, technology, and business journals; German, Brazilian, Japanese, Thai, French, and Hebraic periodicals; popular government documents such as the Budget of the United States and the Congressional Record; and United States Agriculture Decisions and Social Security Rulings from 1960 to 1975.

Document preparation will entail: 1) creating an index record through data entry in LOCIS (The Library of Congress Information System database); 2) scanning the document with a high-speed scanner to digitize it at 300 lines per inch resolution; 3) reviewing the keyboarding accuracy and scanning precision; and 4) writing to optical discs. The high resolution digitized image will be stored on the disc in much greater detail than can be displayed on even high-resolution terminals.

To use the system, the user will enter the appropriate identification at an optical disc terminal through which the appropriate optical disc from the jukebox carousel is retrieved and the black-and-white image displayed. The user stations will be located in several Library reading rooms. High-resolution terminals will be used to request and display full pages of stored text. Single page printouts from slave printers or off-line remote printing will be available for a fee.

The Non-Print Project

The analog videodisc is being used to store LC's image materials. Up to 54,000 separate black-and-white or color images may be stored on one side of a 12-inch videodisc to be viewed frame by frame. The first public disc contains the following materials: 875 lantern slides containing views from around the world gathered on the World Transportation Commission Trip (1894-1896); 25,000 photonegatives (displayed as positives) from the Detroit Publishing Co. Glass Photonegative Collections; 2,900 transparencies from the Detroit Publishing's Glass Transparency Collection; 58 lithographically colored large format photoprints from the Detroit Publishing Company; 241 lithographically colored photoprints from the Detroit Publishing's color photo album, the Abdul-Hamid Collection of 1,825 black and white photos of the Ottoman Empire; 645 color slides and transparencies from the U.S. Farm Security Administration Color Slide and Transparency collection; 965 color slides and transparencies from the U.S. Office of War Information Color Slide and Transparency Collection; 3,615 political and propaganda posters from the Yanker Colleges; and 440 items (plans, details, sections, renderings, measured drawings, etc.) from the Architectural Drawings for the Library's Jefferson and Adams Buildings. Viewers operate the workstation by depressing a button which will cause the images in the chosen collection to display at a rate of several per second. The rate at which images appear may also be controlled manually by the viewer.

Five other analog discs will contain: 10,000 images from the Prints and Photographs Division; almost 100,000 motion picture publicity stills from the Motion Picture, Broadcasting, and Recorded Sound Division; a selection of seven color films and film segments; a selection of around thirty titles from the paper print collection of pre-1910 motion picture films; and, two television newscasts from July 3-4, 1976.

The videodisc is created by filming the images on 35mm motion picture color film, transferring them to videotape, then onto videodisc. Images display in color on standard television monitors. The discs are intended to act as service copies to prevent wear and tear on the original items. The originals will be accessible only for specialized research needs. LC is also considering a micro-based system which will index images and their captions to be viewed together or separately.

LC's collections of over 80 million items increase at the rate of over 7,000 a day. Access to resources while preserving the fragile and historical original sources is of vital importance at the Library of Congress. Both the digital and analog disc systems help the Library provide such access.

Authorized overviews of the print and nonprint projects and detailed system specifications can be found in several Library of Congress publications (Hahn, 1983; Price, 1984; Fleischauer, 1985). While the role of optical disc technologies in resource sharing activities is yet to be defined, it is likely that in years to come the library and information community will benefit from LC's accomplishments in this area. To date, the pilot project has yielded information and built expertise in three main areas of optical media: the development and use of optical technology; file construction, indexing and bibliographic control; and staff and user reactions.

One of the objectives of the print project is to examine the effects of optical disc technology and applications on copyright royalties and the publishing community. Copyright and data ownership are major constraining factors. Publishers are understandably concerned about a technology that has the capability of serving many users with only one copy. LC is working closely with publishers to assure the integrity of copyright for the pilot project. Many publishers are beginning to adopt the technology themselves, exploring a number of mechanisms to protect revenues, including the "metering" of document use at the public workstation, with subsequent billing of the library for accumulated usage in a given period of time.

A recent news item (Library Journal, October 15, 1986, p.17) announces the formulation of a new policy governing the use of print materials in optical disc format. The policy has been developed by an advisory committee to LC consisting of representatives from libraries, publishing, and trade associations. Guidelines defined in the policy place restrictions on LC's dissemination of published information using optical discs, and thus are indicative of future constraints that are likely to be placed on other libraries and network organizations. The recommendations demonstrate LC's sensitivity to commercial concerns for copyright, profits, and royalties.

The statement emphasizes the preservation potential of the new technology as well as its capability for widespread dissemination of materials to the public. LC sees these capabilities as opportunities waiting for the commercial sector to grab. However, LC is currently limited to use its discs internally or for the Congress. Also, the Library will only create or disseminate disc materials if the commercial does not , especially to other locations.

The Linked Systems Project (LSP)

A wide variety of computer systems support the automation of library functions in North America, from the large mainframes of LC and the utilities, to the mini- and micro-based systems that support one or more local functions like circulation control or the online public access catalog. Until very recently, these different computer systems have not been able to interconnect and communicate directly, computer-to-computer. Such an interconnection is desirable for these reasons: two or more local systems could be linked to widen resource sharing activities without requiring the use of the _same_ automated system by the participants, or the use of a separate, intermediate computer facility to facilitate the interfacing of two different systems; the bibliographic utilities could access each other's and LC's databases directly; and data transfer between local systems and the utilities could take place almost instantly.

Although computer-to-computer interconnection between different automated library systems was not achieved in the U.S. until late 1985, two other methods of interfacing systems have been common in practice: tape-to-computer, and terminal-to-computer. Local system files are typically created or updated by loading the results of cataloging or recon activity received from a vendor or utility on magnetic tapes. Libraries subscribe to this "archive" tape service on a weekly or monthly basis. Records are also passed directly into a local system from a utility's cataloging terminal, on a record-by-record basis, utilizing the terminal's printer port and interface software or hardware designed to capture and reformat the utility's displayed MARC record for entry into and processing by the local system.

The existence of a standard format for machine-readable bibliographic records (MARC) has facilitated these modes of exchange of bibliographic data. Direct computer-to-computer linkage to support intersystem transactions and data transfer requires the adoption and implementation of additional standards. Because different computer systems receive, represent, and process data differently, without standardized procedures on which to base intersystem interconnection, each linking of different systems would require special purpose interface facilities, as would each purpose (application; i.e., ILL, cataloging, etc.) for linking. A non-standardized approach to linking is too chaotic and costly and is usually limited to no more than two systems for a single purpose. Such an environment is still closed, ruling out the interconnection of a third, or fourth, system, and so on. The nonexistence of standard data communications procedures until very recently largely accounts for the limited number of computer-to-computer linkages achieved in the library networking environment to the present. However, other obstacles lie in the path of widespread implementation of an open, linked systems environment. These obstacles include claims to the ownership or copyright of data, costs, and administrative concerns.

To overcome these obstacles and make major progress toward a fully-linked library systems environment, the Linked Systems Project (LSP) has been established and developed in the United States. The current partners in this cooperative effort to link the utilities with LC and one another are LC, RLG, WLN, and OCLC. Work on LSP began in 1980 with the assistance of funding from the Council on Library Resources (CLR). The first goal set by the participants was to create online communications links and data retrieval, maintenance, and transfer mechanisms among their systems to support a shared file of authority records.

LSP can trace its roots to the early days of NAC, and CLR's and LC's efforts (through its Network Development Office, NDO) to coordinate the development of a national network. Studies were commissioned in the late 1970s to recommend an architectural framework for linking the existing bibliographic systems and networks. Technical requirements for linking these systems were identified, the decision was made to adopt ISO standard communications protocols where possible, and general criteria for linking the large automated bibliographic services were established. CLR and NDO staff drafted a program document to assist in acquiring the funds needed for such a large undertaking. Criteria established for the planned linkage facility stipulated that it 1) could be implemented on any type or make of computer system; 2) would accommodate initial as well as new applications; 3) could expand to accept new participants with no negative impact on current members; and 4) comprised two major elements, namely, a) the communications link supporting the transmission of any kind of data, and b) a variety of applications in existence or to be developed. (For a brief overview of this period, 1976-1980, See Avram, 1986.)

CLR did receive funding and LSP began in 1980 as a project largely supported by these funds administered within CLR's Bibliographic Services Development Program (BSDP). Initially called the Linked Authority Systems Project, it became the Linked Systems Project to extend the scope of the project beyond authority data. In phase one, the LSP participants, LC, RLIN, OCLC, and WLN, are to build a shared name authority file through a linking of their systems. The authorities project was chosen to implement first because authority creation and maintenance is a costly effort for libraries due to the time and intellectual effort involved. Implementation of bibliographic and location records exchange will come later.

LSP consists of the communications facility and the applications facility. The communications facility is the Standard Network Interconnection (SNI) which allows data exchange for all record types. SNI is based on the ISO Open Systems Interconnection (OSI) Reference Model . OSI and LSP consist of seven layers of the procedures necessary for intersystems communication with each layer building on the layer below. Standards for the lower five layers exist. Standards work continues on the upper two layers. The applications facility supports data sharing, initially for authority records, later for bibliographic and locations records.

The two basic LSP components are record transfer between systems of any type and any number of records, and information retrieval for search and response between systems. The requesting terminal sends a message to its computer, down the seven layers, across the LSP communications link (TELENET in the the case of LSP), and up the seven layers to the queried computer. The user will be able to access another system through his own, query it, and get an understandable response to his query.

The Linked Systems Project makes use of the LC Name Authority Cooperative (NACO) project which adds authority records to the LC master file by: 1) direct online input by the contributing institution and 2) mail shipment for online input at LC. Only the University of Chicago and Harvard University have online access for both searching and input. The 35+ remaining NACO participants may have search only online access or may have to use the manual tools, the National Union Catalog and the Name Authorities on microform. The time delays of manual verification and paper shipment of authority records can lead to duplication. Therefore, with LSP, LC catalogers will check the LC online file for an existing record. If a new record is needed, it will be created and then distributed to the LSP partners. NACO members belonging to a participating bibliographic utility will search the LC file on their own utility. If a new record is needed, they will add it to their utility's authority file for transmission to LC, then for transmission by LC to the other LSP participants.

The frequency of record transfer, at least every 24 hours between LC and the other participants, reduces the possibility of duplication. Also, LC's early notice records, brief records consisting of the heading and a work cataloged citation give warning of the authority records which are in process by LC catalogers.

LSP is currently operational only for record transfer between LC and RLIN. OCLC should begin contributing records to LC by late 1987. WLN should be ready to participate by 1988. LC's work on information retrieval should be implemented with RLIN by late 1987. Information retrieval or intersystem searching allows utility member libraries to search on another utility. This allows non-NACO libraries on other utilities to use library contributed authority records which are not part of the LC file. NACO libraries could modify these records or transmit them to LC via the Linked Systems Project. LC will preside over quality control by viewing records on the original utility for LC standards conformance before adding them to the LC master file.

Anticipated extensions to the authorities implementation of LSP over the next two to three years include intersystem online retrieval and system-to-system transfer of bibliographic and holdings records. Design work is underway for the intersystem bibliographic search implementation. The current participants in LSP are beginning to promote the implementation of LSP protocols and applications by vendors and designers of local library systems. The LSP principals have recently agreed to use LSP standard protocols for network/utility-to-local system linkages. On their part, vendors of local systems will have to develop interfacing software incorporating LSP-OSI standard protocols for their computer systems, but this will only have to be done once in order to link with other systems that also support the standard protocols. This investment will allow a system to link with any of the 3 national network participants, OCLC, RLG/RLIN, WLN. This will be an opportunity for systems such as GEAC, NOTIS, LS/2000, CLSI, etc., and for any library or consortium developed system.

GEAC is the leader in implementing such linkages. The 1986 Beta test to transfer records and link New York University's (NYU) GEAC system to RLIN has proved successful. NYU's cataloging on RLIN is shown almost immediately in the NYU Bobst Library's online catalog. Northwestern University's NOTIS and UTLAS' T/Series 50 plan to implement similar linkages to RLIN with the standard protocols. Such links would be advantageous to the buyers of these local systems and provide a market advantage for the sellers.

Other local system suppliers will probably take a close look at the significance for their systems and current clients of the LSP standard protocols, in light of recent agreements among the LSP principals. These agreements make it likely that in two to three years LC, the utilities and their members, and local system vendors will all be putting capabilities in place to support LSP-based linkage between utilities and local systems.

Recent LSP agreements

The LSP participants in the Linked Systems Project Policy Group -- the Library of Congress (LC), the Research Libraries Group (RLG), the Western Library Network (WLN), and the Online Computer Library Center (OCLC) have agreed upon the work which will follow completion of phase one, the Authorities Implementation. These new agreements describe what the project will mean, who will see what results when, and what should not be expected of the LSP. The agreements as described by McCoy (Library Journal, October 1, 1986) are:

1. The protocols of the LSP will be used by the participants not only to link their systems or networks but as their standard means of linking with local library systems. The LSP protocols are, or will be, specifically , the Open System Interconnection Protocols (OSI) being developed by the International Organization for Standardization (ISO) with the support and participation of U.S. Standards groups such as X.3 and NISO (Z-39). (Additional information on the LSP protocols is available to those planning to implement them on a computer system in the document: LSP/SNI Protocol Specifications (SNI 30) available from the Network Development and MARC Standards Office, Processing Services, Library of Congress, Washington, DC 20540.)

2. A limited capability for internetwork bibliographic record searching will be implemented. An initial set of users will have access to known-item searching in networks other than their "home" network as needed, for example, for expanded access to records to use in support of shared cataloging.

3. A record transfer capability will be implemented which will facilitate transfer of individual records or groups of records among the networks. This capability will be used to transfer coordinated cataloging records to the Library of Congress for distribution to MARC subscribers and would be used, for example, to transfer preservation microfilm records among the networks (now done by tape exchanges).

4. The capability to exchange interlibrary loan messages in standard form among the networks will also be developed within the LSP. This work is being completed under the direction of the National Library of Canada through the auspices of the Canadian Standards Organization.

5. The LSP participants agree that: a) they will continue to move forward with the current protocols of the LSP so that practical progress can be made with minimum delay; and b) they are committed to the standardization process and to providing the evolving standard protocols as soon as practical after they are formally accepted by national and

<u>international standards bodies</u>. This agreement carries with it the intent to continue active work on the developing standards and to support their broad acceptance by the library community.

Proponents of the LSP protocols as <u>the</u> standard for library intersystem communication in support of cataloging, search and retrieval, ILL, record transfer, etc., extend their enthusiasm to the international arena. The current LSP principals hope for worldwide acceptance and implementation of LSP protocols. For this to occur, new LSP application level protocols, including the current record transfer and retrieval protocols, would have to become ISO-OSI standards.

Realists point to other obstacles that must be overcome if LSP is to continue to achieve its original and expanded goals. Prime among these obstacles are costs -- to develop and operate these linkages ("who pays for what to whom?") -- and copyright or database ownership-based restrictions on the sharing and exchange of data. Ultimately, these issues are a matter of administrative policy; but at this time there has been little enlightened discussion of these crucial issues in the context of an open system, fully-linked, environment. Policy matters will surely be more complicated given the mix of participants: locally-governed libraries, utilities, local system vendors, commercial suppliers of cataloging data, and national libraries. Ironically, the trend at the utilities and national libraries is to restrict the means of data exchange and use beyond their "domains" while, at the same time, progress is being made toward an open, interconnected networking environment, at least, in North America.

New groups are being formed to begin to address these joint economic and policy issues, and others will surely follow from the library and information communities. Two committees have been formed within LSP: the Technical Committee, whose role is to ensure consistent implementations of protocols in existence as well as new ones, based on operating experience and evolving international standards; and the Policy Committee, created to provide policy direction for new standard applications, costs, accounting, and other administrative matters. Currently, executive officers from LC, RLG, WLN, OCLC, and CLR's BSDP program officer constitute the LSP Policy Committee. Included on the Technical Committee are representatives from LC, OCLC, RLG, WLN, the National Library of Medicine, the National Library of Canada, GEAC, NOTIS, and the Triangle Research Libraries Network (TRLN). In January 1986, a concerned group of local system vendors formed AVIAC, the Automated Vendor Interface Advisory Committee, composed of eight members, each representing a different commercial organization. AVIAC seeks to identify vendors' requirements for implementation of LSP protocols, and to have a major voice in the selection and design of new applications. AVIAC's relation to the LSP Committee is not formally defined. Some competitive tension is likely to develop, if LC and the U.S. utilities attempt to control policy matters and "hand-down" their decisions to the rest of the community. This is an increasingly competitive community, as utilities now market or support local systems, and vendors provide networking and cataloging facilities. Each LSP application designed beyond the authorities implementation must be carefully specified, with the correctness of no single approach apparent from the start. In each case, an evolutionary, consensus-building process will be required.

B. The National Library of Canada (NLC)

The National Library of Canada's contributions to the advance of library automation and networking have occurred in two main areas: 1) the coordination of planning and development for a nationwide, decentralized, open and voluntary, library and information communications network; and 2) the development of the DOBIS-based online library system which supports a large online union database and serves as the basis of NLC's bibliographic services to other libraries. Highlights in the history of these contributions and recent developments will be reviewed in this section.

Planning for a decentralized library and information communications network

During the 1970s, the National Library played an important leadership role in an environment of rapidly developing technology and new automated bibliographic systems. In the late 1960s and early 1970s, many Canadian institutions developed their own automated library systems. These developments generally took place in isolation from one another. In most cases, single library functions were automated (e.g., cataloging, circulation, acquisitions), and each system used its own non-standard bibliographic record formats to store and process catalog records. These local computer-based resources could not be shared easily, and thus hindered the development of library cooperation. To facilitate the creation and exchange of machine-readable bibliographic records needed for rational resource sharing in the computer age, the National Library initiated and coordinated several study activities and cooperative bibliographic projects. Starting in the early 1970s, one of the aims of the National Library has been to draw-up plans for a nationwide computerized bibliographic network, while, at the same time, encouraging the development of the network's essential building blocks, such as cataloging standards, standardized record formats, and a national union catalog.

As recommended by the National Conference on Cataloguing Standards in 1970, three task groups were charged to develop standards for the planning and implementation of an automated national library network. First, the Canadian Task Group on Cataloguing Standards (1970–1972) provided the groundwork for the content and format revision of Canadiana, the national bibliography. The task group also developed the Canadian position on international standards development. The report also inspired other programs such as Cataloguing in Publication, the cooperative Universite Laval/National Library subject headings project, the National Library/Library of Congress corporate names agreement, and the CONSER project. The second task group, the MARC Task Group (1970–1972), created the bilingual Canadian MARC format. The third task group, the Canadian Union Catalogue Task Group, established in 1972, studied interlending patterns and union catalog activities for a library network environment.

The National Library Networks Office, created in 1974, complemented the task groups' work on the development of the Canadian library network by conducting planning studies. One study, the Canadian Computerized Bibliographic Centre Study (CCBCS), which included seven sub-studies resulted in the important final report, Towards More Effective Nation-wide Library and Information Networking in Canada.

A comprehensive review of the National Library's role, objectives, and services was carried out in 1976 and 1977. Input was received from associations, institutions, Library staff, and individuals. The review culminated in the 1979 National Librarian's report to the Secretary of State, The Future of the National Library of Canada.

This report, "recommended that the Canadian library network be achieved by voluntary cooperation among institutions enjoying a large measure of autonomy, and that it be neither monolithic nor centrally controlled but managed cooperatively through contractual arrangements between two or more institutions or consortia for the sharing or exchanging of information or services."

This recommendation signalled a major change from the previously embraced concept of a centralized network to that of a decentralized one, a change which has come to be enthusiastically endorsed by the Canadian library community. Ironically, this new stance was announced at the very time that centralized, star-configured bibliographic networks were successfully entrenching themselves (OCLC, RLIN, WLN) in the very fabric of cooperative library activities in the United States.

Until the late 1970s, the Canadian library leaders believed that a "closed" national library network with a centralized file to which all other systems would be connected was the only technologically feasible model. However, the Canadian library community wanted a decentralized approach, not a centralized one which did not recognize Canadian regionalization and wide reaching size and geography. In a centralized network, the National Library would be responsible for the centralized union catalog and its maintenance, a difficult and labor intensive task. An alternative to centralization only became available in the late 1970s with the creation and publication of the Open Systems Interconnection (OSI) reference model by ISO.

OSI

The Open Systems Interconnection (OSI) reference model supplied the compelling rationale for a direction many Canadian librarians urgently wished to pursue. Closed, centralized star networks like DOBIS, UTLAS, and the U.S. utilities were viewed as important participants in a future network, but none of these could serve as the model for its structure and organization. The Canadians preferred an open network model which configures the interconnection of different host computers and simplifies access from one terminal to many different databases. In this model, there is no requirement for a central or "master" database. The network database is a virtual database consisting of all databases available in the network. In addition, the Canadians believed, "each system or closed network could be autonomous in its development as long as it could translate its internal configuration into a network standard configuration when access beyond the system or closed network is needed. The network would thus become an "add-on" to the local/regional system to be accessed as required. The cost of maintaining the conversion to the network standard would be borne locally. In reality, the open network would be a network of closed networks, be they based on macro-, mini-, or micro-computer systems" (Durance, 1982. Canadian Network Papers, No. 2).

In 1980, the National Library adopted the OSI Model as the best means of achieving a decentralized networking environment. This decision had its risks, as OSI had not been fully implemented anywhere. Indeed, most of the standard protocols called for in the model were either under development, or non-existent. Furthermore, full compliance with OSI standards would require partial or full implementation by hardware and software manufacturers, telecommunications firms, and library system designers and vendors. Issues of governance, jurisdiction, ownership, accounting, and management would also have to be faced.

In the early 1980s, the National Library undertook three major initiatives to confront these challenges. First, in March 1981, the National Library Advisory Board created two new broad-based committees to advise it on various requirements for network development. First, the Bibliographic and Communications Network Committee studies policy issues and problems arising from the development and management of a bibliographic network. Second, the Resource Network Committee reviews the most cost-effective provision of Canadian library services and collections for the widest usage. It's areas for examination and policy input include: research collections, interlibrarary lending, document delivery, legal deposit, and conservation. The Committee on Bibliography and Information Services for the Social Sciences and Humanitities, previously the Committee on Bibliographical Services for Canada, oversees support and development of information and documentation services in its subject areas.

Second, the Task Group on Computer/Communications Protocols for Bibliographic Data Interchange was created in December 1980 by the National Librarian to define computer-to-computer protocols specifically to exchange bibliographic data. The task group members gained their expertise from the various fields of library, information, and publishing industry systems, university computer faculties, telecommunications carriers, and federal government telecommunications research and standards development. The task group serves as liaison on protocol development across Canada. Their work is conducted within the OSI model framework and they provide further input to ISO on international protocol development (Canadian Network Papers, No. 2, May 1982).

The third initiative involved the NLC-coordinated participation of sixteen Canadian libraries in the 1982-1983 iNet intelligent gateway/intersystem connection Field Trial mounted by Telecom Canada. The iNet Field Trial was one of the first attempts in the world to implement the OSI concept. Technically, it was not completely a standards-based open network (the upper OSI layers had not been specified yet), but it operated much like one and served successfully as a pilot testing environment for libraries. Different computer systems and library databases were connected, and librarians accessed and shared data for cataloging, reference, and ILL activities in a way never possible before. The iNet field trial proved the technical feasibility of a linked-system environment, and provided invaluable experience to guide the further planning of a library, bibliographic network. Based on recommendations put forth after many evaluations of the iNet trial, the development of standard OSI protocols for bibliographic applications became a top priority at the National Library.

Current initiatives

As explained by Cynthia Durance (1986), Director of the Office for Network Development (OND), the National Library of Canada is currently taking a four-pronged approach to the development of the decentralized bibliographic network: 1) the technical research and development of OSI-based application level protocols. Protocols are the standard specifications of the messages which need to be exchanged by two independent systems for a given application, the format of those messages, and the sequence in which they must be exchanged in order to achieve intersystem communication independent of system hardware or software; 2) the conduct of pilot projects involving libraries and related organizations to test the newly developed protocols; 3) implementation of the resulting products through licensing agreements to both the private and public sectors; and 4) developing mechanisms for drafting networking policy, service progress, and ongoing network support and coordination.

Much work has been done on three application protocols: bibliographic record file transfer, interlibrary loan, and an online directory to services available on the open, decentralized network. The status of these standard protocols, as reported by Durance (1986), is as follows:

The file transfer protocol was the first protocol implemented. Implementation was completed in November 1984 on an IBM, a Honeywell, a CDC Cyber and a GEAC machine. This implementation pre-dated LSP and we are told it was the first implementation anywhere in the world of an OSI application layer protocol. It is the only connection-oriented protocol we have implemented. Since early 1985, three universities have been submitting searches online and transferring MARC records online from the National Library's system into their own three different systems. These implementations are presently somewhat incompatible with the LSP file transfer implementations. This is due to the fact that both the NLC file transfer and LSP protocols were implemented prior to international agreement on the File Transfer Application Management (FTAM) standard and neither LSP nor our implementation at present totally conforms to the ISO standard. There is a Canadian-U.S.A. agreement in principle that both ourselves and LSP will implement the FTAM standard and thereby hope to achieve compatibility sometime in the not-too-distant future.

The second protocol we've developed is that for interlibrary loan (ILL) messaging. This protocol is implemented using the connectionless (for store and forward) method utilizing the nation-wide electronic mail services provided by our two national telecommunications companies. This protocol has now been tested and is in the process of revision. The revisions are based on the combined input of the ten Canadian libraries who participated in the pilot project, plus major Canadian and American vendors and providers of automated ILL services (GEAC, OCLC, RLIN, UTLAS, WLN, etc.). In 1986, this revised protocol will be formally submitted for consideration as a common North American standard. It will be submitted to ISO/TC46/SC4 at the same time as a working document for international standardization. The National Library of Canada is currently developing its own automated system for ILL incorporating the protocol. This system is scheduled to be operating early in 1987.

The third development we are working on is a decentralized directory service. In addition to providing a means of finding out who has what in an open network, it incorporates features recognized internationally for the management of distributed applications in an open network such as security, conditions of systems availability, statistics gathering, etc. The directories project is presently in prototype on a supermicrocomputer. A technical assessment of it is currently being undertaken jointly by ourselves, GEAC, and a Montreal firm called IST Informatheque Inc.

Durance aptly points out that the adoption of international standards may be the only way to achieve the flexibility necessary to attain both goals of retaining local autonomy and large-scale resource sharing. Centrally controlled networks have been rejected by the Canadians, and it is far too costly to build and maintain multiple, customized interfaces to all the different systems in existence. However, because each OSI protocol implementation requires establishing communication between different systems, there is a need for a neutral test facility to ensure each implementation can communicate with any other. This facility may have to be centrally administered.

To achieve its goal of a nationwide network, the National Library of Canada defines its current role as one of developing needed standard protocols and promoting widespread implementation of OSI standards for library networking applications. In these efforts, the National Library has worked closely with library system vendors, telecommunications agencies, and national and international standards bodies. They have set a pattern of openness and consensus-building that may be required in the U.S. to realize widespread acceptance of the Linked Systems Project's accomplishments.

In a recent personal communique received by this author from Ms. Durance of the National Library of Canada (March 18, 1987), she reports that "NLC has abandoned licensing as an interim vehicle for the protocol specifications and instead has a protocol implementation support program to assist implementations in Canada. This support can be technical, financial or both according to circumstances. Along this line, NLC and the National Research Council have just signed a major 18-month to 2-year agreement with Geac Canada to assist them with the implementation of several protocols we have developed. The protocols will be incorporated in new software currently under development at Geac." Durance also reports that NLC's automated protocol-supported ILL system has gone into production and will be operational later in 1987.

Bibliographic services based on NLC's DOBIS online system

In the late 1970s, the National Library and CISTI jointly developed the prototype DOBIS online integrated system into a MARC-based operational system for the use of federal government libraries. In 1982, search-only service of DOBIS' online union catalog was offered to libraries of all types throughout Canada. More than 200 libraries now subscribe to this service. Full-service cataloging and catalog production activities on DOBIS are currently offered only to federal libraries and libraries contributing by special arrangement to national products.

The DOBIS online database contains more than 4.5 million unique bibliographic records for all types of materials representing the holdings of over 300 Canadian libraries. Bibliographic records in DOBIS are maintained online under full name and subject authority control. DOBIS is also a bilingual system: information can be added and searched in both English and French.

In 1983, the National Library began its MARC Record Distribution Service (MRDS). MRDS is a batch record transfer and distribution process. MARCALL, the CAN/MARC database can be purchased on tape. A selected record service is also available for recon purposes. For identified records, NLC provides catalog cards or CAN/MARC records on tape.

Since 1984, online file transfer of bibliographic records directly from DOBIS to each of three different university online systems has been in operation. Using the ISO/OSI-based FTAM (file transfer and application management) protocols, more than one thousand records a week are passed from the DOBIS mainframe computer in Ottawa to the University of Waterloo's GEAC library system, the University of Quebec's Cyber-based system, and Carleton University's locally-developed, IBM-based system. These protocols permit a list of record search requests to be sent to the DOBIS host computer, which then retrieves and transfers a file of matching records to the requesting computer at the remote library. The National Library planning to extend this online file transfer service to additional libraries. It is estimated that it will cost $30,000 for each new implementation of the FTAM protocols at a local site.

4. Data Ownership and Use Restrictions

The policies of the major utilities regarding bibliographic record and database copyright ownership and use of this data by other parties have been reviewed in a preceding section of this book. Position statements on these issues by each of the utilities, OCLC, RLG/RLIN, WLN, and UTLAS may be reviewed in Appendix A.

A. Machine-readable Bibliographic Records: Before and After

The open, almost unlimited sharing of bibliographic data -- catalog records and location information -- has been both the foundation and soul of library cooperation in this century. Pre-automated union catalogs were commonly employed to provide cataloging copy and location information to support resource sharing programs, such as ILL and cooperative collection building. Union catalogs at the local, state, and national levels expanded access to the collections in libraries. Once produced, purchased, or otherwise acquired, few, if any, restrictions were ever placed on the subsequent use, copying, or redistribution of bibliographic records in their pre-automated, print forms. The critical issues most often discussed were those of overcoming physical obstacles to access and sharing, and, in a minor way, the costs associated with producing catalog cards and the maintenance of manual union lists or catalogs.

Economic motives became a primary factor at the very beginning of computerized cataloging and the production and use of machine-readable records. Computer-based, shared cataloging was viewed as desirable because it reduced the costs of cataloging for most libraries. The utilities built large, centralized computer systems for bibliographic applications to take advantage of the inherent economies of scale. Computer applications to library functions did not give birth to library cooperation and resource sharing, or even new kinds of resource sharing. The computer, with its vast stores of machine-readable data and online, time-sharing capabilities, enhanced and expanded library resource sharing activities at proportionately less cost. Simply put, computer-based cooperation was cost-effective.

However, on the road to computerized cataloging and machine-readable records and databases, strange new conditions developed. The utilities built large, costly facilities to support online, shared cataloging. Their facilities, staffs, and databases grew, and so did the costs to maintain these facilities and databases. Libraries create and contribute records to these databases, but utilities bear the large operational, maintenance, and development costs to support the databases. Since they depend on revenues made from the database to meet these costs, the database has become a very valuable asset. Contributing libraries, in isolation, or in alliance, have interests in "their" records. They generally believe they own their records and should be able to do with them as they please. The utilities, and national libraries which distribute machine-readable bibliographic records, have substantial financial investments in their databases. They do not wish to see the value of their databases erode through unauthorized copying, redistribution, and use of substantial amounts of records derived from their databases. Thus, conflicts related to ownership, transfer, and use have emerged, often in a very visible, noisy manner. The issues are not merely those of resource sharing and cooperation, for, or against. All parties -- local libraries, utilities, networks, and national libraries -- have economic interests and motives. Machine-readable bibliographic information has become a resource with clearly identifiable costs and benefits. All parties involved in the creation, processing, and storage of bibliographic records may wish to use these records not only for the initial purposes, but to recover some of their initial investment or to reduce the costs of secondary resource sharing activities (e.g. building union catalogs) which use these records, already created, and already "paid for."

In today's technological environment, both the format and means of making bibliographic data widely available for resource sharing among libraries have changed. In the age of machine-readable records, precisely what constitutes property to be owned or shared is a complex matter. One of the consequences -- unintended, no doubt -- has been the creation of tension and conflicts between the creators and processors of machine-readable records and libraries which believe that bibliographic information should be freely available for sharing, and that no one has the right to place restrictions on any use of their own records. Yet, as more and more data becomes available in new machine-readable media (e.g., optical), and open linkages are established between automated bibliographic systems within and across national borders, the trend is clearly toward the increased placing of restrictions on the copying, distribution, and use of bibliographic data in machine-readable form.

Three of the four major utilities place some restrictions on either the extraction, transfer, or use of all or parts or forms of their machine-readable databases. However, each utility's policy differs considerably from the others. Recently, the national libraries have begun to place restrictions on the redistribution of their MARC records in other countries. The long-range impact of these restrictions on library cooperation based on the sharing of bibliographic information whether at the local or international levels, is a matter of speculation. It seems certain, however, that more control over the distribution and use of machine-readable records will be manifest in the form of copyright claims, contracts, and licensing agreements. For a full and precise discussion of these formal, legal measures and their use by utilities and national libraries in today's environment, see "Copyright, Ownership of, In Machine-Readable Bibliographic Data," an essay by Roddy Duchesne in the Encyclopedia of Library and Information Science, Vol. 40, 1986.

B. Some Current Restrictions

In a recent publication, LC's Avram (September 1986) reviews several recent actions taken to restrict the redistribution or reuse of machine-readable bibliographic records:

1. OCLC felt forced to copyright its database to protect its asset, in particular, to prevent the redistribution of its data to profit-making third-party users.

2. The owners (the British Library, the American Antiquarian Society, English Short Title Catalog/North America, based at Louisiana State University) of the Eighteenth Century Short Title Catalog database housed at RLIN have refused distribution of these records until adequate compensation can be foreseen for their efforts.

3. When the Association of Research Libraries planned their program for retrospective conversion, it was assumed that these records would be made available to LC for distribution via the MARC Service. Because LC would not restrict its distribution service to not-for-profit organizations, however, this data has not been forthcoming in all cases.

4. Phase 2 of the automation of the National Union Catalog (NUC) is the acceptance by LC of reporting libraries' records in machine-readable

form. LC has received agreement from the utilities that these records may be printed in the NUC but permission to distribute these records via the MARC Service has not been authorized in all cases. The value of NUC records from the reporting libraries is that the LC staff modify the name headings to make them consistent with LC headings. This consistency does not necessarily exist in the utility databases.

5. Carrollton Press, Inc., under contract with the Library of Congress, converted the LC shelflist to machine-readable form (REMARC). The records were returned to LC for processing through its format recognition programs and the processed records were submitted to Carrollton Press, and a copy maintained at LC. The LC/Carrollton Press contract included the restriction placed on LC that no more than 15,000 machine-readable records, updated by LC, could be distributed each year by LC. This restriction protected the investment made by Carrollton Press. (Carrollton Press, along with UTLAS, is now owned by International Thomson Organisation, Limited.)

6. Several institutions in this country or abroad have made available for sale in a country other than the U.S. the LC MARC database, either in its entirety or subsets of it. Since the LC Cataloging Distribution Service (CDS) must earn half of its appropriated funding, and in the interest of maintaining viable pricing structures for the community, it was necessary for LC to impose copyright for its records distributed internationally, i.e., only LC has the authority to distribute its database internationally -- the concepts of "public domain" and "no copyright claim" do not exist outside of the U.S. Under certain special agreements made with national libraries of other countries, the LC database may be distributed within the country of a national library.

C. International Developments

The exchange of records between national libraries in different countries has been affected by recent events. National libraries in countries outside the U.S. have taken measures which have placed, or could place, restrictions on the distribution of bibliographic data within the recipient's country. As Avram (1986) points out, "Where, in the past, agreements between national libraries included the distribution of the originator's data within the recipient's country, now several national agencies have expressed unwillingness to have their data distributed within the recipient's country to organizations that also provide products and services to other agencies."

The National Library of Canada distributes it CAN/MARC machine-readable bibliographic database under Crown copyright, which in Canada is essentially copyright owned by the government of Canada. But the Canadian Copyright Act permits an owner to "grant any interest in the right by license." A license typically granted by contractual agreement, normally operates as a permission to do certain specified things and does not involve a transfer of ownership. However, in Canada, the grant of an interest in the right is not limited to granting permission to do certain specified things with the data, and may include "the grant of _proprietary_ interest" in the database. (Duchesne, 1986)

The British Library has taken the licensing approach to control the distribution of UK MARC machine-readable records in other countries, including the U.S. For example, LC provides a conversion service to U.S. organizations who wish to obtain UK MARC records converted to USMARC. However, the U.S. customer becomes a customer of the British Library; LC merely provides the conversion service. On the other hand, if an organization desires LCMARC records in UK MARC formats, that organization becomes a customer of the Library of Congress; the British Library provides the conversion service.

Clearly, there is a growning concern for the economic and quality control problems associated with the exchange and redistribution of bibliographic data in machine-readable form. Work is underway at the international level which recognizes these problems and their potential impact on the future of international cooperative programs. IFLA and the International MARC Network Committee are currently working on the development of compatible approaches among members to agreements that will govern the international exchange of data. (See "International Transfers of MARC Records : Guidelines for agreements relating to the transfer of national MARC records between national MARC agencies," IFLA, August 1986.)

The ability of utilities like UTLAS and OCLC to bypass the national libraries in their home countries, and provide access abroad to USMARC, REMARC, and CAN/MARC records, as well as to acquire records directly from other countries' national libraries, dims the prospects that a uniform approach to contracts and agreements governing the exchange of data among countries can be developed. However, the work of the International MARC Network Committee will be valuable if it leads to a common understanding and shared definitions of the kinds of property involved in this new machine-readable environment, the rights associated with these properties, and the activities or uses associated with these properties that may form a part of future contracts and licensing arrangements.

PART III

AUTOMATED SYSTEMS AND SERVICES IN LIBRARIES

1. Integrated, Multifunction Library Systems

The integrated, multi-function, local library system at its most minimal includes functions of: 1) circulation control, 2) bibliographic control for cataloging locally, and through a bibliographic utility, and 3) the public access catalog. Additional functions offered by some system suppliers are acquisitions, serials control, electronic mail, interlibrary loan, and materials booking. Integration may be achieved by running all functions on a single computer or linking and/or interfacing with other computers. These computers may be of varying sizes: mainframe, minicomputers or microcomputers. Many integrated systems are available in modular form offering libraries the opportunity to automate function by function. Single function software is also available but it gives libraries neither the flexibility or growth options that integrated systems do. However, libraries are automating using both methods. A market study done for the barcode industry by International Resource Development Inc. estimates that 26% of the 32,995 U.S. libraries have been partially automated (Library Hi Tech News, May 1987).

Integrated library systems are generally classified into two categories based on how they were developed: turnkey systems and library developed software systems. Turnkey systems have "been designed, programmed, and tested by an organization or company, then offered for sale or lease to libraries, ready to be installed and operated" (Corbin, 1985). The advantages of the turnkey system have made it the overwhelming choice for over 90% of the libraries with integrated systems. These advantages include: 1) relatively short installation, 2) elimination of library development, 3) access to the vendor's computer specialists, 4) system tailoring to meet most library requirements, 5) vendor responsibility for installation, software, and hardware, 6) need for reduced library in-house computer knowledge, and 7) less initial (developmental) and ongoing costs (Corbin).

Most turnkey vendors offer libraries a complete package of software and hardware, including total support of both. A few turnkey systems are software only systems, such as Northwestern University's NOTIS, and TECHLIB products from Information Dimensions, Inc., a subsidiary of Battelle. Some "total package" vendors (e.g., OCLC, VTLS, IBM) do offer libraries the choice of purchasing the vendor's software to run on library maintained hardware.

Library developed software has been designed, tested, programmed, and installed at a particular library, usually by in-house staff. This software is offered to other libraries for purchase in hope of recovering developmental costs and producing profit revenue. These systems' obvious advantage to the developing library is total customization to meet that library's needs. An advantage to the purchasers of software systems is that they may customize the software more than is allowed in systems offered by vendors.

Both turnkey vendor and library developed software systems may be used by single institutions with more than one location (e.g., main library with branches), or shared among several institutions. For example, as of December 1986, CLSI's 277 installed systems served over 1200 libraries. Unfortunately most vendors' figures are compared only on the number of systems/installations, not the actual number of libraries using the systems. This belies the very important trend of shared local systems for networking.

MARKET TRENDS

The _Library Journal_'s annual reviews of the automated library marketplace illustrate current trends. Joseph R. Matthews'(1986) review for the calendar year 1985 gives comprehensive statistics covering most of the system suppliers. Robert A. Walton's (1987) review of developments in 1986 is more limited covering only the turnkey vendors, yet still provides valuable data. While the reported statistics cover worldwide installations, primarily North American vendors are included in the surveys. In 1985, of the top seven vendors' 138 installations, only 17 systems (12%) were reported as being installed outside North America. The 1986 survey charts U.S. vs. foreign installations for the leading 10 vendors (plus an "other" category) with approximately 10% being non-U.S. Therefore, we can assume these two reviews give fairly accurate portrayals of American and Canadian automation activity.

By the end of 1985, Matthews reports customers had installed 1,109 turnkey systems, 235 of which were installed during 1985. Other library customers had installed at least 151 library developed software systems, 107 of which were installed during 1985. The number of library developed software systems only represents those eight systems which were actively being marketed for purchase. These systems are by no means the only library developed automated systems in use.

TURNKEY SYSTEMS

The past three years reflect the vigorous growth for vendor supplied automated systems. The 1985 growth rate was 41%, while 1984's grew 69%. Walton reports a 33% increase for 1986 to 193 installations from 145 in 1985. (NOTE: Walton defines a turnkey vendor more narrowly than Matthews. Therefore, he counts only 145 of Matthews' 235 turnkey systems in 1985.) Gross revenues in 1985 were $88,587,000 for the turnkey vendors. The percentage increase shows a decline over the three year period which may be due to a number of factors, including alternatives to the turnkey library market.

Of the new 235 turnkey systems installed in 1985, it is significant to note that seven vendors accounted for 61% of the marketplace: GEAC 11%, CLSI 11%, Battelle 10%, OCLC 8%, Dynix 7%, Innovative Interfaces 7%, and Data Research 7%. Three of the seven (Battelle's Information Dimensions, OCLC, and Dynix) with systems less than five years old are relatively new entries into the marketplace. Of the over 1,109 turnkey systems installed as of 1985, seven vendors accounted for 65% of the marketplace: CLSI 23%, SHL Business Systems 13%, GEAC 11%, Data Phase 6%, VTLS 4%, Innovative Interfaces 4%. These vendors continued to dominate the market in 1986 with strong showings in new systems by CLSI's 32 systems, Battelle's Information Dimensions' 31 systems, OCLC's 28 systems, and Dynix's 27 systems.

The North American marketplace is highly competitive and volatile. Libraries continued to buy from the more established vendors yet many willingly turned to the newer "improved" vendor systems to make OCLC and Dynix leaders in 1986. However, despite some new success stories, 25 vendors in 1985 had to fight for the remaining market which amounted to less than four systems per vendor. Most vendors cannot support their customers based on such low revenues. In a 1984 survey of 14 vendors, only six showed profits for their library division or company (Library Systems Newsletter, April 1984). The year 1986 saw the collapse of Data Phase with its sale to OCLC, as well as reported financial problems for Data Research and GEAC. Biblio-Techniques, a minor competitor having only seven customers, also closed its business in 1986. Two successful vendors showed healthy changes. Battelle's Software Products Center became Information Dimensions, Inc., a wholly owned subsidiary of Battelle and established independent offices.

Dynix was bought by management and staff from its parent company, Eyring Research Institute.

Yet, despite the competition, six new vendors entered the marketplace during 1985/1986. Four of the six, however, marketed systems that had already been tried and tested in a library environment: 1) Eyring Research Institute's CARL developed by the Colorado Alliance for Research Libraries, 2) UTLAS' T/Series 50, the new name for DataPhase's ALIS III, 3) Sperry's PALS developed as the Minnesota State University system, 4) McDonnell Douglas's URICA revised version of the system sold in Australia and South Africa. Of these four, only UTLAS with three installations was considered viable enough for inclusion in Walton's 1986 survey. With UTLAS International currently for sale, this viability may be short lived. Two young companies in the 1986 marketplace were Carlyle with six installations, and Inlex with seven installations. With increased revenues and personnel, these are vendors to watch in 1987. Despite the constant flow of new entrants, many market observers believe that the next five years will bring a real shakedown, reducing the library turnkey automation vendors to a mere handful.

LIBRARY DEVELOPED SYSTEMS

Sales of library developed systems accounted for only 32 system installations during 1985 (13% of all systems). Northwestern University's NOTIS system did remarkably well accounting for 66% of total sales. Through 1984, 18 NOTIS systems had been installed. In 1985, 21 NOTIS systems were installed and in 1986, 26 systems were installed. This fast paced growth, however, has given rise to installation delays and support problems. The sale of NOTIS to the private sector has been unsuccessfully negotiated several times during 1986 and 1987. Late in 1987, NOTIS loosened its ties to the University and was reorganized as an independent commercial library automation firm.

Other library developed systems have not fared as well. Georgetown University Medical Center Library sold six systems during 1986; the total number of installed systems is 19. Appealing to the smaller medical library market, Georgetown's system is a distant second to NOTIS. The Pennsylvania State University is no longer marketing its LIAS (Library Information Automated System) in 1986. It continues to support its two previous installations. The Washington University School of Medicine Library also appears to have dropped out of the market during 1986.

BUYERS

With such strong market activity, who is buying these local automated systems? The answer is all types of libraries as customers of the leading vendors illustrate: GEAC, OCLC, and NOTIS have mostly academic customers; CLSI, Dynix, and Data Research have predominantly public libraries; Battelle's Information Dimensions customers are mostly special libraries. One 1985 trend for all library types was that the systems purchased were relatively small. In 1985, 69% of the turnkey systems (64% of all systems) were configured with 16 or fewer terminals. With improved and more cost efficient hardware, the trend may be turning in 1986. More than half of all installations by CLSI, Data Research, GEAC, NOTIS, and UTLAS have more than 17 terminals. Libraries may initially install fewer terminals to reduce start-up system expenses and then increase the overall number of terminals.

For the very large systems of over 65 terminals, two systems clearly dominated the market in 1986. Among the vendors, GEAC and CLSI accounted for nearly 70% of the large installations. Among the library developed system providers, Northwestern University's NOTIS leads with approximately 20 sites having more than 65 terminals.

As one might expect, it is usually the larger libraries leading the way in library automation. While there are always exceptions, a survey of the leading academic and public libraries in the U.S. clearly shows the nationwide goal: achieving an automated integrated local system. The recently published Automated Library Systems in ARL Libraries (1986) gives a good overview of this trend. It documents the steps from planning to full implementation, with working documents from nine ARL libraries included in the report.

CANADIAN MARKETPLACE

While the above market review includes cumulative data for the vendors' worldwide installations, the vendors represented are mostly American. Reporting on a recent survey of Canadian libraries, Merilees focuses on that country's trends (Canadian Library Journal, June 1987). Merilees' survey includes only vendors that sell integrated library systems. She divides the marketplace into large systems (mainframe, minicomputer, and super microcomputer systems) and small microcomputer systems.

The vendors dominating the large system arena for new systems in 1986 were multiLIS (40%), and Minisis (24%). However, in the overall picture of 133 installations, Minisis' 44 systems (33%) and GEAC's 31 systems (23%) gained the highest shares of the marketplace. Behind them were multiLIS (11%), Sydney (9%), and CLSI (7%). Four of the top five vendors are Canadian; CLSI is the exception. Whether in reaction to local marketing efforts or the realities of system support, the North American marketplace shows a clear division along national lines.

GEAC and CLSI have both successfully crossed the Canadian and U.S. borders. The Canadian GEAC has a total of 107 foreign sales. Other U.S. vendors are trying to strengthen their Canadian marketing efforts. After having won several Canadian contracts, Dynix plans to open an office in Calgary. INLEX and DRA have recently installed their systems àt Canadian sites.

The systems being installed in Canada are comparable in size to their U.S. counterparts, with most supporting between 10-20 terminals. Although the percentage of large systems in the overall community is decreasing each year, 14 Canadian sites each surpass 100 terminals operating on their systems. Merilees notes that the need for systems to support ever higher numbers of terminals and transaction levels is an impetus in the amount of system development taking place. Libraries' demands for OPACs, heavy circulation loads, and community database access are forcing vendors to develop more powerful software and hardware solutions.

CASE STUDIES -- TRENDS

Two recent surveys reflect the market strength of integrated systems. First, the Association of Research Libraries (ARL) reports in 1986 one year increases for its member libraries for: integrated online catalogs -- up 22%, integrated local catalogs up 19%; integrated acquisitions up 18%. The second survey is covered below in more detail. The library consulting group of Peat, Marwick, Mitchell and Co. (San Francisco, CA) conducted a telephone survey of 26 top academic and public libraries across the U.S. to discover their automation experiences and plans (Mann, 1986). The 26 libraries partipating in the survey were:

Public: Boston Public, Chicago Public, Dallas Public, Denver Public, Detroit Public, Houston Public, Los Angeles Public, Los Angeles County Public, Miami-Dade Public, Minneapolis Public Library and Information Center, New York Public Library - The Branch Libraries, Queens Borough Public, St. Louis Public, San Francisco Public.

Academic: Harvard University, Indiana University at Bloomington, Ohio
State University, Stanford University, University of California - Los
Angeles, University of Illinois, University of Michigan, University of
Minnesota, University of Texas, University of Washington, University of
Wisconsin-Madison, Yale University.

The 30 libraries invited to participate were based on two criteria: 1) for
public libraries: the 15 largest based on budget and collection size, 2) for
academic libraries: the top 15 ranked by the Association of College and
Research Libraries. The survey results show that all the libraries are
currently involved in library automation.

The findings show that all 26 libraries have automated cataloging and
bibliographic functions with 73% using OCLC and 27% using RLIN. This is not
surprising given that machine-readable catalog records are the basis of any
automated library function. In addition, 17 (65%) have automated
acquisitions; 15 (57%) have automated circulation; 7 (27%) have automated
serials control. The libraries who have not yet automated these functions
plan to do so. While only three academic libraries are installing online
public access catalogs, 15 libraries (10 public, 5 academic) plan OPAC's.
Turnkey library systems are employed by 17 (65%) libraries (10 public, 7
academic) to automate their functions. While this 65% figure is lower than
the general marketplace trend (88%) for turnkey vendors, it is also a
statement of the unique needs of the very large public and academic
libraries. Only recently have these libraries had system options among the
turnkey vendors in a marketplace where 16 or fewer terminals was the norm.

In addition to the survey statistics, the Peat, Marwick, Mitchell team
examined the four stages of the library automation maturation process:
initiation, expansion, formalization, and maturity (Mann, 1986). As library
managers and staff increase their knowledge, educate their users, and adopt
new technology, they are achieving (or plan on achieving) the integrated
system. The automated library system is becoming synonymous with the
integrated, multi-function, local library system.

CASE STUDIES -- SPECIFICS

The process of choosing, acquiring and implementing an integrated library
system is a complex and lengthy process occurring over a period of years.
Libraries may handle the entire process themselves or use one of the growing
number of library automation consultants. About 50% of libraries go through
the formal RFP (Request for Proposal) process comparing vendors' written
responses to their requirements. The other 50% select their vendors through

other evaluative means. Some libraries may even do massive comparisons. The Jackson-George Regional Library Systems (Pascagoula, Mississippi) conducted an extensive and detailed Comparative Profile of Integrated Online Library Systems over a nine month period of nine available systems. The Jackson-George Regional Library System completed system implementation in September 1986 after two years of automation efforts. The following case studies were chosen as representing current activity among hundreds of libraries.

TURNKEY SYSTEMS:
UNIVERSITY OF GUELPH

The University of Guelph (Guelph, Ontario) is truly one of the pioneers in automation as described by Margaret Beckman (1980). By 1968, the university had completed a retrospective conversion, automated cataloging and processing, and automated circulation . Punched card circulation served Guelph sufficiently for nearly 10 years when the need for online circulation control became evident. Guelph staff established design criteria for their new system with the basic requirement "to remain independent for local processing and to purchase needed bibliographic data from utilities if and when necessary" (Beckman, 1980). The University of Guelph then entered into a joint development project with GEAC. GEAC's online circulation system with its public inquiry module became operational in September 1977. The module was replaced in 1983 by GEAC's online catalog. Catalog capabilities were further enhanced in 1985 when Boolean searching was added as a result of Guelph's joint development with GEAC. As with most integrated systems, Guelph found its services improved with reduced staff and increased efficiency.

UNIVERSITY OF WESTERN ONTARIO

The automation experience at the University of Western Ontario (UWO) library (London, Canada) like Guelph, parallels the historical development of integrated systems (Bhimani, 1986). The university began automating in 1967 to a computer batch-processing system developed in-house. In 1979, the university produced its first COM catalog. Over the years, the system expanded to include independent batch processing for acquisitions, circulation, serials, cataloging, and other housekeeping functions. However, by 1980, the university saw the advantages in a turnkey integrated library system and purchased a GEAC system. Four other academic libraries in the region had already contracted with GEAC. As libraries move toward regional linking of local systems, the Western Ontario library reasoned, "the idea of sharing information sources and resources influenced UWO's decision to adopt

GEAC" (Bhimani). Currently, UWO has implemented GEAC's circulation, MARC cataloging with authorities, and the online catalog. Possible future features include Boolean searching and adding serials holdings. Bhimani concludes that the benefits of the GEAC online integrated system are numerous for staff and patrons with the demand for more terminals increasing every day.

OHIO UNIVERSITY

In 1978, Ohio University (Athens, Ohio) created a Task Force on an Automated Circulation System to:

- Conduct a feasibility study.
- Investigate vendor supplied systems and the option of in-house development.
- Obtain cost comparisons.
- Submit recommendations (Lee, 1984).

The VTLS system was chosen in September 1981 based on its integrated file structures, system features and functions including an online public access catalog. Installation and database loading took until March 1983. In May, the main catalog was deemed "closed." Full implementation began in fall quarter 1983 at which time a hardware update was already in process.

With VTLS fully operational, Ohio University's plans focus on extending VTLS access to separate but linked regional campus databases through microwave communications linkages and to OVAL's (Ohio Valley Area Libraries) 11 public libraries.

LIBRARY DEVELOPED SOFTWARE:

PENNSYLVANIA STATE UNIVERSITY

In 1969, Pennsylvania State University Libraries (University Park, Pennsylvania) established a Department of Systems Development with the charge of computerizing library processes (Carson, 1983). After more than a decade of work, the Library Information Access System (LIAS) is operational as an integrated local system for bibliographic, circulation control, and an online catalog. Acquisitions control is under development. Serials control is provided through a LIAS terminal to the commercial Faxon serials system (LINX). The University Park LIAS computer provides the central point of access to the 21 campuses across Pennsylvania. The university-wide online catalog is in essence a statewide network. Microcomputers are used to download bibliographic records for both reference and student use creating "mini-catalogs." LIAS uses mainframe technology to expand to a multi-institutional system while employing microcomputers for the single user catalog.

COLORADO ALLIANCE OF RESEARCH LIBRARIES

In 1974, the Colorado Alliance of Research Libraries was formed by the five largest libraries in Colorado: University of Colorado (Boulder), Denver Public Library, Colorado State University, University of Denver, and the University of Northern Colorado "to cooperate to the benefit of its users and to the state as a whole" (Culkin, 1985). While Colorado State dropped out; two institutions joined: Auraria Higher Education Center and Colorado School of the Mines. CARL's purpose was refined to "access the collections of member institutions as if they were one collection" (Culkin). CARL accomplishes this through its integrated "network online system: of Public Access Catalog (PAC), Circulation Control System (CIRC), and Bibliographic Maintenance System (MAINT). The CARL system's over 1.5 million bibliographic records and 100,000 patron records are accessed by over 200 terminals at six library sites. Public users also access the system through three dial-up lines. While the CARL system has received much acclaim for its functionality, particularly PAC, it sees itself not only as state of the art local system by as a "network online system."

EXTENDED SYSTEMS

As evidenced in the above case studies, before the integrated library systems fill their initial purposes of improved online access, they are moving beyond it. Local systems are becoming 1) local mini-networks linking several branches/institutions to one computer system for resource sharing, 2) local linked systems connecting several separate systems together for resource sharing, e.g., the LS/2000 systems of Wisconsin which are separate systems with telecommunications links for collection sharing.

Local systems are also serving as the basis for going beyond traditional access to the electronic library. "Maggie's Place" is the integrated local system of Pikes Peak Library District in Colorado Springs, Colorado. Based on the CARL system, Maggie's Place has added "online reference services, electronic mail and publications to the home, a serials system, a new accounting system, and the networking of the home user with publicly-available databases such as Dialog and BRS," according to innovative director, Kenneth Dowlin (1985). Pikes Peak is still in the forefront of extended catalogs, but it is not alone.

The Purdue University Engineering Library's information system provides bibliographic access to its collection supplemented by tables of contents from books (Posey, 1986). The screen display provides a window allowing the user to browse the contents while looking at the bibliographic record.

The Carnegie-Mellon University Libraries have added an information function to their OCLC LS/2000 system (Diskin, 1985). The information function provides users access through the online catalog to library announcements, hours, programs, policies, and bibliographies. The University of Maryland at Baltimore Health Sciences Library has enhanced its LS/2000 system also. The EARS (Electronic Access to Reference Services) is avalable from an introductory screen display on the local system terminals. EARS allows library patrons to request literature searches, photocopies, reference answers, and interlibrary loans from any LS/2000 terminal .

The University of Guelph's GEAC system is seen as a logical center of the education network of the university's information technology program (Beckman, 1987). The network currently gives access to a campus conferencing system and CAI (computer-assisted instruction) modules. Being added to the system are statistical and word processing packages and student management information. Access to database searching through the network is a hopeful addition.

Lehigh University in Bethlehem, Pennsylvania has integrated pathfinders into its GEAC integrated library system (Jarvis, 1986). These subject guides to bibliographic citations have been given a "pseudo-MARC" record to display in the online catalog.

The Polytechnic University in Brooklyn, New York has plans to build ELISP, the Electronic Library and Information System of Polytechnic as outlined by Dean of Libraries and Information Systems, Richard Sweeney (1987). ELISP, to be developed in 3 phases over the next several years, intends to "provide access to locally built databases, remote databases and to locally loaded database subscriptions on Compact Disc Read Only Memory (CD ROM)." The library plans to enhance the turnkey integrated library system it selects with purchased software for electronic mail/conferencing, full text management and retrieval. The university plans to develop its own software for an intelligent gateway, librarian assistance system, article retrieval management system, library expert system, PAC interface, and a current awareness system. To Sweeney, the integrated library system is merely the beginning of information services.

As libraries moved from single function batch processing automation to multi-function, online, integrated local systems the "definition" of an automated library system expanded. This expansion continues as the integrated local systems truly move beyond housekeeping activities to become electronic library information systems.

2. Microcomputer Products

Microcomputers used in library applications are barely five years old. Up until 1981, ten years after the introduction of the microcomputer, libraries had only three manufacturers' choices: Atari, Apple, and Radio Shack. These were plagued by limited storage and lack of good software as well as the public image problem of being from the "hobby" manufacturers. It took IBM, XEROX Corp. and Digital Equipment Corp. entering the marketplace to "legitimize" microcomputers. By 1982, micros were off and running in the library marketplace (Woods, 1983).

To determine the usage of microcomputers in U.S. public, academic, special, and school libraries, McGraw-Hill research conducted a survey in mid-1984 for the R.R. Bowker Company (Berry, 1985) The results are astounding: American libraries possess 190,000 microcomputers. The key survey findings include:

Microcomputers are owned by nearly 5,000 public libraries, 1,600 academic libraries, over 7,000 special libraries, over 140,000 elementary and high school libraries.

Each library owns an average of 4.1 micros with a breakdown of 2.3 per public library; 4.5 per academic library; 3.7 per special library.

These libraries planned to buy a total of 128,000 more micros by the end of 1986 divided as: 13,000 for public libraries; 5,000 for academic libraries; 27,000 for special libraries; 82,700 for school libraries.

The McGraw-Hill survey discovered that Apple computers are the machine of preference. IBM places second, but grew stronger as the survey reached completion.

The distribution is:

Public Libraries - 44.8% Apple; 24.6% IBM

Academic Libraries - 51.2% Apple; 31% IBM

Special Libraries - 35.6% Apple; 46.2% IBM

School Libraries - 65% Apple; 16% Commodore

Nearly half of the public and academic libraries provide public access microcomputers. Only one quarter of special libraries offer their patrons public access, but 77% of high school libraries and 85% of elementary school libraries permit student usage.

According to the 1984 survey, the most popular software applications are administrative: word processing, database management, statistical programs, and spreadsheets. School libraries also favor graphics programs.

A second significant study of microcomputer usage in libraries was conducted by Knowledge Industry Publications in mid-1984 (Milliot, 1985). On a smaller scale than the McGraw survey, 64 questionnaire responses were tallied from both American and Canadian libraries. This library market distributes slightly differently with 84% owning Apples, 38% owning Radio Shack TRS 80's , and 31% owning IBM PC's (including OCLC's M300 workstation, a modified IBM PC). The libraries surveyed indicate high satisfaction and reliability for all three brands of hardware. This survey posed an interesting question to libraries given the proliferation of local systems, "Is your micro part of an integrated system?" (Milliot) The reply was negative (no) for 84% of the respondents and positive (yes) for 16%. Similar to the MCGraw-Hill survey, over half (55%) of the respondents provide microcomputers for patron use. In regards to software usage, nearly half (48%) of the libraries developed their own software. One-third still plan on developing software. While busy programming, libraries are certainly purchasing software with 83% expecting to buy more software.

The Public Library Association's (PLA) 1985 <u>Directory of Microcomputer Users in Libraries</u> includes 381 American and Canadian libraries. Half of the libraries surveyed were public libraries, the primary interest group of PLA. Across all types of libraries, the PLA results show Apple microcomputers to be the dominant brand accounting for 41% of the market. IBM accounts for 25% (IBM compatibles another 7%) and Tandy 10%. Looking at specific library types, the results parallel McGraw-Hill with 46% of public libraries and 65% of school libraries owning Apples. IBM is strong in the academic libraries with a 47% showing versus a 22% showing for Apple.

The most popular applications according to PLA again parallel the McGraw-Hill findings: word processing, database management, and spreadsheets. The next most popular are communications and educational software. User developed software is produced by 36% of the libraries, a slightly lower percentage than the Knowledge Industry survey shows (48%).

The PLA survey contradicts the McGraw-Hill findings on the availability of public access micros. While 57% of the public libraries provide public access machines, only 31% of the academic, 38% of the school, and 21% of the special libraries do. Except for the public libraries figure which shows a higher rate, these other percentages are much lower than the McGraw-Hill survey found.

In a third survey administered in May/June 1986, OCLC interviewed 306 OCLC members and 154 non-OCLC member libraries to determine microcomputer ownership and use. The results show that 73% of OCLC members own microcomputers; up from 35% in 1983. Of non-members, 25% own microcomputers; up from 20% in 1984. IBM is the leading brand choice for both OCLC (33%) and non-OCLC (38%) libraries. Additionally, 57% of OCLC members with microcomputers own an M300 workstation. The growth of IBM's market share as forecasted in the McGraw-Hill survey is demonstrated here.

The OCLC survey results on microcomputer usage, as reported in the OCLC Newsletter, November 1986, parallel both the McGraw-Hill and Knowledge Industry findings . Both OCLC and non-OCLC member libraries use their micros for word processing and spreadsheets. Other popular applications are: interlibrary loan, cataloging, and database searching. These latter uses may be attributed to OCLC products used by the OCLC libraries.

The four surveys concur on the major trends regarding microcomputer use in libraries: the most prevalent type of software is for administrative applications like work processing and spreadsheets; Apple had early market dominance, but IBM has gained across the library market and predominates among academic libraries. Public access to microcomputers in libraries is an established service to patrons. Most importantly, microcomputers are here to stay and continue to increase in all types of libraries. The significance of microcomputers in the local library reaches far beyond using new technology. Micros give the library new computing power, local flexibility and control, and linking capabilities to other micros and to external computer systems. An examination of some of the library applications demonstrate these far reaching effects.

APPLICATIONS OVERVIEW

The administrative micro applications performed in libraries, such as word processing, use general business software. Since these options are discussed in the personal computing literature, we will focus on the library oriented products. Joseph Matthews, in his annual review of the marketplace estimates 300 available micro products for library use in 1985 (Matthews,

1986). Matthews divides the applications into 15 categories: acquisitions, card catalog printing, the online catalog, circulation, overdues, serials, reference, online searching/downloading, bibliographies, indexing, film booking, circulation system backup, retrospective conversion, library skills, and other. These applications fall into two broad categories: technical services and public services. The diversity of software offerings is almost evenly divided between the two areas. The 161 technical services packages distribute as: circulation-36; cataloging-31; card catalog production-31; acquisitions-26; serials-16; overdues-15; retrospective conversion-12 circulation backup-4. It is interesting to note that this pattern of availability corresponds roughly to how libraries automate using integrated local systems with cataloging and circulation as the highest priorities. A difference, however, with microcomputers is that applications are usually single function. The multi-function, integrated systems, in most cases, require the larger capacity minicomputers. The 114 software packages oriented towards library public services distribute as: library skills-49; reference-21; online searching/downloading aids-20; bibliographies-11; audiovisual booking-9; indexing-4.

The dominant vendors providing library microcomputer software are: DataTrek, Follett, Highsmith, Small Library Computing, and Winnebago. With libraries spending approximately $5 million for software and $7 million for hardware, the library market is vigorous. In 1985, Apple software with 146 products still dominated, but IBM with 100 products was very competitive. IBM tripled its number of product offerings from 1984 to 1985.

IBM COMPETES

The microcomputer use surveys point to the increasing gain made by IBM in the library marketplace. IBM's product increases may be the effect of this gain, but they are not the cause. All of the major U.S. utilities, OCLC, RLIN and WLN have chosen the IBM PC family as their new workstations. (UTLAS has software for the IBM PC, though it does not sell workstations.) This decision for OCLC libraries means over 6,000 IBM PC's in libraries in the next few years. Currently, OCLC finds it difficult to keep up with the demands of users for its M300 workstation, a modified IBM PC. In addition, OCLC has implemented its new serials (SC350) and acquisitions (ACQ350) control modules on IBM microcomputers. The users of OCLC's online system acquisitions and serials control must migrate from accessing the mainframe computers in Dublin, Ohio to local control on library microcomputers. While

the utilities are effecting IBM's growth in the marketplace, they also bring
another trend -- the microcomputer as workstation.

MICROCOMPUTER WORKSTATIONS

In three major areas, microcomputers as workstations link to other
computers for: 1) bibliographic utilities 2) local systems, 3) remote online
database searching.

As mentioned above, the major utilities now use microcomputer
workstations. The primary emphasis of the utilities is still access to their
online databases. However, microcomputers as "intelligent" workstations can
reduce the workload of the main computers. Cataloging and ILL bibliographic
record requests can be stored, transmitted, and retrieved in batch files at
non-peak hours for lowered telecommunication and staff costs. Local editing
of records is often easier with more flexible and user friendly interfaces.
Downloading to local systems may be done "in batch" instead of by individual
record. Local record files may also be used with stand-alone micro software
for other uses, such as producing bibliographies. The utilities also offer
micro-based retrospective conversion products.

With a local system, the microcomputer workstation is used in several
ways. As a circulation terminal, it has the capability of running backup
software to continue circulation activity when the local system goes down.
Micro software may offload some screen displays and index management from the
local system to improve response time. Design restrictions on less than
friendly user interfaces may be overcome by employing "friendly and helpful"
front-end software. Additionally, some automated integrated systems are
using microcomputers as single function modules whose data and files are then
"integrated" into the local system. UTLAS, CLSI, and OCLC Local Systems
offer micro-based serials and acquisitions subsystems. For example, when
OCLC's SC350 serials system is linked to the LS/2000 local system, the
serial bibliographic records are downloaded from the LS/2000 system. As
serials activity, such as check-in or bindery occur on the SC350
microcomputer, the information is uploaded into the LS/2000 system to create
item records for use in circulation. Summary and detailed holdings for the
serials display in LS/2000's online catalog. The data appears integrated
to patrons, yet the library gains the advantages on the microcomputer of
cheaper hardware and storage, independent control of system availability, and
hopefully improved response time. Disadvantages, however, include separate
hardware, slower updating of the database, and often different system
commands and user interfaces.

As a workstation for online database seaching, a microcomputer aids the reference librarian in five basic areas: 1) automatic logon to telecommunications networks and host systems 2) creating, storing, and uploading search strategies, 3) search assistance 4) capturing and dowloading of search results and 5) reformatting and post-processing of search results. Automatic logon and stored search strategies help reduce connect time by providing fast access to systems and fast uploading of search strategies. Microcomputer software may provide search assistance for the remote online system through tutorials, documentation, and command system emulations. Downloaded results saved to a floppy or hard disk "print" faster than to paper. Other programs can then be used to manipulate the data. Currently available software includes: DIALOGLINK, EasyNet, iNet 2000, IT, OCLC Link, PC/NET-Link, Pro-Search, Sci-Mate, Search Helper, SearchMaster, and WILSEARCH.

By employing microcomputer workstations, libraries gain not only the above-mentioned capabilities, but also save library space. A microcomputer used as both a terminal and computer eliminates the need for two devices. Micros tend to be efficient investments since their many functions allow for continuous machine usage (Melin, 1985).

CASE STUDY RESOURCES

With the proliferation of 190,000 microcomputers in the United States, it is impossible to give detailed case studies or even choose representative samples. Indeed, there are many monographs devoted to describing libraries' applications and available programs. This list briefly describes a sampling of these books. Jim Milliot's Micros At Work presents a 16 page summary of the results of the 1984 Knowledge Industry Survey (described above). More than half the book, 88 pages, is devoted to 35 library profiles of microcomputer applications. The Librarian's Guide to Microcomputer Technology and Applications by Woods and Pope provides 10 chapters of explanatory text followed by a listing of 59 libraries with their micro applications. Patrick Dewey's Public Access Microcomputers: A Handbook for Librarians focuses on providing microcomputers for patron use highlighted with case studies. The Fall 1984 issue of Drexel Library Quarterly is devoted to microcomputer applications in library and information services. In September 1985, the Technology in Public Libraries Committee of the Public Library Association, a division of the American Library Association published their second edition of the Directory of Microcomputer Users in Libraries. The directory includes 381 American and Canadian libraries with information on the type of library, types of microcomputer applications, kinds of hardware, and services available to the public. Ching-chih Chen's <u>MicroUse Directory: Software</u> and <u>Micro Use Directory: Application</u> are printed products resulting from the MicroUse database developed at the Graduate School of Library and Information Science, Simmons College, Massachusetts. The database contains over 1,500 software packages with a sampling of libraries using them.

For current information, there are several publications devoted exclusively to covering microcomputers in the library environment. These include <u>Access: Microcomputers in Libraries</u>; <u>Microcomputers for Information Management</u>, <u>Microcomputers for Libraries</u>, <u>Online Libraries and Microcomputers</u>, <u>OCLC Micro</u>, and the <u>Wired Librarians' Newsletter</u>.

In the past, the controversy ran fierce as to the place of audiovisual media (A/V) in the library. A/V is now an integral part of every library's collection. The microcomputer revolution has occurred; now we are in the stage of quiet dispersion as microcomputers spread throughout libraries.

3. Public ("End-User") Services

Direct reference service to the public, as defined by Bill Katz (1974), covers two major categories: 1) instruction in using the library, 2) information service. Instruction in library usage, for the most part, still remains a non-automated task performed by librarians. However, as the previous section showed, automation is making headway as many library skills microcomputer programs are now available. Also, the libraries' automated local systems and machine-readable data files are beginning to incorporate library assistance as well as search assistance.

Information services seek to provide an end product to fulfill the information needs of the requestor. In recent years, reference librarians have been assisted in their information providing function by online database services and local automated files. These automated tools have now moved from the librarians' realm to patron public access. Thus, the librarians' role has expanded to include teaching end-users automated systems. Instructing users in complex index methods and the organization of materials is already a challenge for librarians. The addition of another dimension of system commands, functions, and machine indexing creates a supreme challenge for bibliographic instruction.

SOURCES OF SERVICE

The end-user searching available to library patrons falls into two sources of service: remote online database searching and local database access.

REMOTE ONLINE SEARCHING

Through the 1970s, training of end-users in online search services necessitated teaching patrons to become their own "trained intermediaries" (Machovec, 1986). The difficulty and the expense of the search systems did not encourage their widespread use. The introduction of front-end software and intelligent gateways have reduced these limitations in the 1980's.

Carol Tenopir (July 1986) further divides remote online searching into three categories: end-user systems, front-end software, and gateway systems. The two most popular end-user systems, residing on the accessed central computer, are BRS/Afterdark [BRS Information Technologies, Inc.] and DIALOG's Knowledge Index [DIALOG Information Services, Inc.]. Both of these services provide more limited access than the parent system in the number of databases offered and the hours of availability (after 6 p.m. local time). BRS also offers BRS/BRKTHRU, an end-user system to search all of its databases, which is available during the day at a higher price than BRS/Afterdark.

Front-end software may reside on a microcomputer, minicomputer or mainframe. It is the microcomputer front-end software that is offering users the most options. Tenopir's choices for the best front-end microcomputer software are: Sci-Mate Searcher [ISI], Pro-Search [Personal Bibliographic Software, Inc.], and WILSEARCH [H.W. Wilson Company]. The scope of Sci-Mate Searcher is the widest giving the user assistance for accessing BRS, DIALOG, NLM, SDC ORBIT, and Questel. Users can then employ the Sci-Mate Manager software to create a local database and the Sci-Mate Editor software to produce bibliographies. Pro-Search provides searching assistance for BRS and DIALOG databases. The user can then use the Pro-Cit and Biblio-Links packages to manipulate the downloaded data. WILSEARCH is more limited providing access only to the WILSONLINE system. But its low cost and coverage of the Wilson indexes make it suitable for school, public, and undergraduate libraries.

The new product, Grateful Med may soon join Tenopir's choices. Aimed at physicians and health professionals, Grateful Med provides a micro front-end to nearly seven million records of the (U.S.) National Library of Medicine databases. This package allows users to access NLM's MEDLINE and CATLINE which were previously restricted to trained and certified searchers (IRLA, June 1986).

The current gateway "most appropriate for end-user searching in public or academic libraries is EASYNET," according to Tenopir (July 1986). EASYNET assists the user in choosing a database and a search strategy at a reasonable cost. OCLC, Inc. acquired the U.S. license to Canada's iNet which it has implemented as the OCLC LINK gateway in 1987. If OCLC takes advantage of its large user base, it will be a competitor to watch.

LOCAL DATABASES

Locally stored databases are available in two basic forms: 1) locally produced products and 2) commercially produced products, such as diskettes, commercial 12-inch disks, and compact optical disks (CD-ROM).

A library's largest databases is its catalog, usually stored as part of its integrated library system. In addition, libraries create their own single or multi-function databases, such as community calendars, bulletin boards, course listings, etc. These databases may be limited to one library's collection or include data from several libraries. There are as many varieties of local databases as there are libraries. The databases may be stored on different kinds of storage media, such as hard disk drives, diskettes, CD-ROM.

Commercially available databases on floppy diskettes provide small specialized database subsets at relatively low cost for libraries to load on their microcomputers. Available products include BIOSIS, ERIC, MicroComputer Index, Medline. Micro Reviews, the KAware (Knowledge Access, Inc.) produced subset of MicroComputer Index, is the first in a line of 15 planned KAware products (Spigai,1985). Knowledge Access foresees expanding its line to the CD-ROM format.

According to David Miller (1986), CD-ROM titles in late 1986 numbered 97 with 25% categorized as library titles. User friendly search interfaces, large databases, and the wide availability of microcomputers in libraries make CD-ROM products attractive options to offer patrons. Information Access Company's InfoTrac, specifically designed and tested for reference end-users, is the most popular product (the 12-inch videodisk version is being replaced by CD-ROM). Others available include: Silver Platter's ERIC, PsyLit, AV-Online, PAIS, LISA, and Excerpta Medica; DEC'S MITS, COMPENDEX, and Chemical Abstracts; University Microfilm International's INSPEC and Dissertation Abstracts; R.R. Bowker's BIP (Books in Print) Plus, OCLC's ERIC. New products are announced monthly.

CD-ROM products are projected by Miller to reach 7% of U.S. libraries in 1986, 25% in 1988 and 65% by 1990 (Miller, November 1986). The wide and rapid spread of microcomputers in libraries took only five years; CD-ROM products will no doubt do the same.

CASE STUDIES:

University of Ottawa

In 1983, the University of Ottawa (Ottawa, Canada) pioneered end-user searching with the new BRS/After Dark as described by Richard Janke (1983). A three-week pilot project lead to establishing in July 1983 the "Online After Six" service for end-user searching by faculty, students, staff, and the general public. In the first nine months of service, end-user searching accounted for 14.8% of all online searches at the Morisset Library for social sciences (Janke, 1984). Janke compares the implications and limitations of end-user searching against the experience, knowledge, and power of trained intermediary searching . He concludes, however, that end-user searching is here to stay and that it can successfully be integrated into traditional and online reference services.

In addition to the University of Ottawa, Janke (1984) lists 31 American and Canadian libraries which had or were implementing end-user searching in 1984.

Houston Academy of Medicine

In 1983, the Houston Academy of Medicine (which consists of six participating and 14 supporting institutions) Texas Medical Center Library decided to establish a "comprehensive information management education program. This type of program could effectively address the needs of library clients, teaching them the technology, skills, and decision making processes necessary for independent information retrieval and management" (Hubbard, 1986).

In the Texas Medical Center Library, "independence" for library clients means end-user searching and computing. The extensive seminars offered by the library to their patrons includes: introductory and advanced database searching, gateway and communication software, downloading, microcomputing, database management, word processing, and spreadsheets (Hubbard, 1986).

Montgomery County Media Centers

In 1982, the 22 Montgomery County senior high school media centers instituted student access to online databases. "The initiation of this service had two major objectives: to introduce online information retrieval to students and to expand the resources available to them" (Pruitt, 1985). Microcomputers were chosen as workstations with the multi-purposes of online access, educational and management programs, and programming. Montgomery County broadened the library and information retrieval skills required of students to include judgment of database access, contents, selection and descriptors. One can only assume that these high school graduates are requesting end-using searching in their academic and public libraries.

Additional case studies on implementing and training end-user searchers are included in the bibliography: Oregon State University (Brooks, 1982), George Mason University (Grotophortst, 1984), University of Michigan (Crooks, 1985), Eastman Kodak Company (Haines, 1982), and Exxon (Walton, 1983), and Amoco Research Center (Kirk, 1986). Diane Strauss describes the issues and decision making process for adding data diskettes for public access to the University of North Carolina at Chapel Hill library (Strauss, 1986).

Public end-user searching is the least common of the three automated systems and services in libraries: integrated library systems, microcomputer products and public services, though, it overlaps with the other two. However, all three combined are redefining librarians' skills, services, and organizational structure (Gorman, 1985). The electronic library lies ahead with improved access to materials for all.

BIBLIOGRAPHY

1. Abbott, Peter; Kavanagh, Rosemary. Electronic Resource Sharing
   Changes Interloan Patterns. Library Journal; October 1, 1986;
   111: 56-58; ISSN 0363-0277.
   Library networks/Regional networks/ILL.

2. About RLG; The Research Libraries Group, Inc. Stanford, CA: RLG;
   August 1986.

3. Access: Microcomputers in Libraries. Oakridge, OR: DAC
   Publications.
   Note: A quarterly.

4. AMIGOS Claims Co-Ownership of OCLC Online Union Catalog.
   Advanced Technology/Libraries; May 1985; 14(5): 1,8.
   Data ownership/Bibliographic utilities.

5. AMIGOS Plans Microcomputer Software Program. Advanced
   Technology/Libraries; April 1985; 14(4): 4.
   Microcomputers/Regional networks.

6. AMIGOS, SOLINET Oppose OCLC Claim to Database Ownership.
   Advanced Technology/Libraries; January 1985; 14(1): 3.
   Data ownership/Bibliographic utilities.

7. Andre, Pamela Q.J. Full-Text Access and Laser Videodiscs: The
   National Agricultural Library System. Library Hi Tech; Spring
   1986; 4(1): 13-21; ISSN 0737-8831.
   Note: Continuous Issue Number 13.
   Optical media/Microcomputers/Public services.

8. Annual Review of Supported Software Vendors. Library Systems
   Newsletter; May 1986; VI(5): 33-36; ISSN 0277-0288.
   Local library systems.

9. Annual Review of Supported Software Vendors. Library Systems
   Newsletter; April 1987; VII(4): 25-28; ISSN 0277-0288.
   Note: Richard W. Boss and Hal Espo are Contributing Editors.
   Local library systems.

10. Annual Survey of Automated Library System Vendors. Library
    Systems Newsletter; April 1986; VI(4): 25-31; ISSN 0277-0288.
    Local library systems/Turnkey systems/Integrated library
    systems.

11. Annual Survey of Automated Library System Vendors. Library
    Systems Newsletter; March 1987; VII(3): 17-24; ISSN 0277-
    0288.
    Note: Richard W. Boss and Hal Espo are Contributing Editors.
    Local library systems/Integrated library systems/Turnkey
    systems.

12. Association of Research Libraries. Automation Inventory of
    Research Libraries. Washington, D.C.: Association of Research
    Libraries; 1986.
    Note: Available from the Office of Management Studies, ARL,
    1527 New Hampshire Avenue, NW, Washington, D.C. 20036 ($40.00
    in U.S., $45.00 outside U.S.).
    Local library systems/Bibliographic utilities.

13. Automated Library Systems in ARL Libraries. Association of
    Research Libraries, Office of Management Studies. SPEC Kit
    126; July-August 1986; (126); ISSN 0160-3582.
    Note: Includes survey results and case studies.
    Integrated library systems/Turnkey systems/LANs/Distributed
    processing.

14. The Automated Library Systems Industry: A Time of Change.
    Library Systems Newsletter; December 1986; VI(12): 89-93;
    ISSN 0277-0288.
    Note: Richard W. Boss is Contributing Editor.
    Local library systems/Turnkey systems/Integrated library
    systems.

15. Automated Resource Sharing in Massachusetts: A Plan. 1st ed.
    Boston, MA; 1983.
    Note: Available from the Massachusetts Board of Library
    Commissioners, 648 Beacon Street, Boston, MA 02115.
    Library networks/Regional library networks/Local library
    systems.

16. Avram, Henriette D. Current Issues in Networking. The Journal
    of Academic Librarianship; September 1986; 12(4): 205-209;
    ISSN 0099-1333.
    Library networks/NAC/National network/LSP/OSI/Local library
    systems/Data Ownership.

17. Avram, Henriette D. LSP: History, Overview, and Present State;
    1986.
    Note: Paper presented at the LITA Linked Systems Program held
    at the Annual Meeting of the American Library Association,
    New York, June 29, 1986. Available from Henriette D. Avram,
    Library of Congress.
    LSP/OSI/Bibliographic utilities/Distributed processing.

18. Avram, Henriette D. Toward a Nationwide Library Network.
    Journal of Library Automation; 1978; 11: 285-298; ISSN 0022-
    2240.
    Library networks/National network/Bibliographic utilities.

19. Avram, Henriette D.; McCallum, Sally H. Directions in Library
    Networking. Journal of the American Society for Information
    Science; November 1980; 31(6): 438-444; ISSN 0002-8231.
    Library networks/Bibliographic utilities/National
    network/Regional networks.

20. Beckman, Margaret. Online Catalogue Development at the
    University of Guelph. Library Trends; Spring 1987.
    Note: Draft, to be published.
    Online catalogs/Public services/Local library systems.

21. Beckman, Margaret. Public Access at the University of Guelph
    Library. In: Divilbiss, J.L., editor. Public Access to
    Library Automation. Urbana-Champaign, IL: University of
    Illinois; 1981: 37-48; ISBN 0-87845-065-3.
    Note: Clinic on Library Applications of Data Processing,
    April 20-23, 1980, University of Illinois at Urbana-
    Champaign.
    Public services/Online catalogs/Local library systems.

22. Berry, John. Library Use of Microcomputers: Massive and
    Growing. Library Journal; February 1, 1985; 110: 48-49; ISSN
    0363-0277.
    Microcomputers/Public services/Local library
    systems/Distributed processing.

23. Bhimani, Nazlin. Automation at the University of Western
    Ontario Libraries: A Review. PROGRAM; July 1986; 20(3): 320-
    322; ISSN 0033-0337.
    Local library systems/Integrated library systems/Turnkey
    systems.

24. Boss, Richard W. Interfacing Automated Library Systems. Library
    Technology Reports; September-October 1984; 20(5): 615-703;
    ISSN 0024-2586.
    Note: Includes extensive Glossary.
    LSP/OSI/Library networks/Integrated library systems/LANs.

25. Boss, Richard W. Technology and the Modern Library. Library
    Journal; June 15, 1984; 109: 1183-1189; ISSN 0363-0277.
    Bibliographic utilities/Turnkey systems/Library networks.

26. Bowden, Virginia M.; Swanner, Sallieann. Implementing Change: the Installation of an Integrated System at UTHSCSA. Bulletin of Medical Library Association; July 1985; 73(3): 271-277. Integrated library systems/Turnkey systems/Local library systems.

27. Brooks, Kristina M. Non-Mediated Usage of Online Retrieval Systems in an Academic Environment. In: Proceedings of the Third National Online Meeting, 1982; March 30-April 1, 1982; New York. Medford, NJ: Learned Information; 1982: 35-39; ISBN 0-938734-04-0. End-user services/Public services.

28. Brown, Rowland C. W. The National Network and OCLC: A Vision and a Role. Dublin, Ohio: OCLC; February 1986. Library networks/Bibliographic utilities/National network.

29. Brown, Rowland C.W. OCLC: Present Issues, Future Directions; A Report to the Membership. Dublin, Ohio: OCLC; 1985. Library networks/Bibliographic utilities/Data ownership.

30. Brown, Rowland, C. W. OCLC: Present Issues, Future Directions: A Report to the Membership. Dublin, Ohio: OCLC; February 1985. Library networks/Bibliographic utilities.

31. Bryan Jane C.; Woodward, Wade M. A Comparative Profile of Integrated Online Library Systems. Pascagoula, MS; May 31, 1985. Note: Available from: Jackson-George Regional Library, 3214 Pascagoula Street, Pascagoula, MS 39567. Integrated library systems/Turnkey systems/Local library systems.

32. Buchinski, Edwin; McCallum, David. Network and Protocol Development. Canadian Library Journal; 1985; 42(3): 131-134. Library networks/National network/OSI.

33. Buckland, Michael K.; Lynch, Clifford A. The Future of Bibliographic Networks and Systems in the Light of the Linked Systems Protocol; June 1986. Note: Paper presented at the LITA Linked Systems Project Program, Annual Conference of the American Library Association, New York, June 29, 1986. Copies available from the authors: Office of the President, University of California, Berkeley, CA. LSP/OSI/Bibliographic utilities/Distributed processing.

34. Calmes, Alan. New Confidence in Microfilm. Library Journal;
    September 15, 1986; 111: 38-42; ISSN 0363-0277.
    Optical media.

35. Canadian MARC: A Report of the Activities of the MARC Task
    Group Resulting in a Recommended Canadian MARC Format for
    Monographs and a Canadian MARC Format for Serials. Ottawa:
    Information Canada; 1972.
    Cataloging standards/MARC formats.

36. Canadian Union Catalogue Task Group. Final Report to the
    National Librarian. Ottawa: National Library of Canada; 1976.
    Library networks/National network/Cataloging
    standards/Cataloging sources/ILL.

37. Carson, Sylvia MacKinnon; Freivalds, Dace I. MicroLIAS: Beyond
    the Online Public Access Catalog. Library Hi Tech; Fall 1986;
    4(3): 83-90; ISSN 0737-8831.
    Note: Continuous Issue Number 15.
    Online catalogs/Microcomputers/Distributed processing/Public
    services/Local library systems/End-user services.

38. Carson, Sylvia MacKinnon. LIAS: Online Catalog at Penn State
    University. Cataloging & Classification Quarterly; Winter
    1983; 4(2): 1-15; ISSN 0163-9374.
    Local library systems/Online catalogs/Public services.

39. Chen, Ching-Chih; Bressler, Stacey E. editors. Microcomputers
    in Libraries. New York: Neal-Schumann Publishers; 1982.
    Microcomputers/Local library systems.

40. Cimbala, Diane J. There Goes the Neighborhood. Technicalities;
    June 1985; 5(6): 9-16; ISSN 0272-0884.
    Microcomputers.

41. Clark, Sharon E. Implementation and Operation of
    Linked/Interfaced Systems at the Library of the University of
    Illinois at Urbana-Champaign. In: Association of Research
    Libraries, Office of Management Studies. Automated Library
    Systems in ARL Libraries. SPEC Kit 126; July-August 1986;
    (126): 68-76; ISSN 0160-3582.
    Note: Overview of use of University's online catalog system
    as basis of ILLINET statewide union catalog and computerized,
    multi-type library network.
    Regional networks/Local library systems/Online
    catalogs/Microcomputers.

42. CLASS Data Base Task Group. The CLASS Data Base Network.
    Information Technology and Libraries; March 1982; 1(1): 63-
    68; ISSN 0730-9295.
    Regional networks/Library networks.

43. Cook, Colleen; Payne, Leila. DataPhase ALIS II: Implementing
    the System at Texas A&M: A Case Study. Library Hi Tech; 1985;
    3(4): 87-98; ISSN 0737-8831.
    Note: Continuous Issue Number 12.
    Turnkey systems/Integrated library systems/ Local library
    systems.

44. Corbin, John. Managing the Library Automation Project. Phoenix,
    AZ: Oryx Press; 1985; ISBN 0-89774-151-X.
    Note: Includes Glossary and Bibliography.
    Integrated library systems/Turnkey systems.

45. Costa, Betty; Costa, Marie. Micro Handbook for Small Libraries
    and Media Centers. Littleton, Colorado: Libraries Unlimited;
    1983.
    Microcomputers/Local library systems.

46. Crooks, James E. End User Searching at the University of
    Michigan. In: Proceedings of the Sixth National Online
    Meeting, 1985; 1985; New York. Medford, NJ: Learned
    Information; 1985: 99-110.
    End-user services/Public services.

47. Culkin, Patricia; Shaw, Ward. The CARL System. Library Journal;
    February 1, 1985; 110(2): 68-70; ISSN 0363-0277.
    Regional networks/Local library systems.

48. D'Anci, Marjorie. Acquisitions With an Apple. Technicalities;
    August 1984; 4(8): 9-11; ISSN 0272-0884.
    Microcomputers/Local library systems.

49. Davison, Wayne E. The WLN/RLG/LC Linked Systems Project.
    Information Technology and Libraries; March 1983; 2(1): 34-
    46; ISSN 0730-9295.
    LSP/Bibliographic utilities.

50. De Gennaro, Richard. Integrated Online Systems: Perspectives,
    Perceptions, and Realities. Library Journal; April 1, 1985;
    110: 37-40; ISSN 0363-0277.
    Integrated library systems/Turnkey systems/Local library
    systems/Distributed processing/Bibliographic utilities.

51. De Gennaro, Richard. Library Automation & Networking:
    Perspective on Three Decades. Library Journal; April 1, 1983;
    108: 629-635; ISSN 0363-0277.
    Library networks/Bibliographic utilities/Integrated library
    systems/Turnkey systems/National network.

52. Denenberg, Ray. Linked Systems Project, Part 2: Standard
    Network Interconnection. Library Hi Tech; 1985; 3(2): 71-79;
    ISSN 0737-8831.
    Note: Continuous Issue Number 10.
    LSP/OSI.

53. Denenberg, Ray. The LSP/SNI Test Facility. Library Hi Tech;
    Spring 1986; 4(1): 41-49; ISSN 0737-8831.
    LSP/OSI.

54. Denenberg, Ray. Open Systems Interconnection. Library Hi Tech;
    1985; 3(1): 15-26; ISSN 0737-8831.
    Note: Continuous Issue Number 9. Includes Glossary.
    OSI/LSP.

55. Denenberg, Ray. Vendor's Interest Group Discusses Networking.
    Library Hi Tech News; July/August 1986; (29): 1, 6-7.
    Note: Report on meeting of Automated Vendor's Interface
    Advisory Committee (AVIAC).
    LSP/AVIAC/OSI.

56. Denenberg, Ray; McCallum, Sally H. RLG/WLN/LC Computers Ready
    to "Talk". American Libraries; June 1984: 400,402,404; ISSN
    0002-9769.
    LSP/OSI/Bibliographic utilities.

57. Dewey, Patrick R. Public Access Microcomputers: A Handbook for
    Librarians. White Plains, NY: Knowledge Industry
    Publications; 1984.
    Microcomputers/Public Services.

58. Directory of Microcomputer Users in Libraries, Second Edition:
    Public Library Association, Technology in Public Libraries
    Committee, American Library Association; September 1985.
    Microcomputers.

59. Diskin, Gregory M.; Michalak, Thomas J. Beyond the Online
    Catalog: Utilizing the OPAC for Library Information. Library
    Hi Tech; 1985; 3(1): 7-13; ISSN 0737-8831.
    Note: Continuous Issue Number 9.
    Online catalogs/Public services/End-user services/Local
    library systems.

60. Dowlin, Kenneth E. The "Integrated Library System". The
    Electronic Library; December 1985; 3(5): 340-345.
    Integrated library systems/Local library systems/Turnkey
    systems.

61. Drabenstott, Jon, editor. What Lies Beyond the Online Catalog.
    Library Hi Tech; 1985; 3(4): 105-114; ISSN 0737-8831.
    Note: Continuous Issue Number 12.
    Online catalogs/Public services/Local library systems.

62. Du Breuil, Laval (Vice President of Communications, University
    of Quebec, 2875 Laurier Boulevard, Sainte-Foy, Quebec G1V
    2M3). The University of Quebec Library Network: A Reality in
    the Emerging Canadian Open Network. La Premier Reunion
    Nationale des Reseaux de Bibliotheques; 12-16 March 1986;
    Saltillo, Mexico; March 1986; 14 pages.
    Note: Available from University of Quebec, Communications
    Office (Comptes rendus, No. 40).
    Library networks/Distributed processing/Local library
    systems/Online catalogs/End-user services.

63. Duchesne, R.M.; Guenter,D.A.; Islam, M. Towards More Effective
    Nationwide Library and Information Networking in Canada.
    Ottawa: National Library of Canada; 1980.
    Library networks/National network/Regional networks/OSI.

64. Duchesne, Roddy. Copyright, Ownership of, In Machine-Readable
    Bibliographic Data. In: Encyclopedia of Library and
    Information Science. New York: Marcel Dekker; 1986; 40(5):
    33-43. (Kent, Allen, Executive editor).
    Data ownership/Bibliographic utilities.

65. Dugan, Robert; Bjorner, Susan. Automated Resource Sharing in
    Massachusetts: A Plan. Library Hi Tech; Spring 1984; 1(4):
    73-82; ISSN 0737-8831.
    Library networks/Distributed processing/Regional
    networks/Local library systems.

66. Duke John K.; Hirshon, Arnold. Policies for Microcomputers in
    Libraries: An Administrative Model. Information Technology
    and Libraries; September 1986; 5(3): 193-203; ISSN 0730-8831.
    Microcomputers/Local library systems.

67. Durance, Cynthia J. Exploiting Technology to Build a Canadian
    Library and Information Network; 1985.
    Note: Presented at the IFLA General Conference, Chicago, IL,
    1985. Available from the National Library of Canada, Office
    for Network Development.
    Library networks/Bibliographic utilities/OSI.

68. Durance, Cynthia J. Initiatives Toward a Bibliographic
    Communications Network for Canada. Canadian Network Papers;
    May 1982; (Number 2); ISSN 0226-8760.
    Library networks/National network/OSI.

69. Durance, Cynthia J. OSI-Based Library Networking in Canada. In:
    Ravenna nel Servizio Bibliotecario Nazionale, Convegno
    Internazionale; April 17-19, 1986; Ravenna, Italy. Ravenna,
    Italy; 1986: 23-31.
    Note: "Tavola Rotonda Internazionale: Relazioni".
    Library networks/Bibliographic utilities/OSI.

70. Dyer, Hilary; Brookes, Alison, compilers. A Directory of
    Library and Information Retrieval Software for
    Microcomputers. 2nd ed. Hampshire, England: Gower Publishing
    Company; 1986; ISBN 0-566-03561-8.
    Microcomputers/Public services.

71. Epstein, Susan Baerg. Problems of Integration. Library Journal;
    September 1, 1985; 110: 144-145; ISSN 0363-0277.
    Integrated library systems/Local library systems/Turnkey
    systems.

72. Fleischhauer, Carl. A Report on the Nonprint Project. Library
    of Congress. The Library of Congress Optical Disk Pilot
    Program. Washington, D.C.: Library of Congress; December
    1985; 4 pages.
    Optical media.

73. Freund, Alfred L. A Regional Bibliographic Database on
    Videodisc. Library Hi Tech; 1985; 3(2): 7-9; ISSN 0737-8831.
    Library networks/Cataloging sources/Regional networks/Optical
    media.

74. Friend, Linda. Identifying and Informing the Potential End-
    User: Online Information Seminars. ONLINE; January 1986;
    10(1): 47-56; ISSN 0146-5422.
    End-user services/Public services.

75. Givens, Beth. Montana's Use of Microcomputers for Interlibrary
    Loan Communications. Information Technology and Libraries;
    September 1982; 1(3): 260-264; ISSN 0730-9295.
    Regional networks/Microcomputers/ILL.

76. Gorman, Michael. The Impact of Technology on the Organisation
    of Libraries. London: CLSI Publications; 1985.
    Integrated library systems/Turnkey systems/Public services.

77. Gorman, Michael. Online Access and Organization and
    Administration of Libraries. In: Aveney, Brian; Butler,
    Brett, editors. Online Catalogs, Online Reference: Converging
    Trends. Chicago, IL: American Library Association; 1984: 153-
    164; ISBN 0-8389-3308-4.
    Local library systems/Online catalogs.

78. Gorsline, Jr., George; Powell, Wyley L. UTLAS-Japan
    Communications Link. Information Technology and Libraries;
    March 1983; 2(1): 33-34; ISSN 0730-9295.
    Bibliographic utilities.

79. Grateful Med - Software Simplifies Computer Access to NLM.
    Information Retrieval and Library Automation; June 1986;
    22(1): 7.
    End-user services/Microcomputers/Public services.

80. Griffith, Jeffrey, C. Why Can't I Do It? Emerging Training
    Concerns of End Users and Online Professionals. In: Online
    '83 Conference Proceedings; 1983. Weston, CT: Online; 1983:
    77-81.
    End-user services/Public services.

81. Grosch, Audrey N. Distributed Computing and the Electronic
    Library: Micros to Superminis. White Plains, NY: Knowledge
    Industry Publications; 1985; ISBN 0-86729-145-1.
    Note: Includes Glossary and Directory of Installed
    Distributed Systems.
    Distributed systems/Turnkey systems/Integrated library
    systems/Microcomputers/Online catalogs.

82. Grotophorst, Clyde W. Training University Faculty as End-User
    Searchers: a CAI Approach. In: Proceedings of the Fifth
    National Online Meeting, 1984; 1984; New York. Medford, NJ:
    Learned Information; 1984: 77-82.
    End-user services/Public services/Microcomputers.

83. Hahn, Ellen Z. A Report on the Print Project Activities.
    Library of Congress. The Library of Congress Optical Disk
    Pilot Program. Washington, D.C.: Library of Congress; October
    31, 1983; 3 pages.
    Optical media.

84. Haines, Judith S. Experiences in Training End-User Searchers.
    ONLINE; November 1982; 6(6): 14-23; ISSN 0146-5422.
    End-user services/Public services.

85. Hegarty, Kevin. Myths of Library Automation. Library Journal;
    October 1, 1985; 110: 43-49; ISSN 0363-0277.
    Local library systems/Turnkey systems/Integrated library
    systems.

86. Heinemann, Luba. Auto-Graphics' AGILE II. Library Hi Tech;
    Spring 1986; 4(1): 91-103; ISSN 0737-8831.
    Bibliographic utilities/Cataloging sources/Library networks.

87. Hildreth, Charles R. Online Public Access Catalogs. In: White
    Plains, NY: Knowledge Industry Publications; 1985: 233-285.
    (Williams, Martha E. Annual Review of Information Science and
    Technology; 20); ISBN 0-86729-175-3.
    Public services/Online catalogs.

88. Hildreth, Charles R. Pursuing the Ideal: Generations of Online
    Catalogs. In: Aveney, Brian; Butler, Brett, editors. Online
    Catalogs, Online Reference: Converging Trends. Chicago, IL:
    American Library Association; 1984: 31-56; ISBN 0-8389-3308-
    4.
    Online catalogs/Public services/End-user services.

89. Hubbard, Abigail; Wilson, Barbara. An Integrated Information
    Management Education Program... Defining a New Role for
    Librarians in Helping End-Users. ONLINE; March 1986; 10(2):
    15-23; ISSN 0146-5422.
    Public services/End-user services/Microcomputers.

90. Hunter, Janne A. What Did You Say the End-User Was Going to Do
    at the Terminal, and How Much is it Going to Cost? In:
    Proceedings of the Fourth National Online Meeting - 1983; New
    York. Medford, NJ: Learned Information; 1983: 223-229.
    End-user services/Public services.

91. ILLINET Limits New OCLC Services. Library Journal; June 15,
    1985; 110: 15; ISSN 0363-0277.
    Regional networks/Bibliographic utilities.

92. Implementation of the Linked Systems Project: A Technical
    Report. Library Hi Tech; 1985; 3(3): 87-107; ISSN 0737-8831.
    Note: In four separate parts, representatives from LC, RLG,
    WLN, and OCLC describe their unique LSP/SNI implementations.
    LSP/OSI/Bibliographic utilities.

93. Information Systems Consultants Inc. Videodisc and Optical
    Digital Disk Technologies and Their Applications in
    Libraries. A Report to the Council on Library Resources.
    Washington, D.C.: Council on Library Resources; January 1985.
    Optical media.

94. International Resource Development, Inc. Releases Study on Bar
    Code Systems and Library Automation. Library Hi Tech News;
    May 1987; (38): 2; ISSN 0741-9058.
    Local library systems/Turnkey systems.

95. Janke, Richard V. BRS/After Dark: The Birth of Online Self-
    Service. ONLINE; September 1983; 7(5): 12-29; ISSN 0146-5422.
    Public services/End-user services.

96. Janke, Richard V. Online After Six at the University of Ottawa.
    In: Online '83 Conference Proceedings; 1983. Weston, CT:
    Online; 1983: 124-129.
    End-user services/Public services.

97. Janke, Richard V. Online After Six: End User Searching Comes of
    Age. ONLINE; November 1984; 8(6): 15-29; ISSN 0146-5422.
    Public services/End-user services.

98. Jarvis, William E.; Dow, Victoria E. Integrating Subject
    Pathfinders Into a GEAC ILS: A MARC-Formatted Record
    Approach. Information Technology and Libraries; September
    1986; 5(3): 213-228; ISSN 0730-9295.
    Public services/End-user services/Online catalogs/Turnkey
    systems/Local library systems.

99. Johnson, Gretchen L. Search Helper. RQ; Fall 1983; 23: 96-97;
    ISSN 0033-7072.
    End-user services/Public services/Microcomputers.

100. Jones, C. Lee; Gwinn, Nancy. Bibliographic Service
     Development: A New CLR Program. Journal of Library
     Automation; June 1979; 12: 116-124; ISSN 0022-2240.
     National network/Bibliographic utilities.

101. Katz, William A. Introduction to Reference Work, Volume 1:
     Basic Information Sources. Second ed. New York: McGraw-Hill
     Book Company; 1974. (Gates, Jean Key, Consulting Editor.
     McGraw-Hill Series in Library Education); ISBN 0-07-033353-X.
     Public services.

102. Kesselman, Martin. Online Update. Wilson Library Bulletin; May
     1984; 58(8): 652-653; ISSN 0043-5651.
     Public services/End-user services/Microcomputers.

103. Kirk, Cheryl L. End-User Training at the Amoco Research
     Center. Special Libraries; Winter 1986; 77(1): 20-27.
     End-user services/Public services.

104. Kruger, Betsy. NELINET: A Case Study of Regional Library
     Network Development. Information Technology and Libraries;
     June 1985; 4(2): 112-121; ISSN 0730-9295.
     Library networks/Bibliographic utilities/Regional networks.

105. Kuhlman, James R.; Lee, Everett S. Data Power to the People.
     American Libraries; November 1986; 17(10): 757-760, 778; ISSN
     0002-9769.
     Public services/Optical media/End-user
     services/Microcomputers.

106. LC Begins Conversion Service for British Library MARC Records.
     Advanced Technology/Libraries; September 1985; 14(9): 5.
     Bibliographic utilities/Cataloging sources.

107. Lee, Hwa-Wei; Mulliner, K.; Hoffmann-Pinther, E.; McCauley,
     Hannah. Alice at One: Candid Reflections on the Adoption,
     Installation, and Use of the Virginia Tech Library System
     (VTLS) at Ohio University; 1984.
     Note: Paper presented at the Integrated Online Library
     Systems (IOLS) Second National Conference, September 13-14,
     1984, Atlanta, Georgia.
     Integrated library systems/Turnkey systems/Local library
     systems.

108. Levert, Virginia M. Applications of Local Area Networks of
     Microcomputers in Libraries. Information Technology and
     Libraries; March 1985; 4(1): 9-18; ISSN 0730-9295.
     Microcomputers/LANs.

109. Library of Congress. Network Development Office. A Glossary
     for Library Networking. Network Planning Paper; 1978; (2);
     ISSN 0160-9742.
     Note: Prepared by Dataflow Systems Inc.
     Glossary/Library networks.

110. Library of Congress. Network Advisory Committee. Key Issues in
     the Networking Field Today. Network Planning Paper; 1985;
     (12); ISSN 0160-9742.
     Note: Proceedings of the Library of Congress Network Advisory
     Committee Meeting, May 6-8, 1985, Library of Congress,
     Washington, D.C.
     Library networks/Bibliographic utilities/National network.

111. Library of Congress. The Library of Congress Optical Disk
     Pilot Program. Washington, D.C.: Library of Congress.
     Note: For information, contact the Library of Congress Office
     of Planning and Development, Washington, D.C. 20540.
     Optical media.

112. Library of Congress. The Role of the Library of Congress in
     the Evolving National Network. Washington, D.C.: Library of
     Congress; 1978.
     National network/ Library networks/Bibliographic utilities.

113. Library of Congress. Network Advisory Committee. Toward a
     Common Vision in Library Networking; 1986.
     Note: Proceedings of the Library of Congress Network Advisory
     Committee Meeting, December 9-11, 1985, Library of Congress,
     Washington, D.C.
     Library networks/Bibliographic utilities/National network.

114. The Linked Systems Project: A New Dimension in Library
     Networking; 1985.
     Note: Printed leaflet gives overview of LSP and list of
     official participants.
     LSP.

115. LSN Local Systems Market Survey. Library Systems Newsletter;
     April 1984: 25-29.
     Local library systems/Turnkey systems/Integrated library
     systems.

116. Luce, Richard E. IRVING: Interfacing Dissimilar Systems at the
     Local Level. Library Hi Tech; 1984; 2(3): 55-61; ISSN 0737-
     8831.
     OSI/Regional networks/Library networking.

117. Lynch, Clifford A.; Brownrigg, Edwin B. The Telecommunications
     Landscape: 1986. Library Journal; October 1, 1986; 111: 40-
     46; ISSN 0363-0277.
     LSP/OSI/LANs.

118. Machovec, George S. Administrative Issues in Planning a
     Library End User Searching Program. Online Libraries and
     Microcomputers; June 1986; 4(6-7): 1-3.
     Public services/End-user services/Microcomputers.

119. Malinconico, S. Michael. Network Trends in North America. In:
     Ravenna nel Servizio Bibliotecario Nazionale, Convegno
     Internazionale; April 17-19, 1986; Ravenna, Italy. Ravenna
     Italy; 1986: 44-52.
     Note: "Tavola Rotonda Internazionale: Relazioni".
     Library networks/Bibliographic utilities/Turnkey systems.

120. Mann, Thomas,; Chao, Yuan Tsien Dolly; Hughes, K. Scott.
     Library Automation: A Survey of Leading Academic & Public
     Libraries in the United States. San Francisco, CA: Peat,
     Marwick, Mitchell and Co.; February 1986.
     Local library systems/Turnkey systems/Integrated library
     systems.

121. Markuson, Barbara Evans. Issues in National Library Network
     Development: an Overview. In: Library of Congress. Network
     Planning Paper; 1985; (12): 9-32; ISSN 0160-9742.
     Note: "Key Issues in the Networking Field Today," Proceedings
     of the Library of Congress Network Advisory Committee
     Meeting, May 6-8, 1985.
     Library networks/National network/Bibliographic
     utilities/Regional networks.

122. Markuson, Barbara Evans; Woolls, Blanche, editors. Networks
     for Networkers: Critical Issues in Cooperative Library
     Development. New York: Neal-Schuman Publishers; 1980; 444
     pages; ISBN 0-7201-01599-X.
     Note: Conference on Networks for Networkers, May 30-June 1,
     1979, Indianapolis. Includes networking glossary and list of
     acronyms.
     Library networks/Bibliographic utilities/Regional networks.

123. Martin, Susan K. Delivery Systems: Hurry Up and Wait. In:
     Aveney, Brian; Butler, Brett, editors. Online Catalogs,
     Online Reference: Converging Trends. Chicago, IL: American
     Library Association; 1984: 165-177; ISBN 0-8389-3308-4.
     Document delivery/ILL.

124. Martin, Susan K. Library Networks, 1986-87: Libraries in
     Partnership. White Plains, NY: Knowledge Industry
     Publications; 1986; ISBN 0-86729-127-3.
     Note: Includes list of acronyms and directory of networks and
     members.
     Library networks/Bibliographic utilities.

125. Maruyama, Lenore. The Library of Congress Network Advisory
     Committee. Washington, D.C.: Library of Congress; 1985; ISBN
     0-8444-0511-6.
     NAC/National network/Library networks.

126. Mason, Robert M. The Library Microconsumer; MRC's Guide to
     Library Software. Atlanta, Georgia: Metrics Research
     Corporation; 1986.
     Microcomputers/Local library systems.

127. Matthews, Joseph R. Choosing an Automated Library System.
Chicago: American Library Association; 1980; ISBN 0-8389-
0310-X.
Note: Includes Glossary and Bibliography.
Turnkey systems/Integrated library systems/Distributed
processing.

128. Matthews, Joseph R. Growth & Consolidation: The 1985 Automated
Library System Marketplace. Library Journal; April 1, 1986;
111: 25-35; ISSN 0363-0277.
Integrated library systems/Turnkey systems/Microcomputers.

129. Matthews, Joseph R. Unrelenting Change: The 1984 Automated
Library System Marketplace. Library Journal; April 1, 1985;
110: 31-39; ISSN 0363-0277.
Local library systems/Turnkey
systems/Microcomputers/Integrated library systems.

130. McAninch,Glen. Bibliographic Utilities and the Use of
Microcomputers in Libraries: Current and Projected Practices.
Microcomputers for Information Management; September 1986;
3(3): 217-231.
Microcomputers/Bibliographic utilities/Local library systems.

131. McCallum, Sally H. Linked Systems Project in the United
States. Washington, D.C.; 1985.
Note: Paper presented at the IFLA meeting, August 1985, at
the Library of Congress.
LSP/Bibliographic utilities.

132. McCallum, Sally H. Linked Systems Project, Part 1: Authorities
Implementation. Library Hi Tech; 1985; 3(2): 61-68; ISSN
0737-8831.
Note: Continuous Issue Number 10.
LSP/OSI.

133. McCoy, Richard W.; Davison, Wayne E. Building Networks for
Scholarly Information. EDUCOM Bulletin; 1985; 20: 2-5,8.
Library networks/Bibliographic utilities/LSP/Integrated
library systems.

134. McCoy Richard W. The Linked Systems Project: Progress,
Promise, Realities. Library Journal; October 1, 1986; 110:
33-39; ISSN 0363-0277.
LSP/Library networks/Bibliographic utilities/OSI.

135. McQueen, Judy; Boss, Richard W. Sources of Machine-Readable
     Cataloging and Retrospective Conversion. Library Technology
     Reports; November-December 1985; 21(6): 601-732; ISSN 0024-
     2586.
     Note: 22 vendors are listed, along with prices for their
     services.
     Cataloging sources/Recon.

136. Melin, Nancy. Enlarging Micros: the Mainframe Connection.
     Wilson Library Bulletin; January 1985: 315-318; ISSN 0043-
     5651.
     Microcomputers/Local library systems.

137. Merilees, Bobbie. A Survey of the 1986 Canadian Library
     Systems Marketplace. Canadian Library Journal; June 1987;
     44(3): 135-139; ISSN 0008-4352.
     Local library systems/Integrated library systems/Turnkey
     systems/Microcomputers.

138. Microcomputer Applications in Library and Information
     Services. Stirling, Keith, Issue editor. Drexel Library
     Quarterly; 1984; 20(4).
     Microcomputers/ Local library systems.

139. Microcomputers for Information Management: An International
     Journal for Library and Information Services. Norwood, NJ:
     Ablex Publishing Co.
     Note: A quarterly.

140. Microcomputers for Libraries. Powell, OH: James E. Rush
     Associates.
     Note: A quarterly.

141. Miller, David C. Running With CD-ROM. American Libraries;
     November 1986; 17(10): 754-756; ISSN 0002-9769.
     Optical media/Microcomputers/Public services.

142. Miller, Ronald F. The Impact of Technology on Library Networks
     and Related Organizations. In: Key Issues in the Networking
     Field Today; Proceedings of the Library of Congress Network
     Advisory Committee; May 6-8, 1985: 49-60; ISSN 0160-9742.
     Note: Network Planning Paper, Number 12.
     Library networks/Bibliographic utilities/Regional
     networks/Distributed processing.

143. Milliot, Jim. Micros at Work: Case Studies of Microcomputers in Libraries. White Plains, NY: Knowledge Industry Publications; 1985; ISBN 0-86729-117-6.
Note: Includes Glossary.
Microcomputers/Distributed processing.

144. National Commission on Libraries and Information Science. Toward a Federal Library and Information Services Network. Washington, D.C.: NCLIS; 1982.
National network/Library networks.

145. National Library of Canada. The Future of the National Library of Canada. Ottawa: National Library of Canada; 1979.
Library networks/National network/Cataloging sources/ILL.

146. National Library of Canada. Office for Network Development. Linking: Today's Libraries, Tomorrow's Technologies. Canadian Network Papers; March 1984; (Number 7); ISSN 0226-8760.
Note: Report of the Bibliographic and Communications Network Pilot Project.
Library networks/OSI/Distributed processing.

147. National Library of Canada. Office for Network Development. Optical Disk Technology and the Library. Canadian Network Papers; May 1985; (Number 9); ISSN 0226-8760.
Optical media.

148. National Library of Canada. Office for Network Development. Task Group on Computer/Communications Protocols for Bibliographic Data Interchange: Second Report. Canadian Network Papers; December 1985; (Number 10); ISSN 0226-8760.
OSI/Library networks.

149. Nicita, Michael; Petrusha, Ronald. The Reader's Guide to Microcomputer Books. White Plains, NY: Knowledge Industry Publications; 1984.
Microcomputers/Local library systems.

150. OCLC Annual Report - 1985/86. Dublin, Ohio: OCLC; Summer 1986.

151. OCLC Micro; ISSN 8756-5196.
Note: Bi-monthly. Dublin, OH: OCLC Online Computer Library Center.

152. OCLC: Questions and Answers. Dublin, Ohio: OCLC; June 1987.

153. Online Libraries and Microcomputers. Phoenix, AZ: Information Intelligence.
Note: A monthly.

154. Parker, Elizabeth Betz. The Library of Congress Non-Print Optical Disk Pilot Program. Information Technology and Libraries; December 1985; 4(4): 289-299; ISSN 0730-9295.
Optical media.

155. Peat, Marwick, Mitchell and Co. Library Automation: A Survey of Leading Academic and Public Libraries in the United States. San Francisco, CA: Peat, Marwick, Mitchell and Co.; February 1986.
Local library systems/Turnkey systems/Integrated systems.

156. Pezzanite, Frank A. The LC MARC Database on Video Laserdisc: The MINI MARC System. Library Hi Tech; 1985; 3(1): 57-60; ISSN 0737-8831.
Note: Continuous Issue Number 9.
Optical media/Cataloging sources.

157. Piele, Linda J.; Pryor,Judith; Tuckett, Harold W. Teaching Microcomputer Literacy: New Roles for Academic Librarians. College & Research Libraries; July 1986; 47: 374-377; ISSN 0010-0870.
Microcomputers/Public services/End-user services.

158. Pope, Nolan F. Library Planning for Future Networks. Resource Sharing & Library Networks; Fall 1981; 1(1): 11-18; ISSN 0270-3173.
Library networks/Bibliographic utilities/Regional networks.

159. Posey, Edwin D.; Erdmann, Charlotte A. An Online UNIX-Based Engineering Library Catalog: Purdue University Engineering Library. Science & Tecnology Libraries; Summer 1986; 6(4): 31-43.
Online catalogs/Local library systems/Public services/End-user services.

160. Potter, William Gray. Creative Automation Boosts ILL Rates. American Libraries; April 1986: 244-246; ISSN 0002-9769.
Library networks/ILL/Microcomputers.

161. Price, Joseph. The Optical Disk Pilot Program at the Library of Congress. Videodisc and Optical Disk; November-December 1984; 4(6): 424-432.
Optical media.

162. Pricing of Online Cataloging Support. Library Systems
     Newsletter; December 1985; V(12): 89-92; ISSN 0277-0288.
     Cataloging sources.

163. Principles and Guidelines for Transfer of OCLC-Derived
     Machine-Readable Records. Dublin, Ohio: OCLC; May 1986.
     Bibliographic utilities/Data ownership.

164. Pruitt, Ellen; Dowling, Karen. Searching for Current
     Information Online...How High School Library Media Centers in
     Montgomery County, Maryland are Solving an Information
     Problem by Using DIALOG. ONLINE; March 1985; 9(2): 47-60;
     ISSN 0146-5422.
     Public services/End-user services.

165. Reich, Victoria Ann; Betcher, Melissa Ann. Library of Congress
     Staff Test Optical Disk System. College & Research Libraries;
     July 1986: 385-391; ISSN 0010-0870.
     Optical media/Public services/End-user services/Document
     delivery.

166. Research Libraries Group. The Linked Systems Project: Toward a
     Universe of Discourse. Research Libraries Group News; 1985;
     7(8): 11-14.
     LSP/Library Networks/Bibliographic utilities.

167. The Research Libraries Group, Inc. The Research Libraries
     Group News; May 1987; (No. 13); ISSN 0-196-173X.
     Note: Reviews programs and progress of RLG/RLIN in 1986.

168. Reynolds, Dennis. Library Automation: Issues and Applications.
     New York: R.R. Bowker; 1985; ISBN 0-8325-1489-3.
     Library networks/Bibliographic utilities/Cataloging
     sources/Local library systems/Turnkey systems/Online
     catalogs/Public services/End-user services.

169. Robinson, Barbara M. Cooperation and Competition Among Library
     Networks. Journal of the American Society for Information
     Science; November 1980; 31(6): 413-424; ISSN 0002-8231.
     Library networks/Bibliographic utilities/Regional networks.

170. Salmon, Stephen R. TOMUS: The System's Design and Features.
     Library Hi Tech; Fall 1986; 4(3): 51-64; ISSN 0737-8831.
     Note: Continuous Issue Number 15.
     Online catalogs/Local library systems/Turnkey
     systems/Microcomputers/Distributed processing.

171. Schlatter, M. Warren; Duvis, Shelley, E.; Mims, Dorothy H.
Microcomputers in the Library: A Health Sciences Library Case
Study. Library Hi Tech; 1985; 3(4): 101-104; ISSN 0737-8831.
Note: (Continuous Issue Number 12).
Microcomputers/Local library systems.

172. Segal, Jo An S. Networking and Decentralization. In: White
Plains, NY: Knowledge Industry Publications; 1985; 20: 203-
231. (Williams, Martha E. Annual Review of Information
Science and Technology; 20); ISBN 0-86729-175-3.
Library networks/Bibliographic utilities/Distributed
Processing/Regional networks.

173. Sloan, Bernard. Sharing Resources in Illinois: Statewide
Library Computer System. Wilson Library Bulletin; December
1984; (59): 259-261; ISSN 0043-5651.
Library networks/Regional networks/ILL.

174. SOLINET's New Program Will Support Networks. Library Journal;
April 15, 1985; 110: 12; ISSN 0363-0277.
Library networks/Regional networks/Distributed processing.

175. Spigai, Fran; Butler, Matilda; Paisley, William. Databases on
Floppy Disks: New Publications for Libraries. Library Hi
Tech; 1985; 3(4): 11-19; ISSN 0737-8831.
Note: Continuous Issue Number 12.
Optical media/Public services/End-user
services/Microcomputers.

176. Strauss, Diana. A Checklist of Issues to be Considered
Regarding the Addition of Microcomputer Data Disks to
Academic Libraries. Information Technology and Libraries;
June 1986; 5(2): 129-132; ISSN 0730-9295.
Microcomputers/Public services.

177. Sweeney, Richard. The Electronic Library and Information
System of Polytechnic; April 2, 1987.
Note: Unpublished paper available from the author, Dean of
Libraries and Information Systems, Polytechnic University,
333 Jay Street, Brooklyn, New York 11201.
Integrated library systems/End-user services/Optical media.

178. Taylor, James B. Integrated Systems & Vendor Survival. Library
Journal; October 1, 1985; 110: 50-51; ISSN 0363-0277.
Turnkey systems/Integrated library systems/Local library
systems.

179. Tenopir, Carol. Four Options for End User Searching. Library Journal; July 1986; 111: 56-57; ISSN 0363-0277.
Public services/End-user services/Microcomputers.

180. Tenopir, Carol. Infotrac: A Laser Disc System. Library Journal; September 1, 1986; 111: 168-169; ISSN 0363-0277.
Optical media/End-user services/Microcomputers/Public services.

181. U.S. National Commission on Library and Information Science. Toward a National Program for Library and Information Services: Goals for Action. Washington, D.C.: U.S. Government Printing Office; 1975.
National network/ Library networks.

182. Van Young, Sayre. Where to Find Answers to Questions About Microcomputers. Littleton, Colorado: Libraries Unlimited; 1986.
Microcomputers/Local library systems.

183. Walton, Kenneth R./Dedert, Patricia L. Experiences at Exxon in Training End-Users to Search Technical Databases Online. ONLINE; September 1983; 7(5): 42-50; ISSN 0146-5422.
End-user services/Public services.

184. Walton, Robert. Microcomputers and the Library: A Planning Guide for Managers. Austin, Texas: Texas State Library, Library Development Division; 1982.
Microcomputers/Local library systems.

185. Walton, Robert. Microcomputers: A Planning and Implementation Guide for Libraries and Information Professionals. Phoenix. AZ: Oryx Press; 1983.
Microcomputers/Local library systems.

186. Williams, Martha E. Transparent Information Systems Through Gateways, Front Ends, Intermediaries and Interfaces. Journal of the American Society for Information Science; ISSN 0002-8231.
Note: Prepublication draft from the author.
End-user services/Public services/Microcomputers.

187. The Wired Librarian's Newsletter. Sioux City, IA: Micro Libraries.
Note: Monthly.

188. Wismer, Donald. Microcomputers With a Bold Face; or You've Got
     to Begin Somewhere. ONLINE; September 1983: 52-59.
     Microcomputers.

189. Woods, Lawrence A.; Pope, Nolan F. The Librarian's Guide to
     Microcomputer Technology and Applications. White Plains, NY:
     Knowledge Industry Publications; 1983; ISBN 0-87629-044-7.
     Note: Includes Glossary and Bibliography.
     Microcomputers/LANs/Public services/Distributed processing.

APPENDIX A

Five-Part Questionnaire for North American Bibliographic Utilities
(Responses of the Chief Executive Officers provided in the fall of 1986)

1. There is a growing view that the large, centralized online databases of
RLG, OCLC, WLN, and UTLAS will not be needed in the future to support
cataloging and ILL activities. All libraries will have their own automated
systems (with cataloging modules), interconnected in an open systems
environment, enabling direct library to library communication for the search
and transfer of bibliographic records, and for ILL transactions. Please
comment on this view.

ANSWER: In the 1985/86 OCLC Annual Report, Rowland Brown, President of
OCLC, commented on the situation described in the first question:

> Through the implementation of new policies, programs, services and
> system support, OCLC has been directing its attention to emerging
> local, regional, state, national and international needs. In reports
> I have made during this past year to the OCLC Membership, to our Users
> Council, to network participants meetings, to library associations and
> to the Network Advisory Committee to the Librarian of Congress, I have
> emphasized the fact that the increasing number of technologically
> driven, and frequently commercially available, options for local
> processes may lead many librarians to abandon national (let alone
> international) networking and to ignore the vital importance of the
> resource-sharing structure that they themselves have so painstakingly
> built over the last two decades. Certainly, distributed processing is
> a boon to librarianship, but librarians may be implementing their
> options in ways that will result in fragmentation rather than orderly
> and logical distribution. Most distinguished library leaders view
> this situation with alarm.

> We acknowledge that libraries and the institutions responsible for
> library funding face a critical dilemma: how to use their limited
> resources to accommodate the pressing local needs and interests of
> their immediate constituencies and at the same time meet their
> responsibility to share resources with the broader information
> community. But we cannot allow ourselves to view local and global
> needs of library users as mutually exclusive. Indeed, the resource
> sharing that OCLC facilitates by national and international networking
> is not only cost-effective and practical for libraries, but it also
> inestimably enriches the intellectual resources of the nation and the
> world. One librarian has aptly described this process of looking to
> one's own needs while not ignoring the common good as "standing alone,
> together."

> OCLC is facilitating this interrelatedness through new pricing and new
> membership options, creative collaborative arrangements and a new
> system design that links centralized with distributed processing to
> empower the individual library user at the workstation. We are
> concentrating on economic value and cost effectiveness at every level
> and in every operation.

ONLINE COMPUTER LIBRARY CENTER (OCLC)

APPENDIX A

Five-Part Questionnaire for North American Bibliographic Utilities
(Responses of the Chief Executive Officers provided in the fall of 1986)

1. There is a growing view that the large, centralized online databases of
RLG, OCLC, WLN, and UTLAS will not be needed in the future to support
cataloging and ILL activities. All libraries will have their own automated
systems (with cataloging modules), interconnected in an open systems
environment, enabling direct library to library communication for the search
and transfer of bibliographic records, and for ILL transactions. Please
comment on this view.

---

1. It is true that there will be installed over the next several
years, at rates and times influenced by the size and type of
library and the rate of product development in the market place,
automated systems as you suggest: with cataloging modules.

For smaller and simpler libraries their cataloging work, when
viewed from a short term and local perspective, may require
neither "utility" nor open system network connection. However,
any widespread choice of such go-it-alone options will, in the
longer term and broader perspective (regional, national,
international) produce costly and most unpleasant results. A
retreat from a cooperative environment will threaten ILL, shared
cataloging, National Union Catalogs and other activities that
rely on sharing.

For larger, more complex libraries the need to share is
compelling even when viewed as a largely local question.
Further, these libraries tend to recognize more clearly that a
portion of their mission includes their contribution to the needs
of the broader library and scholarly communities, not just their
own patrons or institution. Thus, the risk of, and the
incentives for a reduction in sharing is moderated.

RLG and its member institutions have determined and stated
explicitly, that for the next five years (at least) they will
need to maintain for the consortium and its programs, a single,
physical, and comprehensive union data base of member
bibliographic records. We expect, even during this time, that
open system networking will encourage and support the sharing of
those records - for mutual benefit - with others. Beyond this
five-year horizon, technology may change the means of storage and
communication of such data; certain fundamental tasks will
remain, however, including establishing standards, creating
systems of organization of data, and arranging for access. These
fundamental roles now carried out by the organizations you are
surveying will need to be supported by someone -- probably a
group including at least some of the same players.

(more)

THE RESEARCH LIBRARIES GROUP (RLG)

APPENDIX A

Five-Part Questionnaire for North American Bibliographic Utilities
(Responses of the Chief Executive Officers provided in the fall of 1986)

1. There is a growing view that the large, centralized online databases of RLG, OCLC, WLN, and UTLAS will not be needed in the future to support cataloging and ILL activities. All libraries will have their own automated systems (with cataloging modules), interconnected in an open systems environment, enabling direct library to library communication for the search and transfer of bibliographic records, and for ILL transactions. Please comment on this view.

(1. Contd.)

There are interesting technological models not only for distributed processing, but for distributed data bases which would comprise a logical union data base whether of a consortium, a region or beyond. The technology is not sufficiently developed, particularly in an environment of heterogeneous and independent choices of local system, purpose, etc., to support this kind of data base in the near term. Open systems protocol standards, still undergoing the usual debate and change characteristic of the standards process should not be understood as providing, ipso facto, such a solution.

Open system network interconnection (of which in the library world only the limited operational examples of RLIN-LC and RLIN-NYU connections exist) will offer substantial benefits. Most of these benefits will be accessible, however, to libraries who access them through a host network of some kind. In North America these are, at present, principally OCLC, RLIN, UTLAS, WLN and the Library of Congress. Individual library or workstation connections to an OSI network (like those being worked on in the proposed Canadian ILL protocol), for example, will serve only limited purposes without access to information (a data base) revealing where a message should be sent. It will not do, for example, to replace a search of OCLC with searches run redundantly at dozens or hundreds of local systems. That's all that would be available at present without more advanced technology and a greater degree of control over the environment.

OSI should not be sold short, however; it has the potential to allow a result-not-found search in one network to be extended easily to another, and it offers, perhaps, the best hope for resolving the "electronic tower of Babel" problem created by the differences in searching protocols among the literally thousands of data bases of interest to scholars and researchers.

###############

THE RESEARCH LIBRARIES GROUP (RLG)

APPENDIX A

Five-Part Questionnaire for North American Bibliographic Utilities
(Responses of the Chief Executive Officers provided in the fall of 1986)

1. There is a growing view that the large, centralized online databases of
RLG, OCLC, WLN, and UTLAS will not be needed in the future to support
cataloging and ILL activities. All libraries will have their own automated
systems (with cataloging modules), interconnected in an open systems
environment, enabling direct library to library communication for the search
and transfer of bibliographic records, and for ILL transactions. Please
comment on this view.

———————

Although the major bibliographic utilities provide libraries with a variety of
products and services, shared cataloging and interlibrary loan activities
comprise the core services of each network. While strong economic pressures
cause libraries to perform circulation, acquisitions and serials control on
local systems, most still rely on the utilities as their source for cataloging
and interlibrary loan data and functionality. And yet, as your question
suggests, even these core network services could be replaced by rapidly
expanding local system capabilities.

Current trends taken to their logical extreme support this conclusion.
Factors contributing to this view include the following:

1) Local systems are certainly on the increase. The wide variety of system
capacities, capabilities and price mean systems exist which meet at least some
of the needs of nearly all sizes and types of libraries.

2) Tight budgets and rising telecommunications costs have forced libraries to
seek local solutions to problems once solved exclusively at the network level.
A fixed price resource such as a local system becomes very appealing.

3) The telecommunications portion of the Linked Systems Project (the Standard
Network Interface or SNI) could become a standard for interconnecting automated
library systems, facilitating links beyond the network level. A fixed price
resource such as a local system becomes very appealing.

4) Inexpensive alternative sources for MARC records continue to appear.

Notwithstanding these pressures, a number of factors work against bypassing
networks for cataloging and interlibrary loan:

1) Primarily for economic reasons, not all libraries will be able to acquire
local systems in the forseeable future.

2) Not all local systems will be sophisticated enough to support
interconnection. Even if SNI becomes a telecommunications standard, interconnection presents a significant set of technical problems involving database
and record structures, search capabilities and techniques, etc. An equally
significant set of policy issues would present itself - one library at a time.

(more)

WESTERN LIBRARY NETWORK (WLN)

APPENDIX A

Five-Part Questionnaire for North American Bibliographic Utilities
(Responses of the Chief Executive Officers provided in the fall of 1986)

1. There is a growing view that the large, centralized online databases of
RLG, OCLC, WLN, and UTLAS will not be needed in the future to support
cataloging and ILL activities. All libraries will have their own automated
systems (with cataloging modules), interconnected in an open systems
environment, enabling direct library to library communication for the search
and transfer of bibliographic records, and for ILL transactions. Please
comment on this view.

(1. Contd.)

3) Telecommunications costs can hardly be called stable. Interconnection at
the local level could cost libraries a great deal more than a single connection
to a utility.

4) Because of its authority control system, WLN provides essential catalog
file maintenance services for its members. Libraries acquiring a local system
for cataloging purposes must count the cost of continuing this maintenance
function locally.

It is our view that, at least for the forseeable future, the library community
will be hard pressed to find a superior method for cataloging and interlibrary
loan than that currently provided by the utilities. There is a tremendous
economy of scale inherent in the union catalogs that will be difficult to
surpass at the local level. As a recent Peat, Marwick & Mitchell survey of 26
top public and academic libraries in the U.S. concluded, "Even libraries with
catalog maintenance on a local system don't view enhancement of their local
systems as a substitute for participation in national bibliographic systems." *

That economy of scale, however, is supported by revenues from the other
products and services made available by the networks, many of which can now be
performed economically at the local level. As these secondary sources of
revenue erode, the networks will be attempting to replace them with income from
new products and services. Their ability to succeed in this arena is more
likely to determine their survival than an erosion of cataloging and
interlibrary loan activity.

*"Peat, Marwick, Mitchell Tracks Automation Trends" in Library Hi Tech News,
July/August 1986, p.4.

################

WESTERN LIBRARY NETWORK (WLN)

APPENDIX A

Five-Part Questionnaire for North American Bibliographic Utilities
(Responses of the Chief Executive Officers provided in the fall of 1986)

1. There is a growing view that the large, centralized online databases of RLG, OCLC, WLN, and UTLAS will not be needed in the future to support cataloging and ILL activities. All libraries will have their own automated systems (with cataloging modules), interconnected in an open systems environment, enabling direct library to library communication for the search and transfer of bibliographic records, and for ILL transactions. Please comment on this view.

While the open systems environment will bring many benefits, Utlas' view is that it does not lend itself efficiently or economically to cataloguing and ILL functions. The centralized database structure now employed by Utlas and other utilities entails a single connection and a single transaction for each user seeking cataloguing or location data; the aggregated data so obtained allows the user to choose the record or location best suited for the situation at hand. On the other hand, the separate-but-interconnected structure will entail multiple connections and transactions for each user and each bibliographic entity; and moreover, it entails a return to the guesswork of earlier decades. Libraries seeking a location from which to request an item (or a catalogue from which to derive a record) are likely to target their inquiries in a more-to-less-likely sequence, thus causing a disproportionate amount of the request and inquiry traffic to converge on the largest libraries. The multiple transactions and connections necessary to complete each ILL request or cataloguing record derivation will place an unmanageable load on library communications facilities and on staff resources. Distributed databases (such as regional union catalogues) may be efficient tool for interlibrary cooperation; but a complete fragmented database of bibliographic data would invite more difficulty than it provides solutions.

##################

Utlas International Canada

APPENDIX A

Five-Part Questionnaire for North American Bibliographic Utilities
(Responses of the Chief Executive Officers provided in the fall of 1986)

2. OCLC, RLG, WLN, and UTLAS now offer many of the same products and services to member or client libraries. What key factors (e.g., financial bases, operating philosophy/goals, governance structure, database content/structure, etc.) best account for your organization's unique role and mission vis-a-vis libraries and library users?

ANSWER: OCLC's unique role derives from its broad public purpose as stated in its charter:

> The purpose or purposes for which this Corporation is formed are to establish, maintain and operate a computerized library network and to promote the evolution of library use, of libraries themselves, and of librarianship, and to provide processes and products for the benefit of library users and libraries, including such objectives as increasing availability of library resources to individual library patrons and reducing rate-of-rise of library per-unit costs, all for the fundamental public purpose of furthering ease of access to and use of the ever-expanding body of worldwide scientific, literary and educational knowledge and information.

OCLC is a nonprofit membership organization comprised of approximately 6,000 libraries in the United States and 16 other countries. It is self-sustaining and does not depend on grants or foundation support for either its daily operation nor its future planning and development. Member libraries are directly represented by both the Board of Trustees and the OCLC Users Council.

The OCLC Board of Trustees is composed of 16 individuals, nine of whom are librarians. Six of the Trustees are elected by and from within the Users Council. Other Board members are selected for their expertise in technical and business areas. The Board's major responsibilities are to ensure the financial well-being of OCLC and to make policy decisions that support the purpose of the organization as stated in its charter.

The OCLC Users Council is a body of sixty delegates elected by the member libraries. The Users Council serves to reflect and articulate the interests the member libraries, and in addition to electing six Trustees, must approve any change in the corporation's documents of·governance.

(more)

ONLINE COMPUTER LIBRARY CENTER (OCLC)

APPENDIX A

Five-Part Questionnaire for North American Bibliographic Utilities
(Responses of the Chief Executive Officers provided in the fall of 1986)

2. OCLC, RLG, WLN, and UTLAS now offer many of the same products and services to member or client libraries. What key factors (e.g., financial bases, operating philosophy/goals, governance structure, database content/structure, etc.) best account for your organization's unique role and mission vis-a-vis libraries and library users?

(2. Contd.)

By working with libraries, OCLC has already become an integral part of that information infrastructure, but it has also done so in other ways. For example, it has facilitated or offered crucial support to a number of important national level programs including CONSER, the NFAIS abstract and indexing project for CONSER, Library of Congress cataloging activities, the U.S. Newspaper Project and the Major Microforms project. These programs, along with many others, have implications for the user, the scholar, the historian and the public policy maker. OCLC is also supporting major programs of ARL, preservation initiatives that are under way with the help of the Council on Library Resources, the Linked Systems Project, library-related and computer assisted educational research efforts that are under way on campuses, in both the U.S. and abroad, and a research partnership with ALA to launch a regular series of statistical reports on the state of the nation's academic, public and school libraries.

With 314 languages, over 14 million bibliographic records, and over 250 million location listings, the OCLC database is an unrivaled international online union catalog. But OCLC is more than just a bibliographic database. When its new computer system is in place, with its menus and easier user interfaces and help screens, easier dial-up access and particularly subject search capability, OCLC will be more widely accessed by scholars and other library users worldwide. In its strategic planning, OCLC sees its role and that of libraries in the broader world of education and information. OCLC is moving "beyond bibliography"--not, _away_ from bibliography--and is becoming, like libraries, a more integral part of the larger national and international educational infrastructure.

################

ONLINE COMPUTER LIBRARY CENTER (OCLC)

APPENDIX A

Five-Part Questionnaire for North American Bibliographic Utilities
(Responses of the Chief Executive Officers provided in the fall of 1986)

2. OCLC, RLG, WLN, and UTLAS now offer many of the same products and services
to member or client libraries. What key factors (e.g., financial bases, oper--
ating philosophy/goals, governance structure, database content/structure,
etc.) best account for your organization's unique role and mission vis-a-vis
libraries and library users?

From RLG, this question requires two responses; one for the
consortium which is the Research Libraries Group and one for the
Research Libraries Information Network RLIN which is more clearly
a counterpart to OCLC, WLN, or UTLAS.

A. RLG is a consortium whose legal form is a corporation owned
by 36 (at present) universities and research institutions. These
members are joined by some 45 Associate and Special Members who
join in some, but not all, of the consortium's programs. The
latter group includes major art museums and archival
repositories. Membership (and ownership) in RLG is limited to a
small number of relatively large institutions; the total which
would qualify is at present 67. The membership is made up of
institutions, not their libraries; there is active participation
in setting the direction of RLG at the institutional level by,
for example, their presidents, their chief information technology
officers, and others representing all parts of the institution.
The consortium is "program driven" and operates four cooperative
core programs and an array of others targeted toward specific
needs, disciplines, or resources, as well as toward more general
concerns of improving access to scholarly and research
information.

In these characteristics one cannot generally compare RLG with
"bibliographic utilities." Comparisons would be more likely
with other kinds of organizations.

B. RLIN, in contrast is a bibliographic network; comparisons can
be more readily made between this component of RLG activity and
the other networks surveyed. The first major differences which
would be evident stem from the fact that the development of RLIN
has focused on support for the Consortium's programs and on
features oriented toward the needs of its owner/members, large
and frequently complex research institutions.

Special data bases support the Collection Development and Art and
Architecture programs, for example, and special features and
enhancements offer critical support to preservation; these are
but three examples of a general programmatic orientation of the
network.

(more)

THE RESEARCH LIBRARIES GROUP (RLG)

APPENDIX A

Five-Part Questionnaire for North American Bibliographic Utilities
(Responses of the Chief Executive Officers provided in the fall of 1986)

2. OCLC, RLG, WLN, and UTLAS now offer many of the same products and services to member or client libraries. What key factors (e.g., financial bases, operating philosophy/goals, governance structure, database content/structure, etc.) best account for your organization's unique role and mission vis-a-vis libraries and library users?

(2. Contd.)

Other special characteristics of RLIN important to RLG members include the on-line support of full library-specific records, allowing maintenance of these records, and supporting catalogers and reference librarians with access to multiple, varied records when needed.

RLIN's design from the outset was intended to offer strong public service support; one reflection of this is found in its large number of indexes and in the searching flexibility offered through the broader capabilities and features of the searching interface.

RLIN is not intended to be a data base-of-record for the nation or the globe, but simply a comprehensive union data base of RLG members' materials or those of special interest to members. It is, therefore, focused in content as well as in features. These characteristics have helped to support a strong quality control capability and to achieve a higher standard of record quality than would otherwise be the case. While RLIN does not seek a comprehensive national or global role, the members of RLG have set for RLIN the objective of leading in the development of standards, technology, and agreements among potential contributors, which will permit open access and exchange of bibliographic records, and to do this in a manner which will allow RLIN to contribute to a larger "logical" (not physical) national and international data base. Policy, technology, and economics dictate that it will not be a single physical entity, nor will it, nor should it be under centralized control.

Philosophically the RLIN data base is viewed as a scholarly resource and that provides the basis for sharing it with others; mutual benefit is the major guiding principle.

Other distinguishing features of RLIN could be listed which differentiate it from the other networks, but it is the strong institutionally based commitment to cooperative programs, rather than particular network characteristics, which holds both RLIN and RLG together

###############

THE RESEARCH LIBRARIES GROUP (RLG)

APPENDIX A

Five-Part Questionnaire for North American Bibliographic Utilities
(Responses of the Chief Executive Officers provided in the fall of 1986)

2. OCLC, RLG, WLN, and UTLAS now offer many of the same products and services to member or client libraries. What key factors (e.g., financial bases, oper-ating philosophy/goals, governance structure, database content/structure, etc.) best account for your organization's unique role and mission vis-a-vis libraries and library users?

WLN is unique among the bibliographic utilities in a number of important ways. The most significant of these are listed below.

1) WLN is a regional network. The vast majority of its members are located in the five northwestern states of Alaska, Idaho, Montana, Oregon and Washington. This regional orientation allows WLN to focus its energies on the needs of a very specific clientele. Further, WLN's membership is composed of libraries with a long history of cooperation.

2) Unlike the other utilities, WLN is an agency of state government. Created in the early 1970s by the legislature of the State of Washington, it is overseen by a lay commission appointed by Washington's governor. As an organization then, WLN is in many ways very much like the libraries it serves. This situation engenders a high level of trust and understanding between WLN and its membership.

3) Each utility has unique system capabilities. However, WLN's uniqueness lies at the very heart of its system design. From the beginning WLN emphasized quality control and was designed accordingly. WLN is constructed around a shared database and shared authority file; both integrally and uniquely linked to allow centralized maintenance. As a result, WLN staff maintain the authority file shared by the entire membership and offer a database almost entirely free of duplicate records. This careful attention to database quality is reflected in WLN's products which include COM catalogs, magnetic tapes, cards and labels and printed bibliographies. It also enhances WLN's online search capabilites which include subject, boolean and many keyword searches.

4) WLN is committed to serving libraries of all sizes. Online access has, however, been beyond the reach of many. For nearly a decade WLN has produced a microfiche union listing of all records in the database which contain holdings. This Resource Directory allows smaller libraries to utilize WLN data. Now, development is well underway on a CD-ROM application, called LaserCat. LaserCat will include on compact disks, all WLN records with holdings plus the most recent 200,000 LC records. This will allow WLN to supply a major portion of its database to libraries of all sizes in a much more flexible format and at a very reasonable price. Among Lasercat's capabilities, are the ability to 1) download records, 2) print catalog cards and labels, 3) produce printed bibliographies, 4) search the entire union catalog or only one's own holdings, and 5) upload holdings statements to the WLN database.

5) WLN's entire software package is exportable. Currently, it has been installed at seven sites worldwide, including the British Library, and the national libraries of Australia, New Zealand and Singapore.

WESTERN LIBRARY NETWORK (WLN)

APPENDIX A

Five-Part Questionnaire for North American Bibliographic Utilities
(Responses of the Chief Executive Officers provided in the fall of 1986)

2. OCLC, RLG, WLN, and UTLAS now offer many of the same products and services
to member or client libraries. What key factors (e.g., financial bases, operating philosophy/goals, governance structure, database content/structure,
etc.) best account for your organization's unique role and mission vis-a-vis
libraries and library users?

Utlas is unique among utilities in the following respects:

a. Organizational Philosophy

   Utlas perceives its domain of activity to encompass all areas of
   library management and is committed to apply appropriate, stable,
   reliable technology with a reasonable life expectancy to the
   integration of products and services supporting library
   processes.

b. Range and Quality of Products and Services

   Utlas' range of products and services have extensive flexibility
   in terms of customization and include both centrally based
   services and local systems which are compatible with the former.
   Based on a computer architecture which allows for gradual,
   needs-driven growth, our local systems enable libraries to
   install appropriate hardware without concern about future
   replacements due to capacity ceilings. Among its shared
   cataloguing services, Utlas' authority control service is
   universally acclaimed as outstanding and unique.

c. User Ownership of Records

   Users own their records in the Utlas database and may obtain a
   copy at any time for use in a local system. Users may modify
   their records to reflect local standards; their storage at Utlas
   constitutes an insurance against loss or degradation which may
   occur in a local system.

d. De Facto National Union Catalogue for Canada; Close to 10 Million
   Unique Records

   Representing the holdings of over 2100 libraries in Canada, the
   Utlas database and ILL subsystem constitutes a de facto national
   union catalogue for Canada. Special collections held in the
   Utlas database (such as the Princeton Theological Seminary
   holdings) makes it a comprehensive resource for cataloguing data
   on common and rare items alike.

Utlas International Canada

APPENDIX A

Five-Part Questionnaire for North American Bibliographic Utilities
(Responses of the Chief Executive Officers provided in the fall of 1986)

3. Who owns the machine-readable bibliographic records that comprise the bibliographic database(s) held and maintained by your organization? List the restrictions (if any) placed on the use or distribution of these records by your member or client libraries.

ANSWER: OCLC does not claim ownership of or a copyright interest in any individual records contributed to the OCLC database by libraries. The United States Copyright Office has registered OCLC's copyright of the OCLC Online Union Catalog as a compilation of data.

A document entitled "Principles and Guidelines for Transfer of OCLC-Derived Machine-Readable Records" (May 13, 1986) is primarily a set of policies, promulgated primarily for U.S. libraries, to provide for the continuing enrichment of the database and to facilitate resource sharing within the library community. The principles as stated in that document are as follows:

- The continued growth and enrichment of the OCLC database for the benefit of the OCLC membership and the library world in general is both necessary and desirable.

- The sharing of information in all formats, including machine-readable records, among members of the library world in general is both necessary and desirable.

- OCLC believes that its member libraries and member networks will act with good faith toward OCLC and other member libraries. OCLC will not invoke copyright against any member libraries with which contracts have been executed which incorporate the Principles and Guidelines, but OCLC reserves its right to invoke copyright against uses by third parties not authorized by OCLC under the Guidelines below or under separate agreement.

The guidelines to which U.S. libraries are asked to subscribe provide for essentially unrestricted uses and transfers of OCLC-derived records by and between libraries, whether OCLC member institutions or not. The use and redistribution of OCLC-derived records by (i) the non-profit network organizations which serve as distributors for OCLC services, (ii) library systems operated under the aegis of state governments, (iii) other large, centralized online databases, and (iv) commercial third-party organizations, are as provided in separate understandings made with OCLC from case to case.

OCLC policies for the use and transfer of OCLC-derived records by institutions located in countries outside the United States are currently being formulated to meet the needs of the library community and of OCLC in each country.

ONLINE COMPUTER LIBRARY CENTER (OCLC)

APPENDIX A

Five-Part Questionnaire for North American Bibliographic Utilities
(Responses of the Chief Executive Officers provided in the fall of 1986)

3. Who owns the machine-readable bibliographic records that comprise the bibliographic database(s) held and maintained by your organization? List the restrictions (if any) placed on the use or distribution of these records by your member or client libraries.

The machine-readable bibliographic records of the RLIN data bases are co-owned by RLG and the institutions which have created them whether through original or copy activity. RLG places no restrictions whatever on the use which the creating institution may wish to make of its own records.

Conversely, the consortium may use the records to serve its purposes, which include exchanging record sets with others for mutual benefit and providing reasonable means of access to others who are not members. The consortium elects not to distribute subsets of records which would comprise primarily the holdings of an individual member (or other RLIN cataloging institution) unless so directed by that institution. It reviews requests for subsets of records with individual institutions which may have a substantial stake in the subset before a decision to share them is made. No individual institution's advice on how to respond to such a request has ever been ignored.

Finally, RLG has sought to lead (in its work toward the development of a nationwide coordinated cataloging program with the Library of Congress, for example, and in its response to the request of the Association of Research Libraries for the sharing of retrospective conversion records) in encouraging wide sharing through the LC MARC Distribution Service of records produced by RLG members, and to do this in a manner which might encourage others to act accordingly.

#############

THE RESEARCH LIBRARIES GROUP (RLG)

APPENDIX A

Five-Part Questionnaire for North American Bibliographic Utilities
(Responses of the Chief Executive Officers provided in the fall of 1986)

3. Who owns the machine-readable bibliographic records that comprise the bibliographic database(s) held and maintained by your organization? List the restrictions (if any) placed on the use or distribution of these records by your member or client libraries.

The following are excerpts from WLN's Principal Member Agreement, the standard contract between WLN and its members:

B.3.c) Ownership. Whereas the Bibliographic Database is compiled, organized, and maintained by the COMMISSION, therefore the Bibliographic Database shall be owned by the COMMISSION. The MEMBER shall have rights in the use of records from the Bibliographic Database, as specified in paragraphs B.3 and C.4 of this Agreement. All rights in the Bibliographic Database not explicitly covered in this Agreement are reserved to the COMMISSION.

C.4. Use of Records from the Bibliographic Database. The MEMBER shall have the right to make any use of Bibliographic Database records to which the MEMBER has attached its holdings symbol, as qualified below:

a) The MEMBER may obtain copies of such Bibliographic Database records, as specified in paragraph B.3.

b) The MEMBER may enter such Bibliographic Database records into a Local System used only by Principal, Associate, or Recon-Only Members without restriction.

c) The MEMBER may enter such Bibliographic Database records into a Local System used by non-members, subject to the provisions of WLN's Cluster Membership policy. Cluster Membership provisions shall be waived for non-members contributing machine-readable bibliographic records to the Local System from another source.

d) The MEMBER may provide such Bibliographic Database records to a vendor or vendors for the purpose of resource sharing or to obtain products or services from that vendor. However, prior to supplying Bibliographic Database records to such a vendor, the MEMBER must provide the COMMISSION with a copy of their contractual commitment with the vendor stipulating that the vendor will not use the Bibliographic Database records for any purpose other than those stated in this paragraph C.4.d.

e) The MEMBER shall not sell, transfer, make available or otherwise convey, or in any manner disclose Bibliographic Database records in machine-readable form to any non-member of WLN, except the MEMBER's own original Cataloging and as provided above, without the prior written permission of the COMMISSION.

WLN offers to license the database to institutions which license its bibliographic system software.

WESTERN LIBRARY NETWORK (WLN)

APPENDIX A

Five-Part Questionnaire for North American Bibliographic Utilities
(Responses of the Chief Executive Officers provided in the fall of 1986)

3. Who owns the machine-readable bibliographic records that comprise the bibliographic database(s) held and maintained by your organization? List the restrictions (if any) placed on the use or distribution of these records by your member or client libraries.

———————————

Each Utlas customer creates its own database of bibliographic records by copying (and modifying at its option) records from other databases held by Utlas, by keying records in directly, or by loading records by magnetic tape. Customers may at any time request an up-to-date copy of their database on magnetic tape in any one of several commonly used versions of the MARC Communications format. Where online interfaces to local library systems exist, the customer's own records may be downloaded online. Customers own the records they create through Utlas' facilities. The records may be loaded for the customer's use into other automated systems which the customer may own or license, or or to which it subscribes.

################

Utlas International Canada

APPENDIX A

Five-Part Questionnaire for North American Bibliographic Utilities
(Responses of the Chief Executive Officers provided in the fall of 1986)

4. What impact will the increasing adoption of new information technologies
(e.g., microcomputer-based workstations, and optical disk data storage,
retrieval, and transfer media) by libraries to support local needs have on
your organization's provision of its products and services for libraries?

ANSWER: Researchers at OCLC are studying systems and strategies for
information retrieval, using bibliographic and full-text databases stored
in optical discs or in online computer databases.

Microcomputers, local area networks, optical disc storage--these
technologies give libraries greater control and flexibility in their
systems than ever before. OCLC is designing its systems to interface with
and support a wide group of user systems and networks in an increasingly
distributed environment. In addition, OCLC is developing an array of
systems that will help libraries meet their own local needs
cost-effectively and take advantage of the benefits of economies of scale
that come from cooperation nationally and internationally.

Compact discs portend an exciting new era for OCLC and libraries as various
subsets of the OCLC database and other library databases are constructed
and stored locally for use in reference or technical processing areas.
Development of prototype CD-ROM based systems for education, medical
information, and cataloging are under way at OCLC.

OCLC is planning to use various forms of optical disc technology, not only
to support the bibliographic system, but also to support document delivery
and to develop the capability for electronic browsing and to access
monographs and journals. These technologies will also form the basis of
international resource sharing where telecommunications costs are a
barrier.

################

ONLINE COMPUTER LIBRARY CENTER (OCLC)

APPENDIX A

Five-Part Questionnaire for North American Bibliographic Utilities
(Responses of the Chief Executive Officers provided in the fall of 1986)

4. What impact will the increasing adoption of new information technologies
(e.g., microcomputer-based workstations, and optical disk data storage,
retrieval, and transfer media) by libraries to support local needs have on
your organization's provision of its products and services for libraries?

For the last four years, RLG has been planning and implementing
changes in the orientation of its network and changes in its view
of programmatic potential related to the increasing adoption of
new information technologies not only by the libraries but more
broadly by the universities and other institutions which are its
members.

The RLIN network is migrating, for example, from a centralized,
star network to a distributed network in which the former central
facility becomes one of many nodes of the network, one with
several special functions including that of data resource.

New RLIN applications development focuses on supporting local
systems, producing transportable software to allow moving some
applications, now run centrally, into the workstation
environment, and on developing (in areas where RLG has special
expertise) contributions to the evolution of the more powerful
"scholars' workstation" now under active development (and limited
use) in the higher education community and by supporting vendors.

To this end, RLG participates in several networks and consortia
with common interests; commits a significant part of its energies
to the development of national and international standards; and
seeks to serve as a forum within which the technological and
library leadership of its member universities can help to forge
necessary links between the new information technologies and "the
old information technologies" which the libraries have been
building for decades and centuries.

RLG's programs have begun to focus more broadly on the needs of
individual scholars and the academic departments and communities
of which they are a part. Links developing now will offer direct
access to RLIN (and other resources) through campus-based
networks and/or local library systems. (This will greatly expand
access over long-standing direct dial-in capabilities.)

The new technologies will bring dramatic changes both to RLIN and
to RLG's programs but will leave intact and will support the
fundamental nature of the consortium: its commitment to
cooperative solutions to information resource challenges which
cannot be solved by individual institutions acting independently.

THE RESEARCH LIBRARIES GROUP (RLG)

APPENDIX A

Five-Part Questionnaire for North American Bibliographic Utilities
(Responses of the Chief Executive Officers provided in the fall of 1986)

4. What impact will the increasing adoption of new information technologies (e.g., microcomputer-based workstations, and optical disk data storage, retrieval, and transfer media) by libraries to support local needs have on your organization's provision of its products and services for libraries?

The rapid pace of technological change affecting libraries makes this a very difficult question to answer. WLN has aggressively pursued two relatively new technological advances. The first, the switch to microcomputer based terminals, has been accomplished. The second, the addition of a significant CD-ROM based capability, is scheduled for delivery to our clientele in January, 1987.

Beginning in 1983, WLN moved to convert its entire leased line network from a relatively unintelligent, single purpose terminal to the IBM PC based WLN PC. This has proven very successful for WLN and its membership. Since the migration to microcomputers has just now been completed, it is impossible to fully assess the impact. Initially, the move has increased the use of network services because it has increased the variety of ways in which the network can be used. The PC has enabled members to more easily manipulate WLN records, it offers more flexibility in downloading records to local systems, it provides countless alternative uses when the PC is not being used for network purposes and it has opened up numerous possibilities for microcomputer based product development by WLN. Further, the number of terminals attached to the network increased 40 percent during the transition, with only a small portion of this amount attributable to new members. In sum, the PC provides WLN with a tremendous opportunity to improve current services and offer a wide variety of new products and services to its membership.

The other side of the PC picture involves those services currently provided by WLN which may be replaced by PC based products not provided by the network. Acquisitions control is an obvious possibility (WLN does not provide serials control, another good candidate for a microcomputer based system). As yet no trend in this direction has begun, but the possibility exists.

More difficult to predict is the impact of CD-ROM and other off-line mass storage technologies. WLN has committed to major development in this area, and will be introducing LaserCat in January, 1987. LaserCat will make available on laser disks approximately one half of the WLN database. LaserCat will contain all WLN records.with holdings attached plus the most recent 200,000 Library of Congress records without holdings. LaserCat will provide complete records in USMARC format for downloading, produce catalog cards and labels, print bibliographies, and contain all WLN interlibrary loan locations.

The fee will be a flat, annual subscription, affordable to many libraries formerly financially unable to acquire WLN products or services. LaserCat will be offered to any library within the WLN service area regardless of its affiliation with WLN or other utilities. While this means significant new business for WLN, it also promises that a large amount of activity formerly done online by current members may now be performed locally. The implications of this will only be fully realized with experience.

WESTERN LIBRARY NETWORK (WLN)

APPENDIX A

Five-Part Questionnaire for North American Bibliographic Utilities
(Responses of the Chief Executive Officers provided in the fall of 1986)

4. What impact will the increasing adoption of new information technologies (e.g., microcomputer-based workstations, and optical disk data storage, retrieval, and transfer media) by libraries to support local needs have on your organization's provision of its products and services for libraries?

Utlas fully supports OSI and is committed to the integration of technologies and sees no threat to its own services as a result of stand-alone products such as optical disk based cataloguing systems. Examples of Utlas' own contributions to the appropriate utilization of technology include a PC-based Public Access Catalogue system and a CD-ROM based retrospective conversion system (the latter to be available in early 1987). From the point of view of an individual library, Utlas sees no conflict between centrally based shared systems and local systems; however, we feel it is imperative not to allow a deterioration of interlibrary loan service to take place as a result of the use of local cataloguing systems which do not provide for the recording of a library's holdings in a regional or national database.

###############

Utlas International Canada

APPENDIX A

Five-Part Questionnaire for North American Bibliographic Utilities
(Responses of the Chief Executive Officers provided in the fall of 1986)

5. OCLC, RLG, WLN, and UTLAS are all currently based in North America. Please summarize your organization's business and service plans or strategies for Europe in the coming years.

ANSWER: OCLC has the objective of building and making available to a broad range of libraries and scholars an international database of not only the records of our own members' holdings together with those of the Library of Congress and other national libraries, but of significant collections of other libraries throughout the world.

The OCLC Board of Trustees authorized OCLC in April 1980 to make its services available to libraries outside the U.S. OCLC Europe, which is based in Birmingham, England, and provides OCLC network support services to libraries in the United Kingdom and Europe, has been in operation since January 1981.

OCLC's international strategy can be summed up in the following points:

- A strategy that is tailored to each national situation but is consistent with a global concept.

- The building of an international database. Not just a "logical" database of linked national and regional systems, but a union catalog of master records and holdings replicated nationally or regionally when the need and technology permits.

- Flexible approaches to relationships and to system and database use that consider the nature of the national political environment and the nature of the parties involved and that take into account the fact that both the environment and the parties may be sharply different from those in the United States.

- Providing access to OCLC's incomparable database, particularly for retrospective conversion agreements.

- Cooperative arrangements with national libraries, library consortia and major universities and large municipal public libraries, which arrangements contemplate an inter-networking relationship, exchange of records, and political cooperation in the encouragement of international standards and the development of format conversion, bibliographic rules conversion and language accommodation.

- Utilizing the new OCLC system environment, new telecommunications and CD-ROM technology to overcome present technical, operational and economic barriers.

(more)

ONLINE COMPUTER LIBRARY CENTER (OCLC)

APPENDIX A

Five-Part Questionnaire for North American Bibliographic Utilities
(Responses of the Chief Executive Officers provided in the fall of 1986)

5. OCLC, RLG, WLN, and UTLAS are all currently based in North America. Please summarize your organization's business and service plans or strategies for Europe in the coming years.

(5. Contd.)

● Adapting our microbased transliteration programs not only to build Romanized and vernacular versions of non-Roman alphabet language collection, but to assist in the development of local stand-alone access systems.

Our fundamental goals in our international initiative are, then, the construction of an international database and the establishment of a variety of linkages that will provide the broadest possible access to the world's intellectual resources. OCLC will be flexible, cooperative and collaborative. Our planning is built on our not-for-profit status. It presumes, in many cases, our building on structures and institutions that presently exist, and it calls for dealing with a limited number of existing institutions and agencies in the countries with which we are working. Such institutions and agencies have generally been ministries of education, culture or science and technology, national library agencies, national libraries and major research university institutions. It avoids establishing local OCLC offices and assumes that our "partners" will provide the continuing support once a central group has been trained.

###############

ONLINE COMPUTER LIBRARY CENTER (OCLC)

APPENDIX A

Five-Part Questionnaire for North American Bibliographic Utilities
(Responses of the Chief Executive Officers provided in the fall of 1986)

5. OCLC, RLG, WLN, and UTLAS are all currently based in North America. Please summarize your organization's business and service plans or strategies for Europe in the coming years.

———————————

RLG recognizes and strongly supports the role of national libraries as appropriate conduits for the exchange of national bibliographies. Based in the U.S., we look to the Library of Congress as a source of such bibliographies for the contribution they can make to our members. Further, we seek to contribute records and products to LC (through coordinated shared cataloging, for example) for eventual LC MARC distribution to others, including other nations.

We believe there are issues of policy, control, and philosophy which many countries will recognize as clear reasons why their bibliographic resources should reside on systems owned and based in their own countries. Surely if the question were to be put in this fashion to U.S. decision makers, we would opt for a home base for such resources. It is RLG's intent, therefore, to operate in ways which: (a) do not compete with national means of bibliographic control, whether under government or other sponsorship, and (b) may produce mutual and supporting benefits, strengthening participants in each cooperating nation. As one direct result, RLG is interested in pursuing links among networks internationally which will be mutually beneficial and serve both programmatic and bibliographic control objectives for each participant. We are generally not interested in offering services supplied from or owned and managed in the U.S. if they would compete with related efforts in other nations.

Where RLIN offers unique capabilities not available in another country we are prepared to share them, perhaps in the interim until they are locally served. Where RLIN is an attractive technical alternative from which others would benefit, we are prepared to support it as the basis for a system to be locally run and managed.

Where RLG, through its programmatic efforts, has developed tools or ideas of potential value to others, we will do whatever we are able within our own resource constraints to share them with other nations and groups. Examples may be found in the RLG Conspectus, a tool for measuring and maintaining an inventory of collecting and collection strengths, and in the work of the RLG Cooperative Preservation Program; aspects of both could be adopted by others. In these two example areas, we are extremely encouraged about the benefits which would accrue to participating institutions and the international scholarly community if broader cooperation were to develop including agreement on common standards.

(more)

THE RESEARCH LIBRARIES GROUP (RLG)

APPENDIX A

Five-Part Questionnaire for North American Bibliographic Utilities
(Responses of the Chief Executive Officers provided in the fall of 1986)

5. OCLC, RLG, WLN, and UTLAS are all currently based in North America. Please summarize your organization's business and service plans or strategies for Europe in the coming years.

(5. Contd.)

The survey to which we respond contains in its introductory material updated information about the actions of the European Parliament calling for "the creation of an electronic clearing house of library holdings across Europe". Developments and experience of RLG which could contribute directly include the Conspectus (and the Conspectus on-line) and our active and early work with the OSI international standards for computer networking. RLG has already shared its experiences in these areas with several groups in Europe and has, in return, learned of their work. Additionally, we have entered into some agreements for more direct working relationships.

In sum, RLG seeks programmatic cooperation; appropriate network interconnections; and the sharing of data, technology, and ideas which would benefit the quality of scholarship and the administration of the information resource complex. We strongly support the role of national libraries in the exchange of national bibliographies, and we seek and are receptive to proposals from them and from universities, consortia or others who share common purpose with us, for mutually beneficial cooperative relationships.

###############

THE RESEARCH LIBRARIES GROUP (RLG)

APPENDIX A

Five-Part Questionnaire for North American Bibliographic Utilities
(Responses of the Chief Executive Officers provided in the fall of 1986)

5. OCLC, RLG, WLN, and UTLAS are all currently based in North America. Please summarize your organization's business and service plans or strategies for Europe in the coming years.

———————————

WLN has licensed its software to the British Library and continues to offer it to all interested organizations.

###############

WESTERN LIBRARY NETWORK (WLN)

APPENDIX A

Five-Part Questionnaire for North American Bibliographic Utilities
(Responses of the Chief Executive Officers provided in the fall of 1986)

5. OCLC, RLG, WLN, and UTLAS are all currently based in North America. Please summarize your organization's business and service plans or strategies for Europe in the coming years.

Utlas has extensive capability in the processing of Asian language cataloguing records and has provided since 1978 shared cataloguing services to a number of Japanese libraries. There are no technological barriers to providing service in Asia and Europe whether by telecommunications or by system replication, and Utlas actively seeks expansion into Europe. Already including British and French MARC records, the Utlas database lends itself well to use by European libraries; the addition of other European MARC files will only enhance its utility on both sides of the Atlantic.

Due to the extensive flexibility and customizability of Utlas' local systems products, they are as applicable in Japan and Europe as they are in North America.

################

Utlas International Canada